# Neil Young

LAUGHIN LADY
R. SOUL / WORLD ON A STRING
OCAHONTAS
STRINGMAN
HURRICANE
TONIGHT'S THE NIGHT
HELPLESS
—
SAMPLE + HOLD
TRANSFORMER MAN
DREAMIN' MAN
HARVEST MOON
UNKNOWN LEGEND
WAR OF MAN
WINTERLONG
LONG MAY YOU RUN

### STERLING
New York

An Imprint of Sterling Publishing
387 Park Avenue South
New York, NY 10016

STERLING and the distinctive Sterling logo are registered trademarks of Sterling Publishing Co., Inc.

© 2012 by Essential Works Limited

Produced for Sterling Publishing by Essential Works
www.essentialworks.co.uk

Publishing Director: Mal Peachey
Managing Director: John Conway
Editors: Laura Jorstad, Nicola Hodgson, Tania Bissell
Designer: Barbara Doherty

ISBN 978-1-4027-9911-2

Distributed in Canada by Sterling Publishing
c/o Canadian Manda Group, 165 Dufferin Street
Toronto, Ontario, Canada M6K 3H6
Distributed in the United Kingdom by GMC Distribution Services
Castle Place, 166 High Street, Lewes, East Sussex, England BN7 1XU
Distributed in Australia by Capricorn Link (Australia) Pty. Ltd.
P.O. Box 704, Windsor, NSW 2756, Australia

For information about customer editions, special sales, and premium and corporate purchases, please contact Sterling Special Sales at 800-805-5489 or specialsales@sterlingpublishing.com.

Manufactured in China

2 4 6 8 10 9 7 5 3 1

www.sterlingpublishing.com

some musical ones (Neil brushed aside most of the questions, about a Buffalo Springfield reunion, about how often Stills seemed to appear in the film, about Crosby, Stills and Nash). Young appeared hyper-excited through the session, like a high-school kid who'd just won in the Science Fair, but still nervous over his first film.

The consensus, from his friends, on the film: a decent first try, even if not exactly Academy. "It was a nice film," said Lou Adler (himself a star of such rock movies as *Monterey Pop*, *Brewster McCloud*, and *A Model Shop*). "Neil's touch is great, as it is in his music." But, Adler added, he'd actually be more enthusiastic to see Neil's second and third tries. "Anyone coming out of one industry and going into another has to still be learning the mechanics of the new one," he said. "And now he'll have something to bounce off of."

Young's co-manager, Elliot Roberts, agreed. "This film is not as proficient as his next endeavor," he said. "But it was made with a lot of care and love."

# Neil Young
## The Definitive History

**Mike Evans**

STERLING
New York

# contents

# INTRODUCTION

One of rock music's true mavericks, throughout a career spanning over five decades Neil Young has consistently challenged every expectation of fans and critics alike. Not even Bob Dylan at his most mercurial has matched the Canadian singer-songwriter in the sheer breadth and boldness of his musical choices.

In a journey taking in folk and country, rock and protest songs, pop-chart triumph and dogged experimentation, through Buffalo Springfield, to Crosby, Stills, Nash & Young, and on to his own sublimely erratic solo career, Neil Young has been nothing if not eclectic. But despite a lifelong refusal to be pigeonholed, Young has remained remarkably in tune with the contemporary music scene of every era— when Pearl Jam's Eddie Vedder inducted him into the Rock and Roll Hall of Fame in 1985, he commented that Young was probably the only artist admitted to the pantheon of rock greats who had remained significantly cutting-edge.

To the point of seeming deliberately perverse, Young has never played it safe if it didn't suit him. An artist who has written and performed some of the classic songs of the past fifty years, he has nevertheless made countless musical, business, and personal decisions that have threatened not only his career but the course of his entire life. After achieving international stardom with the chart-topping "Heart of Gold" and his biggest-selling album *Harvest* in 1972, he followed up with three dark and blatantly uncommercial albums; when Crosby, Stills, Nash & Young were riding high in the mainstream, he quit the band and returned to solo performances; and, as a hero of post-hippie liberals, he shocked fans in 1985 with an apparent shift to the redneck right.

But like his music, Neil Young's position has never been easily classified. His social concerns found their voice in Farm Aid, for instance, which he set up with country star

An image of Neil Young in London in 1970, during a Crosby, Stills, Nash & Young tour, in a house owned by the Rolling Stones.

"I totally have no other talent and I would be totally out of work if I did anything else."

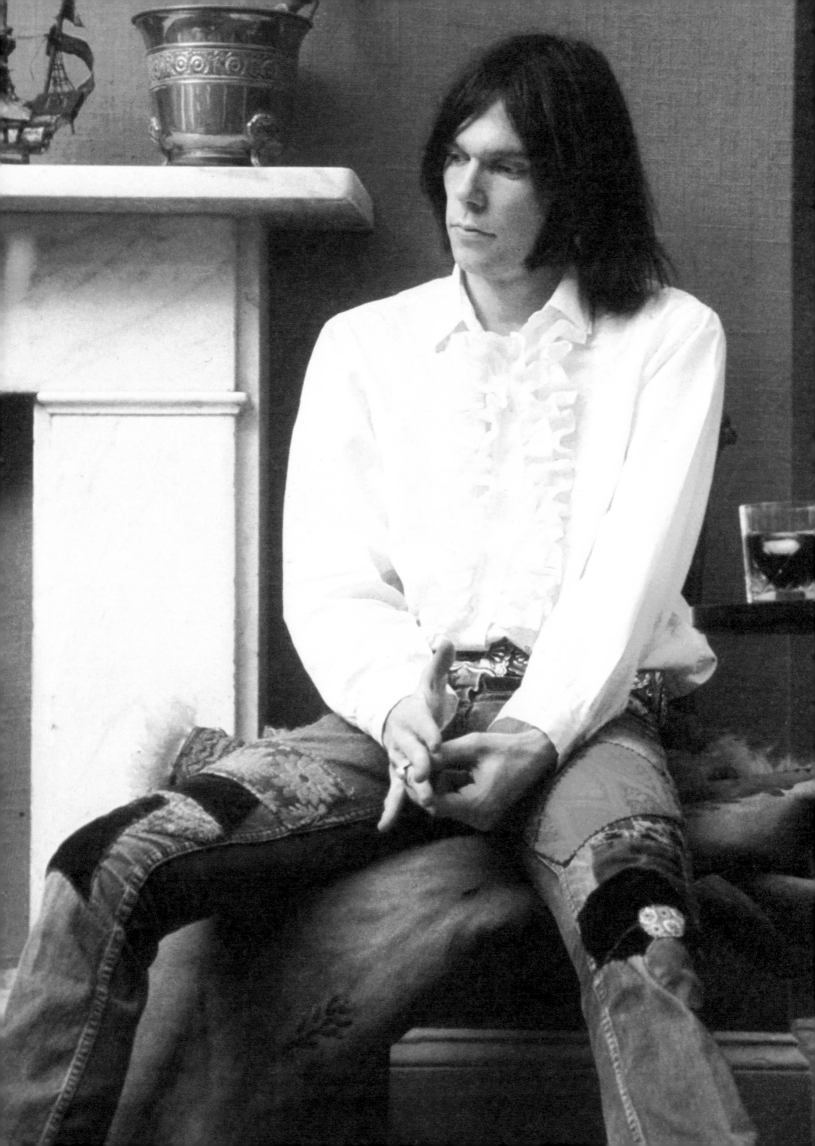

# Neil Young

Willie Nelson in 1985, and which became an annual concert and fund-raising event for struggling American farmers and their families. Closer to home, Neil and his wife, Pegi—with special-needs children of their own—helped found San Francisco's Bridge School, a learning center for children with communication disabilities, which they continue to support with an annual all-star benefit concert.

In 2005 Young was diagnosed with a potentially fatal brain aneurism, but while undergoing treatment he didn't let it slow him down, releasing an album a year between then and 2010. New concerns gripped his attention, including the war in Iraq, which he vociferously opposed both vocally and musically. Likewise environmental issues became a passion, with the design and building of an eco-friendly automobile that would avoid the use of fossil fuel. And 2006 saw the first album release in the ongoing Neil Young Archives project, a series of music and video artifacts

Above: On stage shot during Neil's North American "Music in Head" tour of Fall, 2000.

Opposite: A 1990 press release from Reprise Records promoting Young's *Ragged Glory* album.

drawn from his personal collection featuring remastered past releases, plus long-lost recordings and films made public for the first time.

As Neil Young approaches his seventieth birthday in 2015, the Archive releases mark the amazing scope of his musical history—a story traced in the pages that follow—stretching back fifty years to the early 1960s, and his first tentative recordings with his Winnipeg high school group the Squires.

**Mike Evans, February 2012**

# ONE

Canada

**T**H E Canadian midwestern city of Winnipeg, capital of the sprawling province of Manitoba and not far north of the U.S. border, could never be described as a nerve center of rock 'n' roll. But that was where Neil Young, as a fourteen-year-old, began his musical career. It was there that he formed his first band, played his first solo gigs, and made his first record—although he had already caught the music bug during his preteen years, a thousand miles east across the Great Lakes, in Toronto, Ontario. And it would be to Toronto that he returned during his formative days as a professional musician, torn between the twin influences of folk music and rock 'n' roll, and searching for a musical identity that somehow reflected both.

## Childhood

Neil Percival Young was born in Toronto General Hospital on November 12, 1945. His father, Scott Young, was a journalist and sportswriter who supplemented an unsteady income by selling short stories to newspapers. In June 1940 Scott had married Edna "Rassy" Ragland, who gave birth to their first son, Robert (Bob), in April 1942. There followed a somewhat transient existence for the family, who resided at various locations in and around Toronto, until—not long after Neil was born—they moved to the little rural town of Omemee, Ontario.

As Neil would often later reminisce, his years in Omemee were among the happiest in his early life. The quiet easygoing calm of rural life suited him, as it has ever since; outdoor pursuits like fishing in the summer and tobogganing in the winter made for an idyllic-sounding, quintessentially Canadian childhood.

Near-tragedy struck, however, in 1951, when two months before his sixth birthday Neil—"Neiler," as the family nicknamed him—was hospitalized by a virulent bout of polio. It was during an epidemic that was sweeping Canada, one of the last major outbreaks of the disease. (Coincidentally, singer Joni Mitchell, then nine years old, also contracted the virus.) As Scott Young would recall, "There were people dying every day, the front page of the papers would give a running account of who'd made it through the night."

Neil as a young boy, featured on the back sleeve of his *Prairie Wind* album.

Crucially, although he recovered from the life-threatening illness, it left Neil Young with post-polio syndrome, which included stiffness down the left side of his body and a noticeable limp that in later years became something of a trademark of his onstage image. It also meant that while his brother, Bob, was excelling at school as a typical North American sports jock, Neil began picking up on music as his leisure activity of choice.

Like most youngsters in the Western world during the mid-1950s, at the age of ten or eleven he was attracted by the new sounds of pop music, which for the first time was being aimed specifically at young people. Rock 'n' roll was all around, and Neil would listen to the latest record releases via the local radio station 1050-CHUM; he was a huge fan of Elvis Presley, as well as being mesmerized by the other early pioneers of rock music, including Jerry Lee Lewis, Fats Domino, Little Richard, and Johnny Cash.

Noticing his interest in music, shortly before Christmas 1958, his parents bought him a ukulele, a cheap plastic instrument that nevertheless served to introduce him to actual music making for the first time. Neil immediately took to it with gusto, learning a few chords and simple tunes like "Blueberry Hill" (a prewar oldie, but also a Fats Domino hit at the time). His parents had an old Seabreeze record player, and he would recall how he practiced to it when they were out: "I used to turn that old record player up full volume. I had bought a couple of records the day I got the uke—I'd throw myself around, dancing, and I would have fantasies about winning dance contests."

Neil's childhood home in Omemee, Ontario where the family lived from 1949–53.

In school, meanwhile, Neil had developed into the archetypal class clown, entertaining his fellow pupils with jokes and back talk that simply incensed his teachers. But he did display a remarkable maturity when it came to an entrepreneurial venture he devised—rearing and selling chickens. After setting up a roadside stall selling wild strawberries that grew at the back of the family property, he used the proceeds to buy an incubator and breed chickens, selling their eggs for profit. This was a year or two before the ukulele entered his life, and the financial success of the scheme was such that he seriously thought about going into farming. He wrote of his ambition in a school essay at the time: "When I finish school I want to go to Ontario Agricultural College and perhaps learn to be a scientific farmer."

## Relocation

By this time the Young family had moved yet again, to Pickering, just east of Toronto. The move was an effort by Neil's parents to patch up a rift in their relationship, which Scott had precipitated when he had an affair with a fellow journalist. It was in New York City, where he'd spent some time away from the family writing articles for *Sports Illustrated* magazine. There was talk of a divorce, but Scott and Rassy—probably as much for the boys' sake as anything else—decided to give their marriage another try.

For a while, Scott had seemed settled at last; he took a job away from the hurly-burly of the journalistic world, a well-paid post in public relations with an engineering company. But he still had itchy feet, and in 1957 had begun working for the *Globe and Mail*, a move that would sow the seeds of the final breakup of his marriage.

In the summer of 1960, he became involved with a young PR agent while they were both working on a tour of Canada by Queen Elizabeth. The affair was far more serious than the various dalliances Scott had been guilty of previously, and he announced to his sons (incredibly, over dinner at their favorite restaurant!) that he was leaving their mother. Rassy was furious beyond words, not so much because of her husband's infidelity—she was used to that—but because this time he was actually deserting his family for a younger woman. She immediately upped stakes with her sons and moved west to her hometown of Winnipeg, where she settled in the working-class area of Fort Rouge.

Though it was inevitably traumatic, at fourteen and seventeen, respectively, Neil and Bob were old enough to deal with their parents' separation with a degree of maturity—on the surface, at least. Over the past few years they had become increasingly aware that a split might occur one day, and now that day had come.

But the biggest wrench for Neil, after the initial move to Winnipeg, was when his elder brother decided to return to Toronto, where job prospects were better, and live with their father. (The arrangement wouldn't last long: When Scott decided to move in with his new girlfriend, Bob got an apartment of his own.) Suddenly he was alone, in a strange city, with the added upheaval of having to adjust to a new school.

Earl Grey Junior High was a tough school in a tough part of town. Newcomers are always seen as easy prey by the class bullies, and Neil was

Rassy Ragland (front center) as a panellist on the *Twenty Questions* TV show.

an immediate target when he enrolled in the fall of 1960. The self-confidence he'd displayed previously in school had seemingly disappeared, and the first impression he made at Earl Grey was one of an introverted loner, reluctant to speak to anyone.

But he soon stood up for himself, specifically in an incident recalled many years later in an interview in *Rolling Stone* magazine. The guy sitting in front of him in class had deliberately knocked Neil's books off his desk—"He did it a few times. I guess I wore the wrong color clothes or something. Maybe I looked too much like a mamma's boy for them." Neil asked the teacher if he could borrow a dictionary, and took it back to his desk: "Then I stood up in my seat, raised it above my head as far as I could and hit the guy in front of me over the head with it. Knocked him out."

"Neil was a regular at the weekly hops, along with a group of friends."

The incident led to an immediate day-and-a-half expulsion from school, but at the same time earned Neil some respect among his peers, who quickly got to like the slightly oddball character in their midst. His classmates warmed to his dry humor and lack of pretension, as a female fellow student would remember: "Neil was different, and he made quite an impression on the girls. We thought he was pretty cool because he was tall and very outgoing. He had his hair in a brush cut then. He didn't try to be tough like the other boys and that was unusual."

More impressive to his contemporaries, however, was the fact that the new kid actually played guitar. Neil had long since discarded the ukulele in favor of the banjo, and his recently acquired acoustic guitar was nothing less than a status symbol in school. Most important, it was the key to him joining his first group, a short-lived outfit calling themselves the Jades.

## First Appearances

The catalyst for the formation of the Jades was the Earl Grey Community Club, which held dances in the school canteen most Fridays. By the end of his first term Neil was a regular at the weekly hops, along with a group of friends that included John Daniel, Jim Atkin, David Gregg, and Susan Kelso. Susan and Neil often hung out together, although their relationship never got as far as serious dating.

The community club also encouraged jamming sessions for any budding musicians, and it was there that Young teamed up with Daniel, Atkin, and Gregg to form an impromptu group playing guitar-based instrumentals. (Instrumentals were hugely popular in the charts at the time, thanks to records by the Ventures, Duane Eddy, the Fireballs, and the like.) Dubbing themselves the Jades, the quartet played just one actual gig, a dance at the school canteen during the first week of 1961.

Neil's first guitar was a Harmony Monterey acoustic, fitted with a pickup. He didn't have an amplifier at this stage (for the Jades date he plugged into one of the others' amps), but that didn't stop him auditioning for a vacancy in another band, the Esquires, during the spring. Led by guitarist Larry Wah, the group was well established on the school community club circuit, and Neil's rehearsals with them were a disaster. He just couldn't hack it with a band of some experience, so basic was his guitar playing, and after a few practice sessions the band fired him before he'd managed to play a paid gig.

Neil (center) and schoolfriends who worked together on the 1960–61 Early Grey Junior High Yearbook.

**YEAR BOOK STAFF**

Seated: Jim Atkin, Joann Hagglund, Susan Kelso, Neil Young, Laurelle Hughes, June Hagglund, Ken Koblun. Standing: Mrs. Queen, Richard Clayton, Gerry Soucie, Shirley Lord, Mr. Patterson, Ruth Harris, Joe Vinci, Mrs. Mills.

Still at Earl Grey, Neil struck up a friendship with fellow student Ken
Koblun, who shared an increasing obsession with music. Through the rest of
the year they were virtually inseparable, even when Neil enrolled at Kelvin
High School in the fall of 1961 while Koblun moved to Churchill High.
Inspired by his friend's example, Ken persuaded his father to buy him a guitar
for Christmas, and the two stayed closely in touch through 1962. During that
year Neil played in various short-lived instrumental lineups, including the
Stardusters and the Twilighters (basically the same band), before forming the
Classics—with Koblun on bass—in October 1962.

The Classics were another fleeting affair. Debuting at Churchill High,
they played just six dates before disbanding at the end of the year, Neil later
admitting, "We weren't good enough." By this time, however, both Neil and
Ken were serious about continuing their forays into the (albeit amateur) music
business. Neil had even acquired a new guitar, a secondhand Gibson Les Paul
Junior electric, bought for him by his mother.

Unlike most parents of would-be musicians, Rassy had great faith in her
son's rock 'n' roll ambitions from the start—unlike his absentee father, who
assumed that Neil still had his sights on agricultural college. In short, Rassy
Ragland was Neil Young's first real fan.

# The Squires

Early in 1963, Neil and Ken Koblun played their first gig with the Squires. With Neil and Allan Bates on guitars, Koblun on bass, and Jack Harper on drums, the band had been rehearsing through the closing months of 1962, while the Classics were struggling with their handful of engagements. They practiced in Harper's basement, again developing an instrumental-oriented repertoire, this time heavily influenced by the UK group the Shadows.

Led by guitarist Hank B. Marvin, the Shadows were huge in Great Britain, with a string of chart-topping instrumentals, including "Apache," "Kon-Tiki," and "Dance On." They never figured in North American best-seller lists, but among aficionados of pop guitar they were cult heroes. As well as plundering the Shadows catalog, the band covered most of the many instrumental hits of the era—strident, easily remembered tunes like the Ventures' "Walk Don't Run," the Champs' "Tequila," and "Telstar" by the Tornadoes.

The Squires made their debut on February 1, 1963, at the Riverview Community Club in Fort Rouge, receiving five dollars, not long after which Harper was replaced on drums by Ken Smythe. This would be the only personnel change for some time, as the Squires steadily built a reputation for themselves among teenage audiences in the Winnipeg area.

Most of their bookings were in small venues on the community club circuit, for which their primitive equipment was just about ample, but occasional gigs at larger places like school gymnasiums were becoming a problem. They would often borrow equipment from Chad Allan and the Reflections, Winnipeg's number-one local band at the time. The Reflections included Randy Bachman on lead guitar (later with the Guess Who and, in the 1970s, Bachman-Turner Overdrive), whom Neil would admit to hero-worshipping: "He was definitely the biggest influence on me in the city. He was the best. Back in those days he was years ahead of anybody else."

The band went from strength to strength, as did Neil's confidence in his own ability to succeed in the precarious world of music. It was a passion that eclipsed all others in his life, as his only regular girlfriend of the period, Pamela Smith, would remember: "He had a terrific imagination, it was like dreaming out loud . . . He had a wonderful laugh, but he didn't laugh that often. He was so intense."

His growing dedication to music was bolstered by the unflagging support of his mother, who helped him with equipment— she subsidized the purchase of a flash-looking Orange Gretsch in place of his battered old Les Paul, and replaced his homemade

Chad Allen and the Reflections, Winnipeg's top band circa 1963.

amplifier, which was frequently giving him electric shocks—and let the boys rehearse in the nice suburban house she and Neil had now moved into in the Winnipeg suburbs. Having something of a financial stake in her son's future, she assumed the role of unofficial manager of the group.

A vivacious extrovert who never minced her words, Rassy Ragland had become well-known in the Winnipeg area as a panelist on a local TV version of the popular quiz show *Twenty Questions*. She used her connections to plug the Squires whenever possible, by mid-1963 bringing them to the attention of Bob Bradburn, a DJ on radio station CKRC. Bradburn took an immediate liking to the band, and began to plug their gigs incessantly on his daily show.

This led directly to Neil Young's first appearance on disc, when on July 23 the Squires went into CKRC's small studio and laid down two instrumentals, both written by Young, "The Sultan" and "Aurora." As Ken Smythe would later recall: "I thought you'd go down, do three takes, pick the best one. We didn't just sit down and play the songs—it was put together."

The recordings appeared as a single on the local label V Records; production was credited to Bob Bradburn, although Young would testify that the two-track console was in fact operated by a studio engineer called Harry Taylor. Despite the faux-Arabian feel on "The Sultan" and other kitsch effects, Neil Young realized that this was a valuable beginning—but only a beginning. "It was good to have it out, but I hadn't got the *sound* I was after yet. It was my first recording session and I was just glad to be there for the experience."

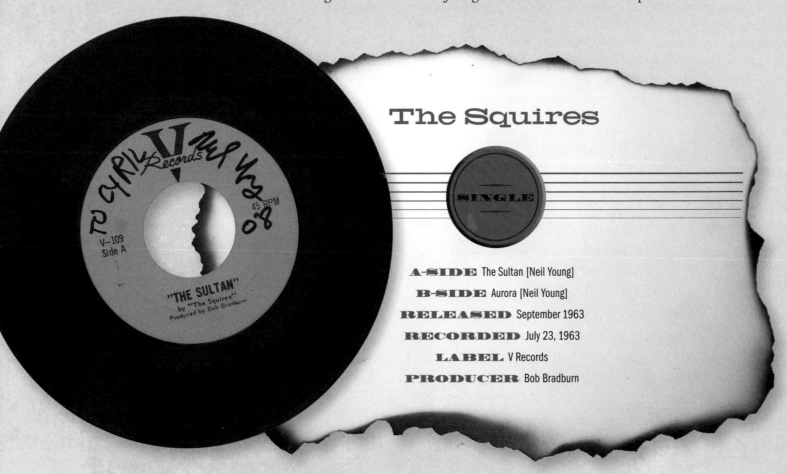

# The Squires

SINGLE

**A-SIDE** The Sultan [Neil Young]

**B-SIDE** Aurora [Neil Young]

**RELEASED** September 1963

**RECORDED** July 23, 1963

**LABEL** V Records

**PRODUCER** Bob Bradburn

## Beat Boom

In the wake of their modest record release, over the next few months the Squires' popularity grew around Winnipeg and its environs. Moving away from a purely instrumental stance, their repertoire now included vocals, with Neil usually assuming the role of lead singer.

The decision to feature vocals was in no small part influenced by events on the other side of the Atlantic, in Great Britain. There, from early in 1963, a musical revolution was taking place, spearheaded by the Beatles. And as the Fab Four's records stormed the UK charts, they were released in Canada within weeks—unlike the United States, where Beatlemania only got a grip in the opening months of 1964. Ken Koblun, who lived with an English family, also had hits from the new British "beat boom" groups shipped over before they appeared in the Winnipeg stores. So when the British Invasion was set to take all of North America by storm in '64, the Squires were ready for the trend—like their local rivals the Reflections, whose leader Randy Bachman even went so far as swapping his Gretsch guitar for a Rickenbacker, just like John Lennon's. According to bass player Koblun, Neil himself wasn't sure that he could take on the job of vocalist with the group, but simple dollars and cents dictated that they couldn't afford another member in the lineup. His high-pitched falsetto wasn't to everyone's taste, and at the first gig that he attempted a couple of Beatles covers (raucous versions of "It Won't Be Long" and "Money") at the Kelvin High cafeteria, one student in the audience heckled, "Stick to the instrumentals!"

No doubt also inspired by Lennon and McCartney, Neil even started experimenting with his own compositions, tentatively getting them transcribed into sheet music, which he mailed to himself, keeping the postmarked envelope unopened—a common device among nonprofessional writers to ensure copyright was protected.

So when the Squires were booked for their second visit to the CKRC recording studios in April 1964, it was with some of his originals, including "I Wonder" and "Ain't It the Truth," on which he sang the lead vocal. The producer was the same Harry Taylor who'd supervised their first session at the studio. He commented to Young afterward, "You're a good guitar player, kid— but you'll never make it as a singer."

Like scores of other Winnipeg groups—and rock 'n' roll hopefuls across the rest of Canada and the United States—the Squires rode the Beatles bandwagon for all it was worth, even donning mop-top wigs at one Riverview Community Club gig, much to the delight of female members of the audience. The boom in British beat meant a spin-off bonanza for the myriad local groups springing up in 1964, and the Squires found themselves playing in a variety of venues outside their regular community club scene, including territory previously out of bounds to rock acts—folk clubs.

V Records

39

45 RPM

V-109
Side B

"AURORA"
by "The Squires"
*Produced by Bob Bradburn

## Folk Scene

Traditionally, folk music and pop were considered poles apart, the followers of each viewing the opposite camp with suspicion and disdain, if not downright contempt. But all that was changing, and alongside the beat boom there was a parallel pop-chart presence of commercially successful folk music. Artists including the Kingston Trio, the New Christy Minstrels, Trini Lopez, and Peter Paul & Mary all had big hit singles with reworkings of standard folk songs, while Joan Baez had no less than five entries in the *Billboard* Top 20 album charts from 1962 through 1964.

In February 1964, the Squires were booked into the Fourth Dimension, a folk music coffeehouse on the outskirts of Winnipeg near the University of Manitoba. It appealed to an arty, beatnik-intellectual sort of crowd, more drawn to poetry readings, folk music, and jazz than electric guitar rock.

But despite the best-selling records, the folk boom was waning for many live venues in the face of beat music. The 4-D (as it was known) wasn't pulling the crowds, and Neil Young managed to convince the proprietor to give the Squires a date. Helped by their loyal local following, they packed the place out, and their Beatle-inclined set raised the roof.

Neil was already familiar with the 4-D; he'd often attend their Sunday-night hootenannies, when anyone could get up and sing—"I got into a Dylan thing in grade nine, playing folk, so I liked going to the 4-D." And it was at the 4-D that Neil first met Joan Anderson, a young singer from Saskatoon who would later find fame as Joni Mitchell. "Neil had just discovered Bob Dylan," she told writer Jimmy McDonough. "He was going from rock and roll to a folkie direction. The concept of writing more poetic lyrics had just occurred to him, so he was checkin' out the coffeehouse scene."

As a budding songwriter, Neil found it was the lyrical quality of folk music—meaningful songs with stories and messages—that sparked his imagination. He would use the 4-D open-mike sessions as a sounding board for new, solo-oriented, and increasingly personal material that would have been out of place in the Squires' exuberant repertoire.

Young described the twin appeal of folk and rock, in many ways an attraction of opposites, during a speech inducting Woody Guthrie into the Rock and Roll Hall of Fame in 1988: "And then I saw Bob Dylan, then I saw so many others, Phil Ochs, Tim Hardin, Pete Seeger, and it all started comin' together for me—but I still couldn't forget about that other guy with the guitar, jumpin' around . . . I saw what I wanted to do with my life."

"Neil was different, and he made quite an impression on the girls"

## School's Out

During the summer of 1964, it was becoming apparent that there was a difference of attitude among members of the Squires that wouldn't be easily reconciled. On the one hand, Ken Smythe and Allan Bates saw the group as great fun, a welcome diversion from their school career and whatever was to follow, but nothing more. Neil and Ken Koblun, on the other hand, saw it as the first step to something much bigger, making music their main occupation—in other words, turning professional.

Things came to a head in August when Neil and a group of friends drove out to the resort area of Falcon Lake for a few days. There he saw a young group like his own playing at the lakeside hotel, and immediately talked the hotel manager into hiring the Squires. But when he rang the others to come up to play the booking, Ken Koblun agreed without hesitation while Smythe and Bates turned the idea down, saying they had other priorities.

Neil was furious, and fired them both—effectively breaking up the band—as soon as he got back to Winnipeg. Although the Squires got on together famously, not just for gigs but hanging out as real friends, clearly the chance of the hotel date—their first real out-of-town appearance—meant a lot more to Neil and Ken Koblun than to the other two.

The following month Neil made an explicit statement of intent when he decided to leave school in favor of pursuing his musical dreams—an ambition that even the headmaster at Kelvin High acknowledged was far more important to the eighteen-year-old than any academic pursuit. And whether he was

A view of Main Street, Winnipeg, in 1965, looking north from Rupert Avenue.

spurred by Neil's decision or not (though it's unlikely that it didn't have some influence), Ken Koblun quit Churchill High School around the same time.

Always one to encourage her son's musical aspirations, Rassy Ragland wasn't at all fazed by Neil's departure from formal education, reflecting later, "You only get one shot at it." Nevertheless, she couldn't resist the opportunity to get in a dig when she sarcastically wrote to inform his father (who believed Neil should have ditched the band and stayed in school): "Dear Scott, Neil has decided to follow your advice and become a dropout."

## Fort William

Neil didn't take long in recruiting replacements for Bates and Smythe. Drummer Bill Edmunsen lived right across the road from Neil and Rassy, attended Kelvin High, and was already a friend. When Neil offered him the job in a new Squires lineup, he, too, quit school immediately. And Jeff Waukert was brought in on piano, although his membership in the band would prove to be short-lived.

The newly constituted outfit started playing around the Winnipeg circuit as a full-time working band. But Neil planned to make his mark farther afield, and to that end purchased (with a loan from his mother) a unique mode of transport—a 1948 Buick Roadmaster hearse. The jet-black monolith of a car was an ideal "band bus" in many ways: There was room for musicians and equipment, the tasseled black curtains concealed what was in the vehicle, and the lift apparatus (designed to gently move coffins in and out) made loading easy. Neil named the car Mortimer Hearseberg, or "Mort" for short. (Whether intentional or not, the wordplay couldn't have gone unnoticed in bilingual Canada, mort being French for "death.")

Although they weren't acquainted with the music scene there, Neil decided that their first trip away from Winnipeg would be to Fort William. "Fort Bill," as it was known, was five hundred miles or so east of Winnipeg, on the shores of Lake Superior near the U.S. border—a considerable distance, with no gigs guaranteed when they got there. Before the group departed, Jeff Waukert's parents had barred him from taking part in what seemed like a foolhardy venture, so the Squires headed east as a trio.

They hadn't been in Fort William long when they were hired for a gig from October 12–17 at the Flamingo Club for $325, plus free lodging at the nearby Victoria Hotel. The venue was far from salubrious, the owner Scott Shields having fallen into debt—"First time we ever played a liquor joint," Bill Edmunsen would recall—but the Squires made an impression, and Shields booked them for a return stint in November, billed as "Rock 'n' Rolling Neil Young and the Squires, Recording Stars under the Vee label."

By the fall of '64, the British Invasion of North America was in full swing, with a host of UK acts making their mark on U.S. and Canadian charts, which in turn impacted homegrown groups like the Squires. With less emphasis on instrumentals than previously, their sound now reflected the harder R&B style of bands like the Rolling Stones and the Animals, as well as the vocal harmonies of the Beatles.

On the second Flamingo engagement, songs such as "Farmer John" (made famous by the Searchers and covered by Neil years later on *Ragged Glory*) were vehicles for barnstorming performances in which Neil Young, on his own admission, seemed to get lost in his own guitar playing for the first time: "We used to break loose in it. That was one of the first times I ever started transcending on guitar. Things just got to another plane, it was gone."

It was also during that return trip to Fort William that Neil wrote his elegy for a vanished adolescence, "Sugar Mountain," on November 12, 1964, his nineteenth birthday. The gentle, heartfelt lyrics—written, as he would recount many times, in the loneliness of his hotel bedroom—were not suited to the Squires' strident R&B, but would feature as a mainstay of Neil Young's solo acoustic sets in years to come.

## Fourth Dimension

During their November visit to the Flamingo Club, Neil and the boys managed to find time to check out the local branch of the 4-D chain, which along with the Winnipeg venue and one in Regina totaled three independently run coffeehouses.

Neil (left) with the Squires as a trio, alongside their faithful transport Mort.

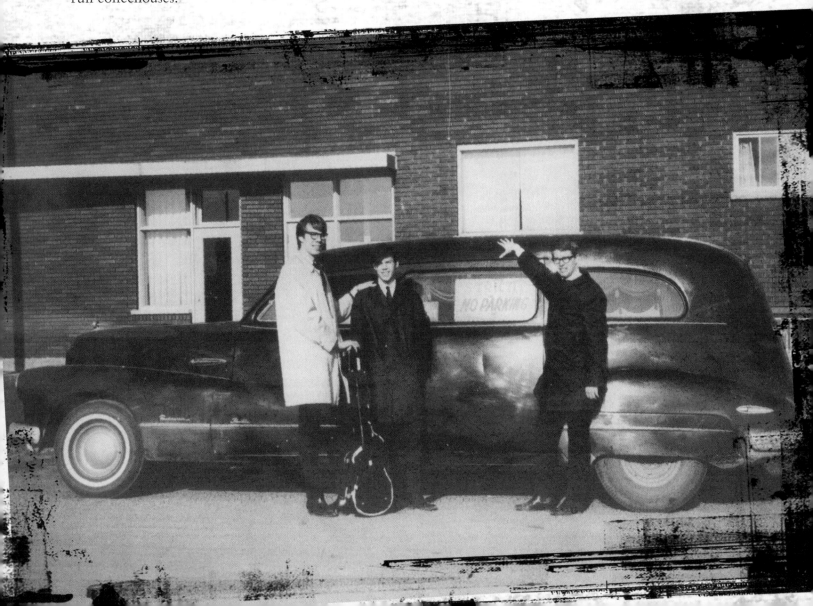

Neil (left) with the Squires as a trio, alongside their faithful transport Mort.

An early shot of Buffalo Springfield, with (left to right) an unknown friend, Richie Furay, Dewey Martin, unknown friend, Bruce Palmer, Neil Young, and Stephen Stills.

Like its Winnipeg equivalent, the Fourth Dimension in Fort William was a fashionably hip music spot and hangout for local musicians; it catered to a more discerning clientele than did the seedy Flamingo. So while appearing at the latter at night, the Squires also played afternoon hootenannies at the 4-D, where they preferred the relaxed atmosphere and attentive audience.

One of those listening was a local DJ, Ray Dee, who worked for CJLX radio station. Talking to Neil Young biographer Jimmy McDonough, Dee would recall vividly when he first came across the band: "There's a band on the stage, three guys whackin' away. Neil's about nine-feet-twelve, all legs and neck . . ." The enthusiastic disc jockey soon got the band into the station recording studio, where he produced two new Young compositions, "I'll Love You Forever" and "Together Alone," plus another version of "I Wonder," which they had recorded previously in Winnipeg.

The DJ quickly became their main contact and ally in the Fort William area.

He began promoting the band, getting them gigs at $120 a time, and even sent a copy of the recordings to the Winnipeg office of Capitol Records, although the company declined to take an interest.

Neil and the band finally returned to Winnipeg early in December. Although Fort William had been a success, there followed a period of unsettling personnel changes, mainly involving drummers. Like Ken Smythe before him, Bill Edmunsen found he couldn't fully commit to the life on the road that was now the only target in Neil's sights. Neil sacked him, something he was learning to do the hard way—"The hardest thing I learned to do was to fire someone. If somebody didn't fit in, I knew I had to tell him." Various drummers followed

Bill, including Terry Crosby, Randy Peterson, Al Johnson, and Bob Clark. Neil also recruited—although by all accounts poached might be a more accurate word—a guitarist, Doug Campbell, who was playing with Ken Smythe and Allan Bates's new group the Dimensions. It was with Campbell, and Randy Peterson occupying the drum stool, that the Squires would make their final recordings. The four-piece laid down a rocker called "(I'm a Man and) I Can't Cry," and had yet another stab at "I Wonder." In retrospect Neil would rave about that particular lineup of the Squires, but it wasn't to last; the two new additions were not able to travel, and by April 1965, Neil had decided he was ready for another trip to Fort William.

Now a trio again with Bob Clark on drums, the Squires headed east for a season at the 4-D nightclub-coffeehouse where they had made an impression some months earlier. This time Neil chose to explore new musical avenues with the latest version of the Squires, challenging the perceived barriers between folk and rock with highly charged electrified versions of old familiar folk songs like "She'll Be Coming 'Round the Mountain," "Oh Susannah," and "My Darling Clementine."

When the Squires opened at the Fourth Dimension on April 18, 1965, it was playing the intermission spot for an American folk outfit who were beginning a tour of Canada. Called the Company, their young guitarist-vocalist was particularly impressed by Neil Young and his group, and their weird treatment of folk music classics. A recent graduate of the Greenwich Village folk scene in New York, like Neil he was searching for something that transcended the pigeonholes of folk and rock. His name was Stephen Stills, and their meeting that night would change the course of American music.

## Stills

Born in Texas in January 1945, Stills had led an itinerant life for most of his twenty years. His father moved around the country from job to job, and the nearest the youngster got to a settled existence was in Florida, where he attended various schools including a military academy and a Benedictine monastery! His parents always encouraged him musically—he was playing the drums by the time he was eight, and while still at high school played in several bands, including the Continentals, whose lineup included future Eagles guitarist Don Felder.

Leaving school, and having caught the folk music bug in a big way, in late 1963 he found himself working in a duo in a New Orleans bar, before deciding to head for the folk mecca of Greenwich Village. There he would meet another hopeful, Richie Furay, with whom he formed the Au Go-Go Singers. Based on the commercial feel-good sound of the New Christy Minstrels, the nine-piece Au Go-Go's (including

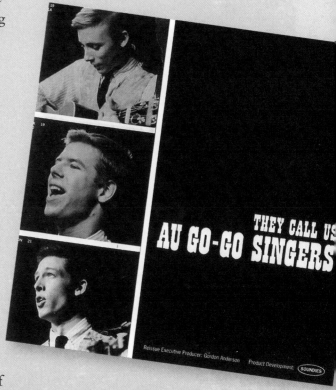

The only album by the Au Go-Go Singers—*They Call Us Au Go-Go Singers*—which featured Stephen Stills and Richie Furay.

two female vocalists) met with moderate success, playing as far afield as Texas, appearing on TV, and even making an album. But the size of the group would soon prove impractical, and Stills wound up with a breakaway five-piece lineup (which didn't include Furay), the Company.

By this time, like millions of other young people around the globe, Stephen Stills was in awe of the Beatles. He would go on record admitting that after watching their movie *A Hard Day's Night* he wanted to reconcile his folk instincts with a rock group sound to produce something totally new. When he saw Neil Young that night at the 4-D, he recognized in the gangly kid on stage a kindred spirit. The two hit it off immediately.

Over the following days Stills and Young spent most of their offstage time getting to know each other—talking music, drinking beer, driving around town in Mort, and generally hanging out. Realizing they had much in common, including their dreams for the future, Stills even considered joining the Canadian's group—it was only the prospect of inevitable work permit problems that prevented him from joining then and there. Determined that they should team up as soon as possible, Stills said he would head for New York once the Company tour was over, fix up some gigs to enable work permits to be granted, and send for Neil and the Squires. Nevertheless, it would be almost a year before they got together again.

## Toronto

As the Company continued on their Canadian tour, Neil and his comrades stuck it out in Fort William for a while, though times were tough. But sensing that their days as minor stars in the town had reached a dead end, with money to match, by July 1965 Neil had opted to move to his hometown of Toronto— with Ken, Bob, and a new member, guitarist Terry Erickson, in tow.

Although not as enthusiastically supportive of his musician son as Rassy Ragland, Neil's father, Scott Young, nevertheless helped Neil and the band get started on the Toronto scene—a much tougher prospect than making their mark in Fort William. Scott set Neil up with a forty-dollar-a-week allowance, found the band somewhere to rehearse, and introduced them to a manager, Martin Onrot.

"Onrot . . . decided that the Squires should change their name to Four to Go."

Onrot was something of an old-school showbiz hustler, but he knew the Toronto scene inside out, and he decided first of all that the Squires should change their name to Four to Go. He struggled to find the band work in the highly competitive clubland of Canada's biggest city, the main problem being that while both folk and rock fraternities were thriving, each had its own distinct style and audience—leaving little chance for the crossover experiments that Neil was forging with his band.

Also, Onrot noted that Neil was spending more and more time hanging out and jamming with local folk artists, and began suggesting he might be better off going it alone as a folk act. Nonetheless, even when Terry Erickson and Bob Clark both left the band out of sheer frustration, Neil continued to pursue his folk-rock dream, bringing in guitarist Jim Ackroyd and drummer Geordie McDonald. But Four to Go would play only one actual gig together—in the United States, at the ski resort of Killington, Vermont. The next day, October 31, he and Ken Koblun were making their way to New York City.

Neil's sudden decision to head for the Big Apple was prompted by the offer of an audition with the leading folk label Elektra for the following week. He also saw it as a chance to catch up with Stephen Stills. They made for the Greenwich Village apartment that Stills had shared with various members of the Au Go-Go singers. There they were welcomed by Richie Furay, who told them that his ex-colleague had moved to California with the idea of forming a

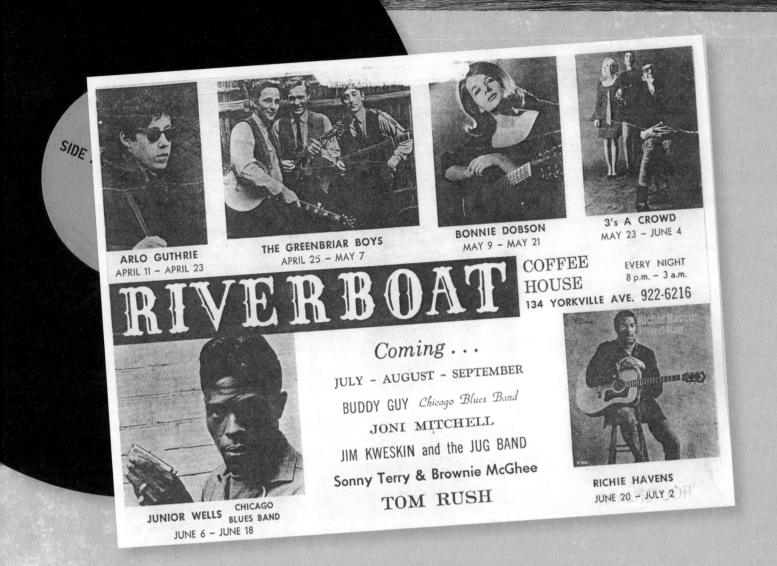

ARLO GUTHRIE
APRIL 11 – APRIL 23

THE GREENBRIAR BOYS
APRIL 25 – MAY 7

BONNIE DOBSON
MAY 9 – MAY 21

3's A CROWD
MAY 23 – JUNE 4

**RIVERBOAT**

COFFEE
HOUSE
134 YORKVILLE AVE. 922-6216

EVERY NIGHT
8 p.m. – 3 a.m.

Coming . . .

JULY – AUGUST – SEPTEMBER

BUDDY GUY *Chicago Blues Band*

JONI MITCHELL

JIM KWESKIN and the JUG BAND

Sonny Terry & Brownie McGhee

TOM RUSH

JUNIOR WELLS CHICAGO
BLUES BAND
JUNE 6 – JUNE 18

RICHIE HAVENS
JUNE 20 – JULY 2

**Flyer for the Riverboat Club, with famous (or soon-to-be-famous) names, including Joni Mitchell, Richie Havens, and Buddy Guy.**

rock 'n' roll band. It struck Young as particularly ironic that while he was heading in a Dylan-inspired solo folk direction, Stills was out west exploring their mutual ambition of a folk-oriented rock ensemble.

As he had with Stills, Neil Young felt an immediate rapport with Furay, the two jamming together and swapping stories and songs. One number, "Nowadays Clancy Can't Even Sing" (which Neil would include in his Elektra session a few days later), was immediately taken up by Furay as part of his regular repertoire on the Village folk circuit.

But despite the potential in "Clancy" and "Sugar Mountain," the seven-song Elektra audition was not a success. Neil delivered a hurried, nervous-sounding performance; as far as the record company was concerned, he was another Dylan wannabe—and Greenwich Village was undoubtedly full of them at the time.

Back in Toronto, Neil threw himself wholeheartedly into the local folk scene centered on the bohemian district of Yorkville, sacking his band in the process. They weren't doing much anyway, and after their vocalist returned tail-between-his-legs, they knew it was all over for Four to Go, almost before it had started. The only person really upset, understandably, was Ken Koblun. He'd stuck by Neil and his ambitions since the earliest days at Earl Grey High, and Young genuinely felt bad about "letting him go." Justifiably or not, Neil laid a lot of the blame for their fate at the door of manager Onrot, whom he felt simply didn't understand what he was trying to achieve.

One person who did understand Neil and his musical vision was Vicky Taylor. A folksinger herself, she was based at the popular Riverboat club in Yorkville, where Neil would hang out and take part in the Monday-night hootenannies. From London, Ontario, Taylor had at just nineteen gravitated to Toronto after a failed marriage, and for a while she shared an apartment with Joan Anderson before the latter married Chuck Mitchell and became Joni Mitchell. Vicky was already something of a name around the Yorkville scene, and as soon as she heard Neil performing she became his self-confessed "number-one fan," promoting and encouraging him at every opportunity.

It was at the Riverboat that Neil had met the attractive raven-haired singer a couple of months after he'd first arrived in Toronto. It was love at first sight, and Neil moved into her apartment that same evening. Taylor helped organize the hootenannies at the Riverboat, and encouraged the manager Bernie Fiedler to give the gangly youth a spot. She was entranced by his voice, saw in his songwriting qualities similar to Bob Dylan, and didn't hesitate to tell anybody who would listen—including Young himself, whose confidence was buoyed by such comparison. So after his disappointment in New York, hers was a perfect—and positive—shoulder to cry on. The couple even teamed up together with a couple of friends to form the Public Futilities, an occasional music-and-satire ensemble that one writer described as a "beatnik review."

**Yonge Street, Yorkville, the hub of Toronto's music scene in the 1960s, with A&A Records, Steel's Tavern, and Sam's Record store.**

## Mynah Birds

Toward the end of 1965, Neil Young had another chance meeting that would change the course of his life. Bruce Palmer was a guitarist playing bass with a local group called the Mynah Birds. They were a rhythm-and-blues band, specializing in Rolling Stones covers and soul music standards, fronted by a flamboyant black vocalist, Ricky James Mathews.

Palmer and Young literally met on the street one day, Bruce remembering Neil as "A tall thin guy carrying an amplifier top on his shoulders and above his head. It was such an odd sight that I stopped him and we talked." The Mynah Birds had just lost their guitar player, and Palmer offered Young the job almost on the spot. The group was being financed by John Craig Eaton, of the multimillion-dollar Eaton retail company that owned stores all over Canada. He saw the band as an investment opportunity—a chance to cash in on the beat group craze—what with their stage uniform of black leather jackets and yellow turtleneck sweaters inspired by their ornithological namesakes. As a consequence, their benefactor poured money into the group, and Neil—at the time playing a folk-style twelve-string semi-acoustic, not suited to amplified lead solos—acquired a shiny new Rickenbacker six-string. With the band grabbing a lot of attention in and around Toronto, it was a new and exhilarating experience for Neil. Although a sideman, he glimpsed real-deal fame when the Mynah Birds landed a recording contract with the mighty Motown Records.

"A tall thin guy carrying an amplifier top on his shoulders, and above his head.

**BRUCE PALMER ON NEIL YOUNG**

## The MYNAH BIRDS

RICK MASON – DRUMS
JOHN TAYLOR – RHYTHM GUITAR
BRUCE PALMER – BASS HARMONICA
RICKIE MATHEWS – VOCAL, MOUTH ORGAN
TOM MORGAN – LEAD GUITAR

A great band, exciting, showy and different. The Mynah Birds released the
Mynah Bird Hop on Columbia. They have appeared on HI TIME, MICKIE A
GO-GO, and other shows throughout Ontario. Their ability to entertain well
is proven each time they step on stage.

The only black-owned major label in the music industry, Motown couldn't
resist the notion of a white rock group with a "black Mick Jagger" up front.
In the Detroit studios, the band members were immediately treated as part of
the famous "hit factory" production line. If something wasn't right, a Motown
session player would correct it; if the vocals were wanting, there were plenty
of house backup singers to fill the gap. As Neil would describe it, "They'd
Motown us!"

The big time at Motown was short-lived, however. While the group was
still working on its debut album, Ricky Mathews was arrested for being absent
without leave from the U.S. Navy—which took everyone in the band by
surprise, as they had all assumed he was Canadian. The singer would reappear
on the Motown label some years later as funk star Rick James, but in the
meantime the Mynah Birds were no more.

So after a brief sojourn licking his wounds back in Toronto, Neil Young's
thoughts turned once again to his deep-seated folk-rock ambitions, and to
Stephen Stills, who was still pursuing the dream out on the West Coast.

two West Coast Dreamin'

An early TV appearance by
Buffalo Springfield, after Jim
Fielder (second from the right)
had replaced Bruce Palmer
on bass guitar.

LTHOUGH Neil Young's musical vision involved a fusion of folk and rock, the details of which even he couldn't exactly envisage early in 1966, "folk rock" as a pop phenomenon had been flourishing for the previous half year or so. Triggered largely by Bob Dylan's first "electric" album (the opening side of *Bringing It All Back Home*), and marked famously by his controversial appearance at the Newport Folk Festival in July 1965, it first hit the singles chart with the Top 40 entry of "Subterranean Homesick Blues" (from *Bringing It All Back Home*) in May 1965.

But it was the cover of another song from that album, "Mr. Tambourine Man" by the West Coast group the Byrds, that topped the charts in June and inspired potential folkies-turned-rockers like Stephen Stills and Neil Young. With Sonny & Cher's "I Got You Babe" hitting #1 in July, Dylan's "Like a Rolling Stone" #2 in August, and the Byrds' "Turn, Turn, Turn," another chart-topper in November, by the end of the year the trend was in full swing. As "California Dreamin'" by the Mamas & the Papas crashed into the Top 5 in February 1966, the song's message of escape from the cold northern winter to West Coast sunshine couldn't have been more timely for Neil Young.

## On the Road

Now without a band, Neil and Bruce Palmer considered what to do next. They spent most of their time hanging out at the Cellar Club, a Yorkville coffeehouse where they'd sometimes performed as a duo prior to the Mynah Birds' Motown fiasco. The club was managed by three young women, out-of-towners who'd all been attracted by the bohemian life in Yorkville. Painter Beverly Davies, aspiring singer Tannis Neiman, and Janine Hollingshead occasionally performed together as Tannis & Two, and would now be party to Young and Palmer's escape plan.

With the forced disbandment of the Mynah Birds, Neil had unofficially inherited the band's equipment, not being inclined to return it to their former backer John Craig Eaton. His idea was to sell or pawn most of it, the proceeds going toward a road trip to California, where he and Palmer had now set their sights. The word quickly spread around the Yorkville scene that the two were preparing to leave for the West Coast, and were looking for fellow passengers to help subsidize their journey. The three girls running the Cellar, all anxious for a change of scenery (and at least two of whom, Neiman and Davies, would admit to having a crush on Neil), were immediate volunteers, along with another Cellar Club regular, Judy Mack.

As with his attitude toward Eaton's investment, Young was quite ruthless when it came to making sure the trip to California was going to happen. The participants all had to pay their way, and when it transpired that Bev Davies had no cash, she was immediately replaced—on the day prior to departure—by a young guy named Mike Gallagher. Not a musician, Gallagher claimed his place purely on the grounds that he had gasoline money to contribute. Neil had acquired a new vehicle for the epic journey—or new to him, at least.

# "Buffalo Springfield was very special in so many ways."

**AHMET ERTEGUN**

The first PR photo of
Buffalo Springfield—with
Neil Young nodding off—
taken in September 1966.

It was another secondhand hearse, this time a 1953 Pontiac. His previous transport, Mort, had finally given up the ghost during the Squires' last days in Fort William, so this one he christened Mort Two. It was snowing as the six adventurers set off from outside the Cellar Club, on March 22, 1966; the West Coast seemed even more appealing than ever.

After persuading customs officials at the U.S. border that they had no visas because they were just making a shortcut to visit his mother in Winnipeg, Neil imagined it would be plain sailing. But the trip quickly developed into a series of near-catastrophes. Their initial optimism and general good vibes soon gave way to petty bickering and seemingly endless arguments, as one delay followed another.

High on amphetamines most of the time, Neil did virtually all the driving while the others got stoned on Bruce Palmer's generous supply of marijuana. Exhaustion soon took its toll, and Neil's increasingly frequent epileptic condition (which had first been diagnosed back in 1963) added to the problem. In Albuquerque, New Mexico, Young was forced to rest for three days. While they waited for him to recover, Janine Hollingshead suffered burns from a gas stove accident, followed by an attack that the hospital said was caused by kidney stones. And to add to an atmosphere of uncertainty, Tannis Neiman secretly suspected she might be pregnant.

By this time Neil was well enough to move on, and insisted they do so right away. But Hollingshead and Neiman opted to stay on in Albuquerque, getting

work in a local coffeehouse. And according to Hollingshead, it wasn't entirely voluntary: "They dumped us in Albuquerque." Mike Gallagher, too, had had enough, and jumped ship at the same time, returning to Toronto after a few days.

Neil, Bruce Palmer, and Judy Mack finally made it to Los Angeles on April 1, April Fools' Day. While Judy became quickly disillusioned with the City of Angels and all that Hollywood offered, wiring home for money for the return bus fare to Canada, the boys spent days seeking out Stephen Stills—the prime objective of their cross-country odyssey. Almost without a cent between them, they slept in Mort Two when the cops weren't moving them on, and earned a dollar a trip using the old hearse as a bizarre unofficial taxi.

All the time, they would ask in bars and coffee shops, up and down Sunset Strip, around Hollywood Boulevard—wherever—if anyone knew of Stephen Stills, or his whereabouts. After a few futile days they decided to give up the search and head north to San Francisco, where they knew there was a vibrant music scene, probably more accommodating to two newcomers with no means of support. It was at that point, as they drove down Sunset Boulevard (legend has it they were actually on their way to the northbound highway out of town), that Neil Young crossed paths once again with Stephen Stills.

Neil, his dress reflecting the Native American look he favored in the late 1960s.

## The Meeting

Inspired by the success story of the Byrds, Stephen Stills had decided to head for California in the fall of 1965, not long before Neil Young had come seeking him out in Greenwich Village. His first days in Hollywood were far from successful. He briefly played with the singer-songwriter Van Dyke Parks, and also failed an audition for the Monkees! (Apparently the company putting the TV series together thought his teeth weren't even enough, so Stills recommended a friend from Greenwich Village, Peter Tork, to take his place.)

But still harboring grandiose ideas about forming a band, he managed to entice his former Au Go-Go partner Richie Furay to join him from New York, with promises of a newly formed group ready to take off. When Furay arrived in LA he found no such thing, but Stills had made some useful contacts nevertheless. He'd even sold a song, "Sit Down I Think I Love You," which became a minor Top 40 hit for the Mojo Men. More importantly, he convinced

record producer Barry Friedman (aka Frazier Mohawk) to sign him and
Furay to a management deal.

Traffic was bad, almost at a standstill, as Richie Furay drove Stills and
Friedman along Sunset Boulevard on that fateful day in early April 1966.
Suddenly Furay spotted a black hearse with Ontario number plates going in the
opposite direction: "I remembered that Stills had told me that Neil drove a black
hearse. So we chased him down." As an excited Stills confirmed that he was
sure it was Young—who else would be driving an old Canadian hearse?—Furay
made a quick U-turn and drew up behind the Pontiac.

Furay honked the horn and Stephen yelled, and in the hearse Palmer turned
around, amazed as he realized that the man they'd been seeking out for days
had now found them. Both vehicles pulled into a parking lot, and within a few
minutes it was clear that here was the nucleus of the band Young and Stills had
dreamed of almost a year earlier.

After the parking lot meeting, Friedman was elated that Stills's proposed
band would at last take shape. He arranged to pay them a dollar a day toward
food, found them somewhere to stay, and let them rehearse in his house on
Fountain Avenue. All they needed now was a name—and, of course,
a drummer.

## Birth of a Band

The speed with which the new band got together musically was astonishing—
just a couple of days' rehearsals, according to Neil Young, before they were
settling into a unified sound. Even the drummer issue was resolved almost
immediately: After three or four days, Barry Friedman brought in Dewey
Martin. Another Canadian, with an impressive track record as a session player
in Nashville, Martin had played behind some of the biggest names in country
music before moving to the West Coast and working with the bluegrass-
oriented Dillards. He was looking for another regular job when he heard about
the new rock group Friedman was managing, and agreed to come over to
Fountain Avenue for an audition. He fit in perfectly, and the bonus was that
he could sing, too.

And it was on the day of Martin's audition that they agreed on a name
for the new band. A day or so before, Neil and Barry Friedman had noticed
a steamroller parked outside the house, with a nameplate that read BUFFALO,
SPRINGFIELD ROLLER CO., SPRINGFIELD, OHIO. They quietly went outside and
removed the sign, which they mounted on the living room wall; when the
drummer arrived and asked the name of the band, they said that was it, showing
him the sign—Buffalo Springfield.

Friedman was well connected on the Los Angeles scene, and almost before
his new protégés had played a gig he had persuaded the Byrds' management
to offer Springfield a support slot on a short tour of Southern California. The
Byrds were the kings of Hollywood as far as rock music was concerned, and

Buffalo Springfield in a
contrived "pop group" shot
typical of record company PR
at the time.

The "Buffolo Springfield" steamroller nameplate from which the band took their name.

their current hit in April 1966, "Eight Miles High," marked their move from folk rockers to psychedelic superstars.

After a couple of open rehearsal showcases—their debut gig was at the famed Troubadour in Hollywood on April 11, 1966—the first major appearance by Buffalo Springfield was at the bottom of a Byrds bill at the Swing Auditorium, National Orange Showgrounds, San Bernardino. It was April 15, just two weeks after Neil Young and Bruce Palmer had hit the West Coast, and only ten days from their meeting with Stephen Stills and Richie Furay.

Things moved just as fast after the brief trek with the Byrds. Chris Hillman, the Byrds' bass player, persuaded the owners of LA's most prestigious rock club, the Whisky a Go Go, to give the band an audition. The seven-week residency that followed, running from early May to mid-June 1966, really helped to raise their profile. Although they were playing support to big-name acts including Captain Beefheart, Love, and the Doors, it was Neil and Stephen's folk rock combined with Richie's country feel and Bruce's soul-tinged bass that created the buzz.

As word spread about the sensational new band, the club was packed every night—and not with just the rock glitterati who came to see them, the Mamas & the Papas, Sonny & Cher, and so on, but more importantly, the talent scouts and A&R men from the major record labels.

In his autobiographical song "Don't Be Denied," Neil would recall the clamor as companies vied with one another to sign them: "There we were on the Sunset Strip, playing our songs for the highest bid." And the bidding did get high. Dunhill Records was first, with an offer of a five-thousand-dollar advance, followed by Warner Bros., which proposed double that amount—but there were more to come.

Meanwhile, Barry Friedman had brought in Richard "Dickie" Davis, a neighbor (and lighting man at top LA clubs, including the Whisky), to advise on the contracts on offer. Conflict arose between the two, however, when Friedman thought the band should settle for a deal with Elektra and Davis felt the band could do better; considering the various bids flying around, he convinced them that the sky was the limit. With Davis driving for the highest bidder, Friedman felt he was being sidelined in the process, and eventually departed. The band would admit they couldn't have done without his help in those early few weeks, but excused themselves on grounds of seemingly necessary pragmatism. Naturally, Freidman didn't take it quite as philosophically, feeling he'd been let down by all sides.

Davis, however, was also beginning to feel out of his depth as the stakes got higher, and called on the advice of Charlie Greene and Brian Stone, the heavyweight management team who looked after Sonny & Cher. Greene and Stone were the personification of 1960s showbiz flash, driving around LA in a shiny black Lincoln limousine or holding court in their plush Sunset Boulevard offices, with money seemingly no object. To the naive youngsters in Buffalo Springfield, this was what the rock 'n' roll high life was all about.

Buffalo Springfield '67 with (left to right) Martin, Fielder, Young, Furay, and Stills.

**The original Springfield lineup in front of a "psychedelic" poster for a gig supporting the Turtles.**

With five singles in the US Top 20 chart in less than a year, plus an album at #2, Sonny & Cher were Greene and Stone's biggest asset. All but one of the hits were on Atlantic Records' subsidiary label Atco, so when Charlie Greene called about a sensational new band they were promoting, Atlantic boss Ahmet Ertegun listened.

Founded by Ertegun with his brother Nesuhi, Atlantic had long been at the forefront of rhythm and blues, jazz, and soul—basically black American music, with names like Ray Charles, Ruth Brown, and the Drifters among its long roster of best-sellers. Sonny & Cher were only the second white act signed to the label since its inception almost twenty years before.

Other than Greene's bluster, all that Ahmet Ertegun had to go on was a demo tape that Buffalo Springfield had made at Capitol studios with Barry Friedman, and the general buzz trickling out of Los Angeles about the band. The Atlantic honcho met with the band in Greene and Stone's office, and there was an immediate rapport between the eager musicians and the politely mannered, well-dressed, but very hip record executive from New York City.

"I guess they were quite impressionable young people," Ertegun would recall, "because they were amazed that I knew a lot of the music they were talking about, and they certainly seemed to feel that I was, in any event, a different kind of record executive. . . . We got on very well, they seemed to be happy with me, so we were able to sign them."

Atlantic agreed to pay a twelve-thousand-dollar advance for Buffalo Springfield's recordings, which were to be made through Greene and Stone's own label York/Pala, the band having signed to the pair in a full management, recording, and publishing agreement.

As a consequence, when they went into Gold Star Studios in Hollywood to begin making their debut recordings in June 1966, it was not with the producer of their choice—Jack Nitzsche—but with the inexperienced Charles Greene and Brian Stone behind the control desk.

## Buffalo Springfield

The first tracks they recorded were destined for a debut single release, with Stephen Stills's song "Go and Say Goodbye" planned for the A-side, and Neil's "Nowadays Clancy Can't Even Sing" for the flip. Right away, under the auspices of Greene and Stone, Neil began to feel sidelined when they decided that Richie Furay should sing "Clancy" on the single. The composer was a little miffed, but reticent to make a big deal out of it—Furay, after all, had been

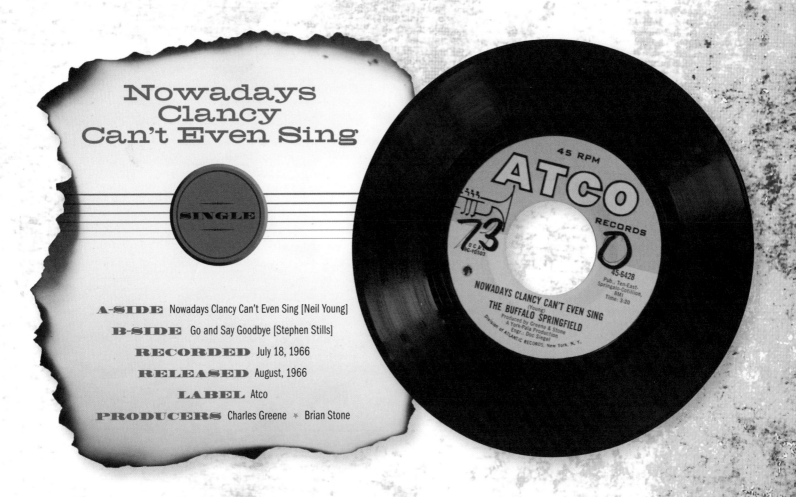

**Nowadays Clancy Can't Even Sing**

**SINGLE**

**A-SIDE** Nowadays Clancy Can't Even Sing [Neil Young]

**B-SIDE** Go and Say Goodbye [Stephen Stills]

**RECORDED** July 18, 1966

**RELEASED** August, 1966

**LABEL** Atco

**PRODUCERS** Charles Greene ✦ Brian Stone

singing the song in his solo repertoire since adopting it after their first meeting in New York. And Young was pleased to see one of his songs going out on the band's first release—especially when Atlantic decided to promote it as the A-side.

On July 25, a week or so before the single's release, Buffalo Springfield played bottom of the bill at a Rolling Stones date at the twenty-thousand-seater Hollywood Bowl. It was a marvelous opportunity to plug the single, which swiftly reached the #25 spot in the local charts, but did nothing elsewhere. Its failure nationwide was put down to the lyrics (a self-analysis on Neil's part) being deemed too "serious" for the pop-single market. Others recognized that such subjective feelings might have been most effectively expressed by Neil Young himself.

As the recording sessions continued through August and September, Neil felt increasingly marginalized as Greene and Stone delegated Richie to sing the majority of his songs. Clearly his own singing voice wasn't as "good," in the conventional sense at least, as that of Stephen or Richie, but he did feel it suited his own songs, which had been written in most cases with his limitations and eccentric delivery in mind.

Neil Young

The two producers, however, thinking more of the commerciality of their upcoming product, deemed Neil's voice "too weird" to handle most of the material, even with songs he had composed. One exception was "Burned," a crowd-pleaser on their live gigs, which would be the first studio recording of Neil Young singing lead. The amphetamine-assisted recording would also be the Springfield's next single, backed with Stills's "Everybody's Wrong" and released at the same time as the album in December '66—only to be withdrawn soon afterward. Neil's other featured track was "Out of My Mind," which highlighted the unique strength of his vocal style and the confessional lyrics that would become a Neil Young trademark.

After completing the album—not without tribulation on the technical side, with Greene and Stone's production techniques leaving a lot to be desired—the Springfield trailed its release with increasingly high-powered live dates. These included a return to the Whisky as headliners, a support date with the Turtles, three nights at San Francisco's all-important Fillmore Auditorium (a key venue of the emerging alternative music scene), followed by another week at the Whisky.

A book of Neil Young sheet music, published by Warner Brothers in 1974.

And as the band became more confident, their growing fan base began to notice, even at those early gigs, visible tensions in the group. It was clearly part of their appeal that each member's individual characteristics came across onstage, but there was also a marked competitive spirit, verging on rivalry, particularly between Stephen and Neil. Stephen obviously wanted to be the archetypal rock star, while Neil—even then, in anticipation of their debut album and the success it might represent—seemed content for his artistic ambitions to be fulfilled, rather than yearning for the trappings of celebrity.

# Buffalo Springfield

ATCO

MONO 33-200

# Buffalo Springfield

**ALBUM**

Although the album has its deficiencies in the production department, at the time it boded well for the future of Buffalo Springfield. Cited here are the track listings before the 1967 re-release (pictured opposite) when "Baby Don't Scold Me" was replaced by "For What It's Worth" in the wake of the latter's chart success. Five of the songs are Neil Young compositions, although he only actually sings on two tracks, "Burned" and "Out Of My Mind." "Nowaday's Clancy Can't Even Sing" was the song that Neil had taught Richie Furay in New York before they teamed up with Stills on the West Coast, and preempted the album as the group's debut single.

### ⇒ SIDE ONE ⇐

Go and Say Goodbye [Stephen Stills] ★ Sit Down I Think
I Love You [Stephen Stills] ★ Leave [Stephen Stills]
Nowadays Clancy Can't Even Sing [Neil Young] ★ Hot Dusty Roads
[Stephen Stills] ★ Everybody's Wrong [Stephen Stills]

### ⇒ SIDE TWO ⇐

Flying on the Ground Is Wrong [Neil Young]
Burned [Neil Young] ★ Do I Have to Come Right Out and Say It
[Neil Young] ★ Baby Don't Scold Me [Stephen Stills] ★
Out of My Mind [Neil Young] ★ Pay the Price [Stephen Stills]

### ⇒ RECORDED ⇐

June—September 1966, Gold Star Studios, Los Angeles;
Columbia Recording Studio, Los Angeles

### ⇒ RELEASED ⇐

December 5, 1966 [re-released April, 1967]

### ⇒ PERSONNEL ⇐

Neil Young (vocals, guitar, harmonica, piano) ★ Stephen Stills
(vocals, guitar, keyboards) ★ Richie Furay (vocals, guitar)
Bruce Palmer (bass guitar) ★ Dewey Martin (drums, vocals)

### ⇒ LABEL ⇐

Atco

### ⇒ PRODUCERS ⇐

Charles Greene ★ Brian Stone

# Burned

### SINGLE

**A-SIDE** Burned [Neil Young]
**B-SIDE** Everybody's Wrong [Stephen Stills]
**RECORDED** August, 1966
**RELEASED** December, 1966
**LABEL** Atco
**PRODUCERS** Charles Greene ✳ Brian Stone

Part of Young's frustration was that his role was primarily that of guitar player rather than vocalist, even though his songs were a key part of the group's repertoire. Onstage Stills would even, embarrassingly for Neil, apologize when the guitarist had the odd vocal spot. Even so, it was very much Stills and Young's band, with Richie Furay the man in the middle, singing Neil's songs while he harbored songwriting ambitions of his own: "I think they had me sing a couple of Neil's songs just to appease me," Furay recalled, "to keep me satisfied, because I had all the songs that made it onto the second album [already] written when we recorded the first one."

Despite the album's shady production, and rumored rifts already appearing within the band, Ahmet Ertegun was convinced the group had a great future, the diversity of talent in Young, Stills, and Furay its main asset. "Buffalo Springfield was very special in so many ways," the Atlantic chief would state many years later. "First of all, the songs they wrote didn't resemble anything that anybody else was doing. They also had three outstanding lead singers who were also great guitar players—Neil Young, Stephen Stills, and Richie Furay. I mean, a rock 'n' roll band is lucky if it has one good singer and one guitar player who can really play—that alone can make them a great band."

Released on December 5, 1966, *Buffalo Springfield* met with favorable reviews, but initially sales were disappointing. As well as praising the beat-group-influenced pop of Stephen Stills's tracks, the newly emergent rock press in magazines like *Crawdaddy* was particularly impressed by Neil Young's compositions, especially the spectacular "Flying on the Ground Is Wrong." But critical plaudits plus a loyal West Coast following were not enough to shift copies nationwide in any great numbers, and chart-wise the album looked like it might well disappear without a trace by the end of the year.

Another publicity set-piece in the 1960s pop publicity mode.

## "For What It's Worth"

By late 1966, the youth-led counterculture was rearing its head across America (and to a lesser extent the rest of the Western world), with California as its epicenter. The loose-knit "movement" (if it could be called such) was united by its relaxed sexual attitudes, the widespread use of mind-altering substances, and music—the subsequently overused slogan "Sex, drugs, and rock 'n' roll" did indeed apply to a burgeoning section of American society. Adding to which, opposition to the war in Vietnam (and the consequent drafting of thousands of young men into military service) often brought the younger generation into direct confrontation with the powers that be.

It wasn't an antiwar protest that had brought thousands of teenagers into conflict with the LAPD police force on November 12, but a growing resentment at general harassment by the cops, and hundreds of arrests for minor offenses like jaywalking and loitering. This worsening of relations was a result of attempts to "clean up" the Sunset Strip area by local businesses, including the threatened closure of various music venues. A mass protest was organized outside one of the clubs, Pandora's Box, and very soon over a thousand kids were facing the police eyeball-to-eyeball. In what observers judged to be a gross overreaction, the police charged the youngsters with batons, beating many to the ground, and arresting many more.

Shocked by the so-called riots, Stephen Stills wrote a song reflecting the passion and frustration of the youthful protesters, and on December 5, the day

## For What It's Worth

**SINGLE**

**A-SIDE** For What It's Worth [Stephen Stills]
**B-SIDE** Do I Have to Come Right Out and Say It [Neil Young]
**RECORDED** December 5, 1966 (A-side)/August 1966 (B-side)
**RELEASED** January 9, 1967
**LABEL** Atco
**PRODUCERS** Charles Greene ✳ Brian Stone

their album was released, the Springfield went into the studios to record it as their next single. With Neil's "Do I Have to Come Right Out and Say It" as the B-side, "For What It's Worth" was released on January 6, 1967, and by the middle of February had entered the *Billboard* Top 40, where it soon climbed to the #7 position.

The single helped raise the band's profile in the UK a little when it was released in February; a review in the influential music paper *Melody Maker* read: "A warm but mumbling performance from this American group. Interesting arrangement, very American guitars and English vocals. Could easily be a hit." Nevertheless the single failed to make an impact in Britain, where the band remained relatively unknown.

But more important, the single's success prompted Atco/Atlantic to withdraw the debut album, replace Stills's track "Baby Don't Scold Me" with the hit single as the opener, and re-release *Buffalo Springfield* in April 1967. This time the record managed a modest improvement in sales, making it to #80 in the album best sellers.

## Manhattan to Monterey

The week "For What It's Worth" was released, early in January, Buffalo Springfield traveled to New York City to play a ten-day residency at Ondine's, a small club with an "in-crowd" clientele of record industry people and recording stars. But what should have been a sensational NYC launching pad for the West Coast band—the great soul singer Otis Redding was among the big names who got up to jam with them that week—soon deteriorated into a series of disasters.

At one show, physical violence broke out in front of an astonished audience when Stephen Stills asked Bruce Palmer to turn his volume down, only to be slapped across the face by the irate bass player. As he would describe in *Rolling Stone* magazine, Stills "put him through the drums" before the rest of the band "just flipped right out."

On another evening at Ondine's, Neil suffered a particularly severe epileptic blackout. He'd been having seizures with increasing frequency since the summer of 1966, the attacks often taking place when he was onstage, sometimes even mid-song. This time, suddenly aware of what was about to overtake him, he ran off the stage, collapsing in a hallway before someone stuck a pencil between his teeth to prevent him from swallowing his tongue. Sometimes the fits would occur without any warning at all—leaving audiences perplexed, wondering whether it was part of some bizarre stage act.

Between the dramas at the club, the band was able to squeeze in some recording at Atlantic's New York studio, cutting an initial version of a new Neil Young song with a view to their next single. "Mr. Soul," addressing the pressures of stardom (though only a recent experience for Young and his

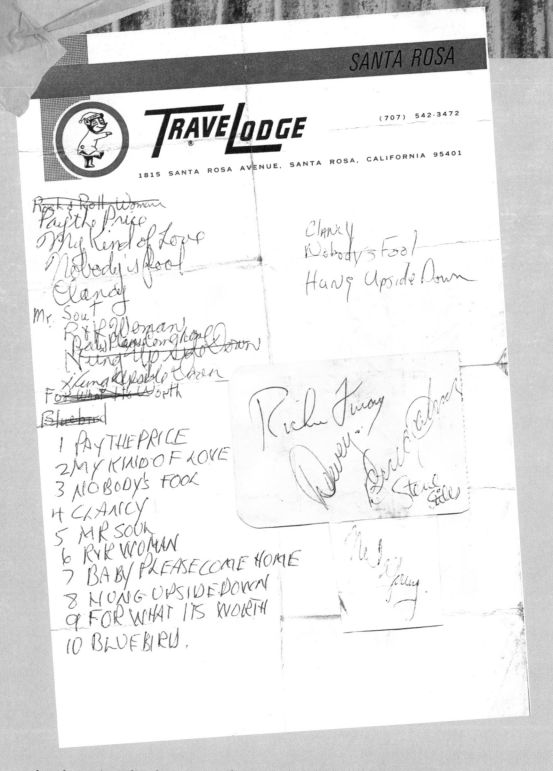

A Buffalo Springfield set list scribbled on motel notepaper during a tour.

Opposite: Bootleg versions of *Stampede*, an album which was never officially released.

bandmates), utilized a guitar riff seemingly lifted straight from the Rolling Stones' "Satisfaction." Otis Redding, who was in the studio during the taping, was about to release his own cover of the Stones song as a single, and suggested he might record Young's number for a follow-up release. Without thinking twice, Neil turned the idea down flatly.

The final catastrophe during their short excursion to the Big Apple occurred at the Wellington Hotel, where the band was staying, when Bruce Palmer managed to get arrested due to possession of a large quantity of marijuana. He was detained in jail, then deported back to Canada. The band, meanwhile, had hightailed it back to California.

Losing a key member was potentially disastrous for the group, and as soon as they hit the West Coast they started the urgent search for a substitute. The situation was so desperate that for one TV date, the *Hollywood Palace* show, Dick Davis (who'd been relegated to road manager since Greene and Stone's takeover) "played" the bass with his back to the camera, while the band lip-synched to a pre-recorded track. Ken Forssi from the band Love sat in for Bruce Palmer on a temporary basis while the group tried to find a permanent replacement. Neil contacted his old comrade Ken Koblun, who joined the group for a series of one-night stands, before being in turn replaced by former Mother of Invention Jim Fielder, whose tenure lasted over three months. Fielder was eventually dropped, completely abruptly—"No notice, no nothing" as he put it—when Bruce Palmer suddenly reappeared. Regardless of whether the errant member's reentry into the United States was legal or not, the band—especially Stills—welcomed him back into the fold like he'd never been gone.

Throughout this period the band members were spending time in a variety of recording studios, ostensibly preparing their next album. Tracks were laid down (though most were never completed) and artwork was prepared, ready for a release later in the year. The forthcoming LP even had a name, *Stampede*, but it was never to be released beyond various bootleg versions years later. One thing that did come out of the studio, however, was the next single.

In the wake of his success with "For What It's Worth," Stephen Stills wanted the A-side to be his new song "Bluebird." Neil, perhaps naturally, felt it was his turn, and had finalized an

amended version of "Mr. Soul" with that in mind. Stills, apart from seeing his song as a follow-up to the recent hit, felt that the Young number sounded too much like "Satisfaction." In the event, Stills won the day, with his song the top side and Neil's the flip. But everyone in the group lost out in the long run, when Neil announced at the beginning of June, as a result of the bickering over the single, that he was leaving the band.

The shock announcement couldn't have come at a worse time. As well as now going out for a thousand dollars a night, the band was enjoying national exposure at last, with prime-time TV slots scheduled, an offer to appear at the upcoming Monterey Pop Festival, and a spot as the only rock group on the prestigious Newport Folk Festival. Initially Neil agreed to fulfill already-booked dates on the East Coast plus a spot on the network *Tonight Show* hosted by Johnny Carson, but just when the band was about to leave he simply disappeared.

The East Coast gigs were a disaster. The kids were shouting "Where's Neil?" and Bruce Palmer had yet to fit back in properly. At one venue in Boston, roadie Dick Davis even agreed to take a reduced fee, the lackluster performance by the four-piece Springfield was so badly received. Back in Los Angeles, as "Bluebird" and "Mr. Soul" hit the stores, the thoughts of the band were not so much on the pop charts as on what they were going to do for the Monterey Festival, which they all agreed they couldn't afford to miss.

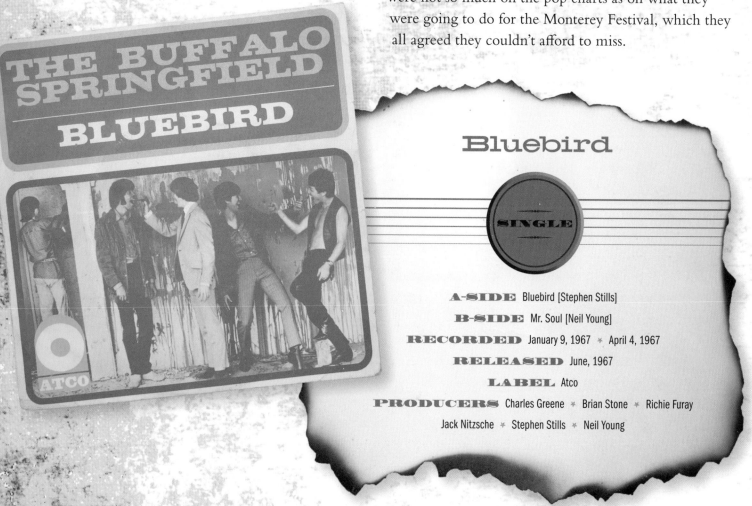

## Bluebird

**A-SIDE** Bluebird [Stephen Stills]
**B-SIDE** Mr. Soul [Neil Young]
**RECORDED** January 9, 1967 ✴ April 4, 1967
**RELEASED** June, 1967
**LABEL** Atco
**PRODUCERS** Charles Greene ✴ Brian Stone ✴ Richie Furay
Jack Nitzsche ✴ Stephen Stills ✴ Neil Young

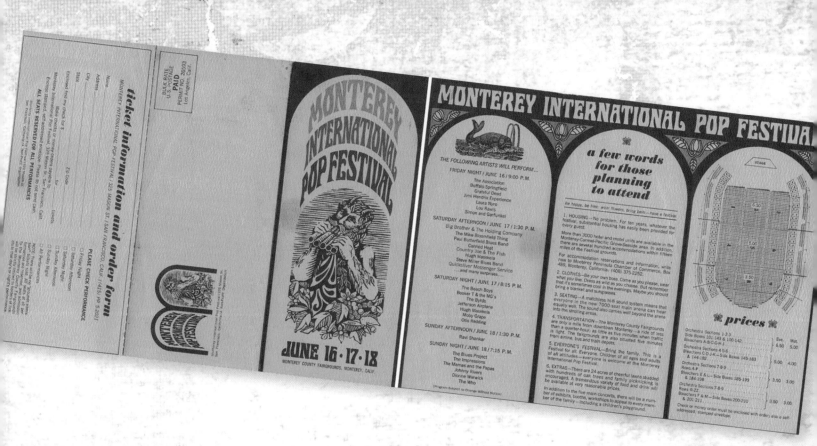

Eventually Buffalo Springfield would take the stage at Monterey as a six-piece, immediately before the Who on the final day, Sunday June 18, 1967. They appeared with Doug Hastings recruited as their new lead guitarist, and David Crosby of the Byrds helping out on rhythm guitar. Crosby made his appearance with the group deliberately low-key, so as not to alienate his fellow Byrds or confuse the audience—or indeed encourage the press to start "Byrd to Buffalo" rumors. Nevertheless, with him up there by the side of Stephen Stills, it augured important things to come.

Flyer and ticket order form for the now-legendary Monterey Pop Festival in 1967, the first great gathering of the "peace and love" hippie era.

## Buffalo Springfield Again

Through June and July, while members of Buffalo Springfield were struggling to find their artistic feet without Neil Young, the latter was developing a close working relationship with producer Jack Nitzsche. A protégé of the legendary Phil Spector, who had gone on to work with the Rolling Stones among others, Nitzsche had begun experimenting with Neil on various tracks before the singer had left Springfield. The collaborations were partly responsible for Young's departure from the band, with the producer encouraging him to branch out as a soloist, and Neil realizing it was a far more creative environment than the studio battleground with Stephen Stills.

One result of their extensive sessions together that summer was "Expecting to Fly," a mystical-sounding epic from Young, introduced with sweeping strings and reflecting the sounds of psychedelia currently swirling around the collective rock consciousness, inspired by the Beach Boys' *Pet Sounds* and the just-released *Sgt. Pepper's Lonely Hearts Club Band* by the Beatles. Although put together prior

to Young's departure from the band, the track involved no other members of Buffalo Springfield, and in that respect was a potent showcase for Neil Young as a solo artist. Nevertheless, the track would appear on the next Springfield album, after Neil had rejoined the band in early August.

Despite Jack Nitzsche's exhortation that he should strike out alone, there seemed no immediate prospect of that happening; Young was still involved contractually with Buffalo Springfield, and with a new album in the offing he decided to try to reinstate himself. According to Dewey Martin, it was a very humble Neil Young who approached the band, sitting in on a couple of gigs, before they finally welcomed him back and fired his replacement Doug Hastings. The band divided its time over the next few weeks between concert dates and adding the final touches to their next album. While more of a compilation of individual contributions than a fully integrated group project, the resulting long-player *Buffalo Springfield Again* was certainly their most accomplished release.

There were three tracks by Richie Furay (now singing his own songs rather than Neil's), and four by Stephen Stills—including his seminal "Bluebird" and "Rock & Roll Woman." Neil Young was represented by "Mr. Soul," the lavishly elegant "Expecting to Fly," and the extraordinary "Broken Arrow," a six-minute sound collage full of tempo changes, special effects, and dubbed instrumental passages. In "Broken Arrow" Young addressed three themes of modern America: the cult of celebrity, teenage angst, and romantic love. He dedicated the song to Ken Koblun, his old colleague since high school, whom he'd sacked from the Springfield a year earlier.

With over twenty guest instrumentalists and vocalists across its ten tracks, including such luminaries as guitarist James Burton, drummer Jim Gordon, Jack Nitzsche on electric piano, and David Crosby singing backing vocals on "Rock & Roll Woman," *Buffalo Springfield Again* was well received and sold steadily after its release at the end of October. Things were looking good for the band once again, but that wasn't to last long.

Opposite: Richie Furay and Stephen Stills fronting Buffalo Springfield onstage.

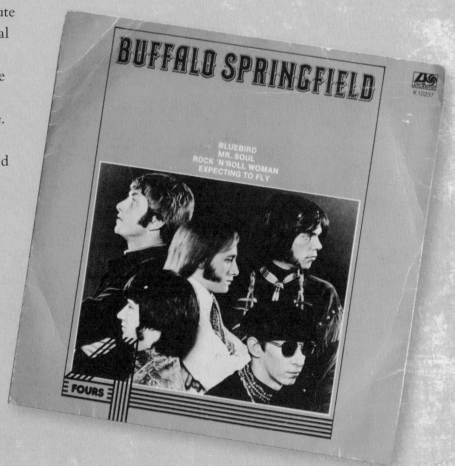

# Buffalo Springfield Again

**ALBUM**

Representing Buffalo Springfield at their peak, Neil Young's contributions—including the masterpieces "Learning to Fly" and "Broken Arrow"—set him as equal to the other members in both the songwriting and vocal stakes. A heavyweight cast of guest personnel, including among the luminaries Elvis Presley's guitarist-to-be James Burton, ensured that Atlantic's faith in the band seemed well placed. Things would not go as planned, of course, but here the only misjudgment is drummer Dewey Martin's vocalizing on Richie Furay's "Good Time Boy." Name checks in the original sleeve notes included Hank Williams, Shadows' guitarist Hank Marvin, Otis Redding, and acid rockers Vanilla Fudge—a testament to the eclectic sweep of influences that informed the band's approach.

## ⋆ SIDE ONE ⋆

Mr. Soul [Neil Young] ⋆ A Child's Claim to Fame [Richie Furay] ⋆ Everydays [Stephen Stills] ⋆ Expecting to Fly [Neil Young] ⋆ Bluebird [Stephen Stills]

## ⋆ SIDE TWO ⋆

Hung Upside Down [Stephen Stills] ⋆ Sad Memory [Richie Furay] ⋆ Good Time Boy [Richie Furay] ⋆ Rock & Roll Woman [Stephen Stills] ⋆ Broken Arrow [Neil Young]

## ⋆ RECORDED ⋆

January–September 1967

## ⋆ RELEASED ⋆

October 30, 1967

## ⋆ PERSONNEL ⋆

Neil Young (vocals, guitar, harmonica) ⋆ Stephen Stills (vocals, guitar, organ, piano, keyboards, rhythm guitar) ⋆ Richie Furay (vocals, guitar, rhythm guitar) ⋆ Bruce Palmer (bass guitar) ⋆ Dewey Martin (drums, vocals)

## ⋆ ADDITIONAL PERSONNEL ⋆

Norris Badeaux (baritone saxophone) ⋆ Hal Blaine (drums) ⋆ Merry Clayton (vocals) ⋆ James Burton (Dobro, guitar) ⋆ Charlie Chin (banjo) ⋆ David Crosby (backing vocal on Rock & Roll Woman) ⋆ Jim Fielder (bass) ⋆ Jim Gordon (drums) ⋆ Doug Hastings (guitar) ⋆ Brenda Holloway (vocal) ⋆ Patrice Holloway (vocal) ⋆ Jim Horn (clarinet) ⋆ Gloria Jones (vocal) ⋆ Carol Kaye (bass) ⋆ Shirley Matthews (vocal) ⋆ Harvey Newmark (bass) ⋆ Gracia Nitzsche (vocal) ⋆ Jack Nitzsche (electric piano) ⋆ Don Randi (piano, harpsichord) ⋆ Chris Sarns (guitar) ⋆ Ryss Titelman (guitar) ⋆ Bobby West (bass)

## ⋆ LABEL ⋆

Atco

## ⋆ PRODUCERS ⋆

Ahmet Ertegun ⋆ Richie Furay ⋆ Charles Greene ⋆ Dewey Martin ⋆ Jack Nitzsche ⋆ Stephen Stills ⋆ Brian Stone ⋆ Neil Young

3856

> ## "They only lasted a couple of years, but in those two years I would have sued to hear them play.
>
> **AHMET ERTEGUN**

## Last Time Around

In January 1968, turmoil ensued when Bruce Palmer was deported, for a second time, after another drug bust. This time he was replaced by Jim Messina, who knew the band well, having worked as recording engineer on some of the recent album. This time Palmer's exit was permanent, but without him some of the internal dynamic that made Buffalo Springfield unique was also gone.

With the departure soon after of longtime aide, right-hand man, and road manager Dick Davis, Neil Young was increasingly disillusioned. He started missing gigs, leaving Stephen Stills to handle all the lead vocals, and after the chart failure of "Expecting to Fly" when it was released as a single, he again considered leaving the band.

Despite the ensuing chaos, through the opening months of 1968 the Springfield were booked into recording sessions, but neither Young nor Stephen Stills was particularly interested in the results. The sessions were supervised by Jim Messina, who complained that he found it impossible to get everyone in the same place at the same time.

As if the fates were contriving the band's destruction—or the members planning their own self-destruction—on March 20 another drug bust took place, this time involving Young, Messina, Richie Furay, and English guitar hero Eric Clapton.

They were holed up in a ranch house that Stills was living in, in rural Topanga Canyon. Clapton had showed up, and a party ensued with everyone getting high and jamming at full volume. Neighbors complained, and when the volume still wasn't turned down, the police were called.

The raid came swiftly and surely a short while later. Dewey Martin had left the party before the cops arrived, and Stephen Stills managed to escape via a back window and alert the band's lawyers. The rest, including various friends

Previous pages: Neil at home in 1967.

Below: Relaxing with Stephen Stills at a roadside meal stop.

and groupies, were arrested and hauled off to the LA county jail. The band's lawyers moved quickly, and everyone got off with a "disturbing the peace" charge and small fine, except roadie Chris Sarns, who was caught red-handed with a bag of marijuana and fined three hundred dollars.

The raid was the final death blow for Buffalo Springfield. Neil Young had already announced he was leaving to take the solo road (yet again), and Stephen Stills was deep in clandestine plans to form a new group with David Crosby. On May 5, 1968, the band played their final gig at the Long Beach Arena, officially announcing their disbandment the following week.

Almost as an epitaph for the group, Furay and Messina busied themselves putting together a compilation of tracks that had yet to see the light of day featuring five songs by Stephen Stills, four by Richie Furay, and one by Jim Messina. Only two tracks—"On My Way Home" (rumored to be a paean to Stills) and the country-flavored "I Am a Child"—were fronted by Neil Young. Released in July, two months after Buffalo Springfield broke up, the aptly titled *Last Time Around* sold in sufficient numbers to make #44 in the charts. But the album's cover said it all, using a picture of the group taken without Neil Young, whose image was pasted on later—significantly, looking in the opposite direction.

# Last Time Around

# three

# Into the Unknown

**T**HE last years of the 1960s saw the flowering of the youth-led revolution that had been heralded by the so-called Summer of Love of 1967. The hippie counterculture was at its zenith, and the pop-oriented beat group boom—which had first inspired bands like the Byrds and Buffalo Springfield—was fast becoming a thing of the past. All around barriers were being broken in musical form, studio production, and lyric writing. On the West Coast, bands like the Doors, Jefferson Airplane, and the Grateful Dead were rewriting the rule book. As Neil Young had spectacularly demonstrated with the audacious "Broken Arrow," it was a time for experiment and change more radical than anything that had gone before. Freed of the constraints and tensions that had made life in the Springfield increasingly intolerable, by the end of 1968 he had taken the first bold step into a new unknown with the completion and release of his first solo album.

## Topanga Canyon

As Buffalo Springfield called it a day, Neil Young made his first move toward a new solo career by signing a management deal with Elliot Roberts. Born Elliot Rabinowitz in 1943 in New York's Bronx, Roberts currently managed Joni Mitchell, through whom he would meet her fellow Canadian singer-songwriter. He had signed Mitchell to the Warner Bros.–owned Reprise Records (founded

Topanga Canyon, Neil Young's home in the late 1960s.

in 1960 by Frank Sinatra), and it wasn't long before Roberts suggested his new client Neil Young for the label.

Neil had decided that, post-Springfield, he wouldn't stay with Atlantic Records. He felt it would be problematic sharing the same label with his ex-colleagues—specifically, Stephen Stills—and Atlantic agreed. So when Reprise offered him a twenty-thousand-dollar advance to go away and write songs for a debut album, he signed without hesitation.

The first thing Neil did with his newfound wealth was seek out a home in Topanga Canyon. Scene of the fateful drug bust that had finally finished off Buffalo Springfield, the Canyon had long been a retreat for artists, political radicals, and various social outcasts. Located just half an hour's drive from the bright lights of Hollywood, with its artist colonies and hippie communes it might as well have been on another planet from Tinsel Town.

His first major encounter as a would-be resident of the Canyon, even before he'd found a place of his own, was with the record producer David Briggs. Briggs's house had been a regular hangout for musicians passing through Topanga since he'd moved there in the mid-1960s, and soon Neil was more regular than most. Young and Briggs got along well from the start, talking

Neil in pensive mode during the late 1960s, when he was working with Buffalo Springfield and enjoying life in Topanga Canyon.

music and running through songs—and smoking copious amounts of pot. It was the start of a major working relationship for both of them.

Friends noticed, as Neil got used to the laid-back lifestyle of the Canyon, that he was far more relaxed than previously, less prone to any stress-related blackouts, and generally more settled in his demeanor. There was plenty of dope-and-booze hell-raising going on among the musicians, of course, especially among the tight-knit Topanga rock scene centered on the Corral Club. But Neil tended to keep it at arm's length; he got high like everybody, but avoided the carousing that often went with it, to the extent that he was often considered something of a loner. As Elliot Roberts and others would observe, Neil Young seemed to grow up during those first months in Topanga Canyon.

"FRIENDS NOTICED AS NEIL got used to the laid-back lifestyle of the CANYON that he WAS far more relaxed than PREVIOUSLY."

In August 1968 Neil moved into his newly purchased house at 611 Skyline Trail, a three-story redwood building hanging precariously on the edge of a hill overlooking the Canyon. Around the same time he'd become involved with Susan Acevedo, an attractive but no-nonsense woman six years older than Neil who ran a short-order diner called the Canyon Kitchen. He saw her as something of a mother figure in his life. Very soon, Acevedo had moved into the Young household along with her seven-year-old daughter from a previous partner.

It was the beginning of a period of benign domesticity for Neil; a welcome calm away from the day-to-day distractions of the LA music business, as he prepared and recorded his first solo album. And on December 7, 1968, the couple were married in what could only be described as an archetypal hippie wedding, by a minister from the cultish-sounding Temple of Man. The hippie "alternative society," while born of freethinking attitudes and liberal values, also encouraged a rash of pseudo-religious cults, dabbling in everything from ancient Egyptian mythology to UFOs and devil worship. At one stage in the fall of 1968, Neil was briefly drawn into the orbit of the most notorious character to emerge from this milieu of quasi-mystics and charismatic charlatans—Charles Manson.

Introduced by another Topanga resident, Dennis Wilson of the Beach Boys (whom Buffalo Springfield had supported on tour shortly before disbanding), Neil was fascinated by Manson's magnetic, if slightly intimidating, presence. The ex-jailbird regaled him with his singing and songwriting, surrounded always by a compliant harem of attractive young females. Sympathetic to left-field attempts at making music, having been rejected himself in the past, Neil met Manson a few times at Wilson's house and was impressed by his weird songs, describing him later as "Great, unreal. . . . He was potentially a poet." Young even recommended Manson to Warner Bros. Records, but nothing came of it.

Less than a year later, after Manson and his cult of female followers, known as "the Family," had moved from the Topanga area, the Sharon Tate murders hit the headlines. Manson had masterminded and helped carry out the ritualistic killing of actress Sharon Tate and six others over three nights in July and August 1969. Manson, age thirty-four when the crimes were committed, remains in jail to this day.

**Charles Manson at the time of his arrest in 1969.**

## Going Solo

Between setting up home and enjoying the domesticity with his new partner, from August through October 1968 Neil busied himself in the studio, cutting the songs he'd been developing most of the summer. David Briggs was engaged as the prime producer—the first of many collaborations with Young—with Jack Nitzsche taking the controls on three of the tracks. Musicians in on the sessions included the young guitar virtuoso Ry Cooder and ex-Springfield bass player Jim Messina, as well as a six-strong roster of backup vocalists.

Opening somewhat unconventionally with a country-fueled instrumental, the eponymous album was an encouraging debut for Neil Young as a solo artist. Some of the songs, such as "The Old Laughing Lady" and most famously "The Loner" (released as his debut solo single in December 1968), would stay in the live repertoire for years to come. Others were definitely of their time, like "I've Loved Her So Long" with its sextet of female voices, and Neil's traumatic ten-minute closer "The Last Trip to Tulsa," in which his lyric "Well I used to be a folk singer/keeping managers alive" hints at his sometimes volatile relationship with Springfield's managers Greene and Stone.

Young deliberately had his vocals played down in the mix, but regretted the decision after agreeing to the use of an experimental system called Haeco-CSG, which was intended to make stereo records compatible with mono record players but had the unfortunate side effect of degrading the sound in both stereo and mono. Unhappy with the result, he had the album partially remixed in January 1969, then re-released with his name added to the cover design—the original '68 release featured just a painting by Topanga artist Roland Diehl.

## The Loner

**A-SIDE** The Loner [Neil Young]

**B-SIDE** Sugar Mountain [Neil Young]

**RECORDED** August—October, 1968

**RELEASED** December 1968

**LABEL** Reprise

**PRODUCERS** David Briggs ✶ Neil Young

Neil's biggest criticism of the album in retrospect was that it was "overdubbed rather than played," referring to the layers of overdubs that Jack Nitzsche painstakingly imposed on the production. Whatever, the textural mix of folk, orchestral pop, and electric rock was perhaps too eclectic for either dedicated Young fans or more mainstream record buyers, and the album never made the U.S. Top 200.

**A quizzical-looking Neil facing the press in 1970.**

STEREO

6317

PRINTED IN U.S.A.

# Neil Young

**A**lthough an encouraging debut for a solo performer, at the time of its release Neil Young was a little too early for the trend toward singer-songwriters, typified by the likes of James Taylor and Carole King, that was just around the corner. Some of the songs here—including "The Old Laughing Lady" and most famously "The Loner" (which Neil released as his debut solo single in December 1968)—would remain as part of his live concert repertoire for many years, while others would soon be discarded. But the main problem with the album lies in the production: the original suffered from the use of an experimental system that played down Neil's vocals in the mix, and even in the later remixed version the sound balance leaves a lot to be desired.

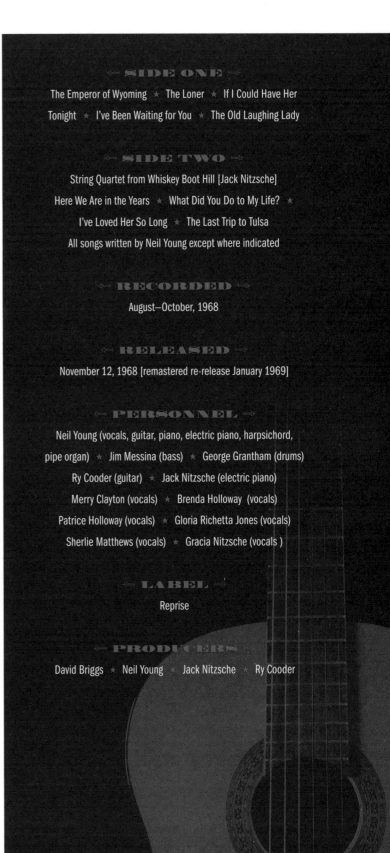

### SIDE ONE

The Emperor of Wyoming ★ The Loner ★ If I Could Have Her Tonight ★ I've Been Waiting for You ★ The Old Laughing Lady

### SIDE TWO

String Quartet from Whiskey Boot Hill [Jack Nitzsche]
Here We Are in the Years ★ What Did You Do to My Life? ★
I've Loved Her So Long ★ The Last Trip to Tulsa
All songs written by Neil Young except where indicated

### RECORDED

August–October, 1968

### RELEASED

November 12, 1968 [remastered re-release January 1969]

### PERSONNEL

Neil Young (vocals, guitar, piano, electric piano, harpsichord, pipe organ) ★ Jim Messina (bass) ★ George Grantham (drums)
Ry Cooder (guitar) ★ Jack Nitzsche (electric piano)
Merry Clayton (vocals) ★ Brenda Holloway (vocals)
Patrice Holloway (vocals) ★ Gloria Richetta Jones (vocals)
Sherlie Matthews (vocals) ★ Gracia Nitzsche (vocals )

### LABEL

Reprise

### PRODUCERS

David Briggs ★ Neil Young ★ Jack Nitzsche ★ Ry Cooder

## The Rockets

Neil had first come across the Rockets back in 1966, when Buffalo Springfield was recording its first album. The rough-at-the-edges rock group consisted of Danny Whitten plus brothers Leon and George Whitsell on guitars, Bobby Notkoff on violin, bassist Billy Talbot, and Ralph Molina on drums. Introduced by a mutual friend, Neil would visit them when the pressure around Springfield got too much, trying out songs and jamming with them at their headquarters, a rambling house in Laurel Canyon. He identified particularly with Whitten, a budding songwriter like himself, and already a spirited guitar player. By March 1968 the Rockets had smoothed their rough edges enough to have an album out, *The Rockets*, released on a small indie label, White Whale. Neil loved it, and when the Rockets were booked into the Whisky a Go-Go for five nights in August, he sat in with them for one of the dates. That night at the Sunset Strip club was to prove fateful; Neil realized immediately he wanted the same loose-knit, rock-heavy sound on his next album, and promptly booked some studio time—not for the entire six-piece, but for the rhythm section of Whitten, Talbot, and Molina.

Initially Young intimated that the trio could record (and perhaps tour) with him as Neil Young & Crazy Horse—named for the legendary Native American warrior chief—while keeping the six-piece going as the Rockets. But it was not to be; as soon as the preliminary jamming sessions gained momentum, it was clear that the Rockets were history.

66 **The numbers were laid down virtually as live, with few takes and a minimum of editing.** 99

## Everybody Knows This Is Nowhere

January 1969 saw the quartet settling into Wally Heider's Los Angeles studio to cut what would be the first landmark album of Young's solo career. Those first sessions produced two of Neil's classic jamming numbers, "Down By the River" and "Cowgirl in the Sand," over nine and ten minutes long, respectively, as well as "Everybody Knows This Is Nowhere" and "Cinnamon Girl." Young had apparently written "Down By the River," "Cowgirl," and "Cinnamon" all in the same day, while convalescing in bed with the flu and a temperature of 103°F, a few weeks earlier.

Neil onstage perfecting his craft in the early 1970s.

The numbers were laid down virtually as live, with few takes and a minimum of editing (although most of the lead vocals were overdubbed)—straightforward no-frills recordings, in contrast with the measured production jobs that characterized Buffalo Springfield's releases and Neil's solo debut. A second visit to the studio in March resulted in three more tracks—the melancholic country song "The Losing End," "Running Dry" (subtitled "Requiem for the Rockets"), with a violin contribution from the Rockets' Bobby Notkoff, and "Round & Round," which featured vocal and guitar by Danny Whitten's girlfriend Robin Lane.

*Everybody Knows This Is Nowhere*, released in May 1969, summed up where Neil Young was right then—he'd left the politics and ego trips of the Springfield behind him and was striking out on his own, wearing his heart on his sleeve.

# Everybody Knows This Is Nowhere

**ALBUM**

The first recorded collaboration with Crazy Horse, the album (which peaked at only #34 in the U.S. charts but went on to sell over a million copies) includes the first hints of what would become Neil Young's future trademarks. With the internal tensions of Buffalo Springfield now behind him, this is Neil as he strikes out to make a highly personalized statement for the first time. His strident, confident guitar playing—with Danny Whitten as a dynamic foil—backs up often minimalist lyrics that are powerful by virtue of their sheer economy. And in the opener "Cinnamon Girl," which marked Neil's first entry in the U.S. singles chart under his own name, the feel of the entire album is condensed into a dynamic three minutes of perfection.

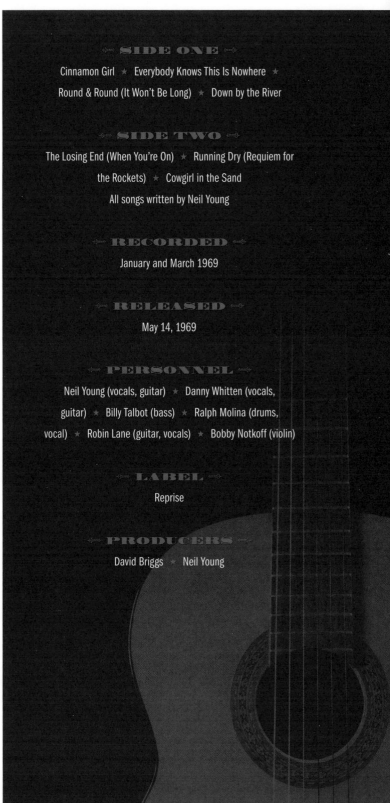

### SIDE ONE
Cinnamon Girl ★ Everybody Knows This Is Nowhere ★ Round & Round (It Won't Be Long) ★ Down by the River

### SIDE TWO
The Losing End (When You're On) ★ Running Dry (Requiem for the Rockets) ★ Cowgirl in the Sand
All songs written by Neil Young

### RECORDED
January and March 1969

### RELEASED
May 14, 1969

### PERSONNEL
Neil Young (vocals, guitar) ★ Danny Whitten (vocals, guitar) ★ Billy Talbot (bass) ★ Ralph Molina (drums, vocal) ★ Robin Lane (guitar, vocals) ★ Bobby Notkoff (violin)

### LABEL
Reprise

### PRODUCERS
David Briggs ★ Neil Young

As always, the songs were part confessional, part private constructs, with often-minimalist lyrics conjuring up a wealth of images. Equally significant, his guitar playing was taking on the strident, authoritative character that would mark him as a major voice on the instrument. The album not only neatly encapsulated Neil Young circa mid-1969 but would be a template for much of his output to come.

It received good reviews and a decent amount of airplay. It turned out to be what the record industry would call a "sleeper," not being bought in huge numbers immediately (it only reached #34 in the weekly-based sales charts), but eventually earning a platinum disc for selling over a million copies. And in the spring of 1970, "Cinnamon Girl" marked Neil Young's first entry under his own name on the U.S. singles chart, albeit at a modest #55.

Between the January and March recording sessions, Neil Young and Crazy Horse went out on some live dates, starting with a week at the Bitter End in the heart of Greenwich Village, and followed by a short season at the Troubadour in LA. At the shows Neil did a brief acoustic set, then was joined onstage by Crazy Horse. After the album was completed they did more dates, all in small venues, including dates to promote its release in May. Neil's performances with the band mesmerized audiences—especially the musical rapport he had with Danny Whitten. The two guitarists were perfect foils for each other, some observers describing their empathy as almost telepathic.

## Cinnamon Girl

**SINGLE**

**A-SIDE** Cinnamon Girl [Neil Young]

**B-SIDE** Sugar Mountain [Neil Young]

**RECORDED** January and March 1969 [A-side]

**RELEASED** April 20, 1970

**LABEL** Reprise

**PRODUCERS** David Briggs ✶ Neil Young

It was while touring with Crazy Horse that Neil would once again share the stage with Stephen Stills, when the latter turned up at several dates, and sat in along with Dallas Taylor—the drummer from his current lineup, the much-heralded "supergroup" of Crosby, Stills & Nash.

## Crosby, Stills & Nash

While Buffalo Springfield was still in the throes of breaking up, Stills had been privately jamming with David Crosby, whose career with the Byrds had come to an abrupt halt when he was fired from the group in September 1967. As Neil Young settled into life in Topanga Canyon through 1968, Stills and Crosby firmed up their plans by recruiting Graham Nash from the British pop outfit the Hollies.

Nash had been increasingly dissatisfied with what he perceived as the bland commercialism of the Manchester beat group, with whom he had found fame in the early 1960s. After a jamming session at one of Mama Cass Elliot's famous parties, at which the trio realized they had a potentially unique vocal sound together, Nash opted to leave his old comrades and join Stills and Crosby in their new venture.

Atlantic Records' Ahmet Ertegun signed the band as soon as contract problems with Crosby and Nash could be ironed out, and their debut album *Crosby, Stills & Nash*—with Stills playing most of the backup instruments, plus Dallas Taylor on drums—came out at the end of May 1969, just two weeks after Neil Young's debut with Crazy Horse. By July it had made it into the *Billboard* Top 40, reaching #6 and earning a gold disc in the process.

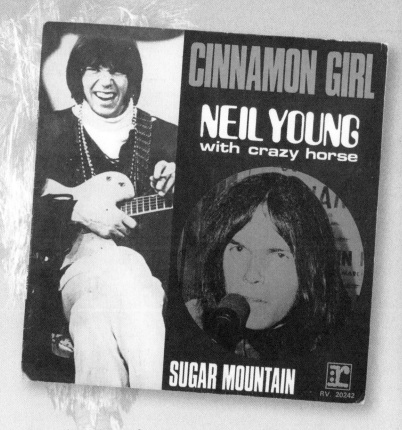

A 4-track Extended Play (EP) release of "Cinnamon Girl," and (above) the single sleeve, with an early picture of a grinning Neil clutching his guitar.

## . . . & Young

Crosby, Stills, and Nash decided they could use a fourth voice, preferably with an electric guitar contribution, to help meat out the undeniably "folksie" texture of their carefully wrought harmonies. After some discussion, they agreed to a suggestion by Ahmet Ertegun that the answer might be found in Neil Young. At first Nash and Crosby were doubtful—they knew of Neil's past reputation for unreliability, and feared the tensions between him and Stephen that had ripped apart Buffalo Springfield might surface again—but Stills was more confident, and approached his former colleague.

After establishing that he would continue a parallel solo career, and ensuring that he was included in the group's "all-star" title rather than being treated as a celebrity sideman, Neil was in—and Crosby, Stills, Nash & Young was born.

After some intense rehearsal, CSNY were set to debut to an eager world at the Fillmore East in New York on July 25, but had to cancel due to Graham

Nash contracting a throat infection. They subsequently appeared for the first time at the Chicago Auditorium Theater on August 16, and such was their instant prestige that Joni Mitchell was actually playing support. The concert was a triumph, and the next day they were due to appear at what came to be regarded as the most celebrated gig in rock music history, the Woodstock Music and Arts Fair, held at Bethel in upstate New York.

## Woodstock

After the delays and chaos that famously characterized the festival, the much–anticipated appearance of Crosby, Stills, Nash & Young at Woodstock took place at four in the morning—sandwiched between Blood, Sweat & Tears and the

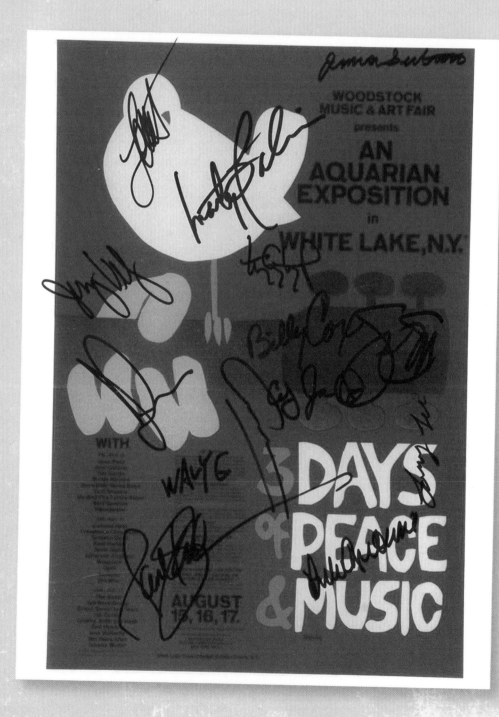

Paul Butterfield Blues Band—in the overrun final few hours of the three-day marathon. To say they were nervous was an understatement—as Stephen Stills famously announced to the crowd, "This is the second time we've ever played in front of people, man. We're scared shitless!"

Adding to their apprehension was the fact that, due to the hype surrounding CSN's current hit album and single ("Marrakesh Express" had entered the charts a month earlier), there was an all-star audience at the back of the stage, wondering what the new lineup was all about, as David Crosby would recall in his autobiography.

"Everybody was curious about us. We were the new kid in the block, it was our second public gig, nobody had ever seen us, everybody had heard the record, everybody wondered 'What in the hell are they about?' So when it was rumored that we were about to go on, everybody came. Every band that played there, including all the ones that aren't in the movie, were all standing in an arc behind us and that was intimidating, to say the least. I'm looking back at

Crosby, Stills, Nash & Young, who made their sensational four-in-the-morning debut as a group at Woodstock.

"'This is the second time we've ever played in front of people, man. We're scared shitless!"

Stephen Stills at Woodstock

**woodstock**
the movie
from Warner Bros.

Neil Young

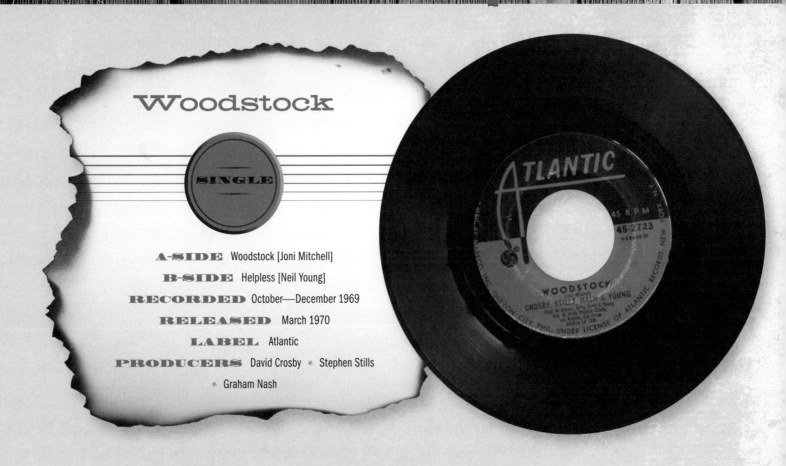

# Woodstock

**SINGLE**

**A-SIDE** Woodstock [Joni Mitchell]

**B-SIDE** Helpless [Neil Young]

**RECORDED** October—December 1969

**RELEASED** March 1970

**LABEL** Atlantic

**PRODUCERS** David Crosby ✴ Stephen Stills
✴ Graham Nash

Hendrix and Robbie Robertson and Levon Helm and the Who and Janis and Sly and Grace and Paul, everybody that I knew and everybody that I didn't know."

After a seven-song acoustic set from just Crosby, Stills, and Nash, Neil Young took the stage for an acoustic duo with Stephen Stills. That was followed by an "electric" set by the whole lineup (including Greg Reeves on bass and Dallas Taylor on drums), then two acoustic closers by the CSNY quartet. Out of the sixteen songs performed, only three were Neil Young compositions, but that seemed to suit Neil, who appeared to be keeping the whole affair somewhat at arm's length.

He would admit not being comfortable with the entire festival "experience" as it played out at Woodstock, and was particularly distracted by the movie cameramen moving about the stage during the set. He even threatened to hit them with his guitar if they came near him—which is why he never featured in the celebrated *Woodstock* movie.

Joni Mitchell—who was in a relationship with Graham Nash at the time—was billed to play at Woodstock, but when Atlantic executive (and CSNY manager) David Geffen heard the news reports of the chaotic conditions, he told her not to go: "I picked up the *New York Times*, and it says, '400,000 people sitting in mud,'" Geffen would recall. "And I thought, no way am I going to Woodstock. And so they [CSNY] went on to Woodstock. And Joni and I went back to my apartment on Central Park South, and we watched it on television. And she wrote the song 'Woodstock' in my apartment on 59th Street!"

The song, with its evocation of the hippie idealism of the festival, became the unofficial Woodstock anthem months after the event, when Crosby, Stills, Nash & Young made it into a hit single in the spring of 1970, and it was used on the soundtrack of the Oscar-winning movie. Ace negotiator Geffen had refused permission for any CSNY footage to be used in the film unless the producers used the group's version of the Mitchell song as its theme tune.

## Déjà Vu

Following Woodstock, CSNY got out on the road with a series of dates that reinforced their status as potential superstars. The upmarket Greek Theater in LA's Griffith Park hosted a week's residency, swiftly followed by their TV debut on the *Music Scene*—where the number chosen was a reworking of Neil Young's "Down By the River" from the Crazy Horse album.

Other memorable dates included the Big Sur Folk Festival (at which Stills got involved in a fight with a hippie heckler in the audience), a taped appearance on the very middle-of-the-road *This Is Tom Jones* TV show, and the ill-fated Altamont festival in December '69, when the Rolling Stones set was the scene of violence and death right in front of the stage. By this time seen as the embodiment of the flower power "peace-and-love" ethic, at Altamont CSNY played as best they could—David Crosby entreating the Hell's Angels in the audience to "Stop hurting each other, man"—as they witnessed the mayhem breaking out in the crowd.

Throughout that time they were in and out of Wally Heider's recording studios, both in San Francisco and Los Angeles, laying down tracks for what would be Crosby, Stills, Nash & Young's debut album. Recorded between October and December 1969, *Déjà Vu* confirmed the concept of CSNY (and indeed Crosby, Stills & Nash before them) as a collection of individuals rather than a fully integrated band.

Contrary to common practice, there was always a tacit understanding that, regardless of how successful the foursome might prove to be, they would also each pursue their own personal projects. All the songs except for Joni Mitchell's "Woodstock" were recorded as specific sessions for each member, the others contributing whatever was needed for that particular track. For dedicated Neil Young fans, the album also reaffirmed their belief that their hero hadn't completely thrown his lot in with the "supergroup" at the expense of his own solo career. Far from it. Even within the tight-knit constraints of the much-lauded lineup, Young seemed something of the outsider, the added ingredient to an already successful recipe.

Many observers wondered about CSN's motives in inviting him to join in the first place; he conspicuously shied away from much of the superstar ballyhoo (while enjoying the financial rewards, of course), his contribution brought an electric rock 'n' roll edge to the sweet-sounding harmonies that some found unnecessary, and his relationship with the others (Stills in particular, as always) could be fractious to say the least. Nevertheless, as the 1970s dawned, Neil was enjoying the wider acclaim afforded via CSNY, including a European tour during which members of the quartet were treated as bona fide rock royalty.

*Déjà Vu* was much anticipated, to the degree that in the U.S. market alone it notched up over two million dollars in pre-release orders. Released on March 11, 1970, it was almost universally applauded, even among those critics who had been skeptical about the whole CSNY project from the start.

Just two tracks on the album were Neil Young songs (apart from Stephen Stills's closing number, a fusion of his "Know You Got to Run" and Neil's

David Crosby, Stephen Stills, Graham Nash, and Neil Young, plus drummer Dallas Taylor (back right), and bassist Greg Reeves (front right).

# Déjà Vu

**T**he only studio album that Neil Young made with Crosby, Stills, and Nash prior to 1988's *American Dream*, *Déjà Vu* was reported to have taken no less than 800 man-hours to record. The effort paid off, with a listener-friendly production that earned seven platinum discs in the United States alone, and contained three U.S. hit singles—"Woodstock," "Our House," and "Teach Your Children." With each member recording their "own" tracks at specific sessions, the album reflects the "individuals within a group" that was the basis for the whole CSNY project, while Neil's contribution to the collective whole brings a raw, gritty edge to the otherwise sweet-sounding harmonies of CSN that could sometimes border on the saccharine.

### ★ SIDE ONE ★

Carry On [Stephen Stills] ★ Teach Your Children [Graham Nash] ★ Almost Cut My Hair [David Crosby] Helpless [Neil Young] ★ Woodstock [Joni Mitchell]

### ★ SIDE TWO ★

Déjà Vu [David Crosby] ★ Our House [Graham Nash] 4 + 20 [Stephen Stills] ★ Country Girl: [a] Whiskey Boot Hill [b] Down, Down, Down [c] Country Girl (I Think You're Pretty) [Neil Young] ★ Everybody I Love You [Stephen Stills, Neil Young]

### ★ RECORDED ★

October–December 1969

### ★ RELEASED ★

March 11, 1970

### ★ PERSONNEL ★

David Crosby (vocals, rhythm guitar) ★ Stephen Stills (vocals, guitar, bass guitar, keyboards, congas, percussion) ★ Graham Nash (vocals, rhythm guitar, keyboards, congas, tambourine) Neil Young (vocals, guitar, keyboard, harmonica)

### ★ ADDITIONAL PERSONNEL ★

Dallas Taylor (drums, percussion) ★ Greg Reeves (bass) Jerry Garcia (pedal steel guitar) ★ John Sebastian (harmonica)

### ★ LABEL ★

Atlantic

### ★ PRODUCERS ★

David Crosby ★ Stephen Stills ★ Graham Nash ★ Neil Young

"Everybody I Love You"), the slow ballad "Helpless," and the three–part "Country Girl"—the latter representing CSN's collaboration with Neil Young at its very best. Crosby and Nash had the same number of tracks allocated on the album, Stephen Stills three, while the Side One closer, "Woodstock," would be the group effort that catapulted CSNY into the singles chart in April 1970. Two other tracks, Graham Nash's "Teach Your Children" and "Our House" would also go on to feature in the Top 40 during 1970.

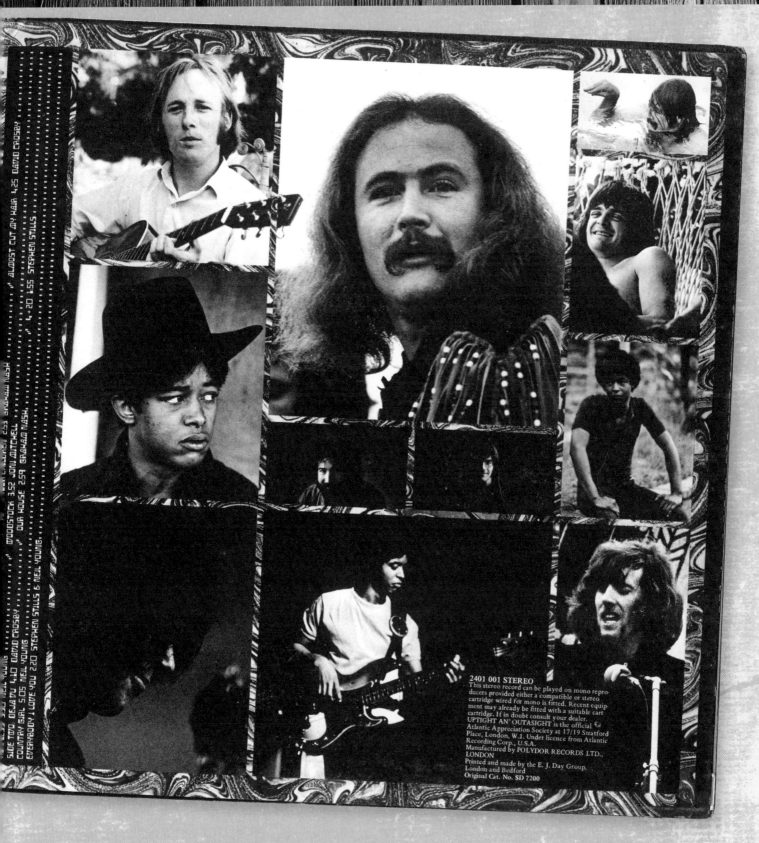

The inevitable chart success of *Déjà Vu*—hitting #1 in America, Australia, and the Netherlands, and eventually earning no less than seven platinum discs for million-plus sales in the United States—also boosted the solo activity that the four principals were still engaged in. Not least Neil Young, who just a few months later would release *After the Goldrush*, one of the most influential albums of his entire career.

The inside gatefold sleeve —a very fashionable format in the late 1960s—for the *Déjà Vu* album.

# JAMMING WITH NEIL YOUNG

I n a career famous for frequent—and often unpredictable—changes of direction, Neil Young has worked together with a vast range of fellow artists, many of whom have acknowledged the influence of the capricious Canadian on their own work.

Most famous of all his collaborations, of course, are as a member of Buffallo Springfield early in his career, his frequent spells fronting Crazy Horse, and the ongoing relationship with Crosby, Stills, and Nash—which still manifests itself in guest appearances, and even reunion tours, from time to time. But over the years Neil has played with scores of other singers and musicians, from support names on tours to one-time appearances on festivals, benefit concerts, and TV shows.

From a seemingly endless list of such encounters, several particularly grab the imagination, those with Bob Dylan being an obvious example. Dylan figured from early on as a huge influence on Neil Young's music—back in his early days around the Winnipeg folk scene, Joni Mitchell (then Joan Anderson) observed how he moved from a rock 'n' roll to "a folkie direction" after having discovered Dylan for the first time. The two have shared the same stage on several occasions over the years, the most auspicious including the Band's farewell "Last Waltz" concert in 1976, and Dylan's own 30th anniversary tribute event in 1992. And a number of Dylan songs have appeared regularly in Neil's concert repertoire, including "All Along the Watchtower," "Just Like Tom Thumb's Blues," and the appropriately titled "Forever Young."

It was at the tribute "Bobfest" that Neil first met Pearl Jam, who were also on the bill. It was probably then that he invited them to play at the 1992 Bridge School benefit, the start of a productive relationship which led to Neil being heralded by Pearl Jam fans as the "Godfather of Grunge." The Seattle rockers have since played Neil's "Rockin' in the Free World" over 100 times at shows, often as the final encore. Plus there was the 1995 studio collaboration Mirror Ball, although Pearl Jam's name didn't appear on the cover due to contractual reasons.

Alongside Bob Dylan, the Beatles were the other major influence on aspiring rock artists like Neil Young in the mid-1960s. With his high school band the Squires, homage to the UK rockers even went as far as wearing "Beatles wigs" on at least one occasion! Over three decades later, it was Neil who presented Paul McCartney with his induction into the Rock and Roll Hall of Fame in 1999, saying "The first song I learned to play was a Beatles song—'Give Me Money, That's What I Want.' Paul McCartney

A poster for the 1995 album *Mirror Ball*, which featured members of Pearl Jam.

is one of the greatest songwriters ever. He'll be remembered hundreds of years from now." The two have joined forces at various concert events, including Neil's annual Bridge School benefit in 2004, and a sensational finale to his London Hyde Park gig in 2009, when McCartney walked onstage to join Young for the Beatles' "A Day in the Life."

A team-up as unlikely sounding as the one with Pearl Jam was when Neil recruited the new wave band Devo for some low-key concerts and his movie *Human Highway* in 1978. One spin-off result of the collaboration was Neil using a phrase borrowed from Devo—"Rust Never Sleeps"—as the title of his next album and tour, in which he incorporated some of the bizarre influences of the Ohio group into his own stage presentation.

One-time appearances where Neil has performed with all manner of fellow rock artists include a memorable David Letterman Show TV jam with veteran rocker Jerry Lee Lewis in 2006, a performance of "Your Song" with Elton John for the fifth annual

Neil Young and Paul McCartney onstage together. The Beatles were an early influence on Neil.

benefit of the AIDS Foundation, and the first of several guest dates with Bruce Springsteen. Neil invited Springsteen to join him at the end of a Sydney benefit concert for the Australian Cerebral Palsy Association in 1985, the pair concluding his mammoth 28-song-set with a remarkable 20-minute version of "Down by the River."

For an artist with a reputation at various stages in his long career as being "difficult," Neil Young has garnered a great deal of goodwill and support from fellow performers over the years—not least because of a generosity of spirit which welcomes the participation of others. Never too precious about his own interpretation of his songs being the definitive version, his open approach to guest appearances, ad-lib encores, or just plain jamming, allows for other artists' input to be continually part of the mix.

Golden
Harvest

A student lies dead after the National Guard opened fire on an antiwar protest at Kent State University, Ohio.

T H E hugely successful *Déjà Vu* would be the first of three chart-topping, million-selling albums for Crosby, Stills, Nash & Young during the early 1970s. With their mellow harmonies and slick production, the records were at the forefront of a trend for easy-listening rock that would be a major part of the pop music market throughout the decade. Variously dubbed by the record industry and media as "soft rock," "adult-oriented rock," and "MOR (middle-of-the-road) rock," the most prominent exponents of the genre that followed in the wake of *Déjà Vu* included the Eagles, Fleetwood Mac, and singers like Billy Joel and Neil Diamond. The open-ended nature of CSNY, however, with each member also traveling down his separate path, meant that the group was always somewhat distanced from the soft rock mainstream. This was especially true in the case of Neil Young, who through the first half of 1970 managed to juggle his time among touring, promoting *Déjà Vu* and two CSNY singles, and finalizing his next solo album.

## "Ohio"

As well as music, the one element that unified the often disparate counterculture, and American youth generally, was opposition to the war in Vietnam. This groundswell of antiwar feeling, manifest in dozens of demonstrations as well as nonpolitical gatherings like Woodstock, was highlighted tragically on May 4, 1970, at Kent State University in Ohio. There, while students protested the U.S. invasion of Cambodia, members of the Ohio National Guard shot dead four unarmed demonstrators and seriously wounded nine others.

Neil Young was with David Crosby not long after news of the shootings shocked the world; seeing a magazine picture of the atrocity, he sat down and wrote a song about it there and then. Young, unlike the other three in CSNY, normally kept any political opinions to himself, and had certainly never penned anything remotely like a "protest song"—until now.

Within a day of the song's completion, Young and Crosby were in the studio—with Stills, Nash, and the new rhythm section of Calvin "Fuzzy" Samuels on bass and drummer Johnny Barbata—cutting the group's next single. With Stills's antiwar message "Find the Cost of Freedom" as the B-side, they made the recording in just a few live takes, giving it to Ahmet Ertegun, who flew with it to Atlantic in New York. Released a week or so later, at the beginning of June, the single seemed to capture the mood of the nation's youth,

### Ohio

**SINGLE**

**A-SIDE** Ohio [Neil Young]

**B-SIDE** Find the Cost of Freedom [Stephen Stills]

**RECORDED** May 21, 1970

**RELEASED** June, 1970

**LABEL** Atlantic

**PRODUCERS** David Crosby ✶

Stephen Stills ✶ Graham Nash ✶ Neil Young

ATLANTIC

BE 650204

CROSBY, STILLS, NASH & YOUNG

OHIO

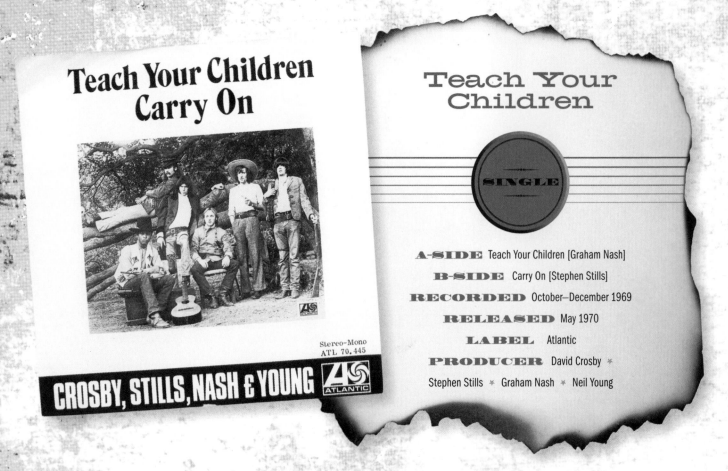

**Teach Your Children / Carry On**

CROSBY, STILLS, NASH & YOUNG

Stereo-Mono
ATL 70.445

**Teach Your Children**

SINGLE

**A-SIDE** Teach Your Children [Graham Nash]

**B-SIDE** Carry On [Stephen Stills]

**RECORDED** October–December 1969

**RELEASED** May 1970

**LABEL** Atlantic

**PRODUCER** David Crosby ✳ Stephen Stills ✳ Graham Nash ✳ Neil Young

climbing to the #14 spot by early July. "Ohio" followed CSNY's previous single, Graham Nash's heartfelt message to parents from *Déjà Vu*, "Teach Your Children," released a few weeks earlier.

## After the Gold Rush

When CSNY weren't actually gigging, Neil had managed to fit in dates with Crazy Horse, the loose countrified feel of the band a long shot from the well-rehearsed perfectionism of the superstar quartet. There had also been studio sessions dating back through the fall of 1969, and by March 1970, just as *Déjà Vu* was storming up the charts, Neil was able to announce that a new album with Crazy Horse was almost finished.

However, things didn't run that smoothly. Crazy Horse guitarist Danny Whitten had been growing increasingly unreliable due to a heroin habit he'd acquired over the previous few months, and when he missed yet another album session, Neil had had enough. He promptly withdrew Crazy Horse from the rest of the project, announcing on the radio that he wouldn't be working with them anymore; the album was effectively shelved.

Not for long, however. When Stephen Stills broke a wrist in an automobile accident, Neil took advantage of the unexpected furlough from a grueling CSNY tour by completing the album with some new names in the lineup.

Before Stills's accident Neil had already enlisted his supergroup partner to help out on some vocals, and also brought in their bass player Greg Reeves in place of the dismissed Billy Talbot. As the sessions recommenced, they were short of a drummer, so after some deliberation Neil re-engaged Ralph Molina from Crazy Horse.

But the newest name to appear on the forthcoming album's personnel listing was that of Nils Lofgren, a young singer-guitarist who had during the previous year befriended both Neil and, after moving to Topanga Canyon, producer David Briggs. Lofgren was an up-and-coming star, with his band Grin on the verge of signing a record contract, when Neil offered him session work on his new album.

A Henry Diltz profile shot of (left to right) Nash, Crosby, Young, and Stills.

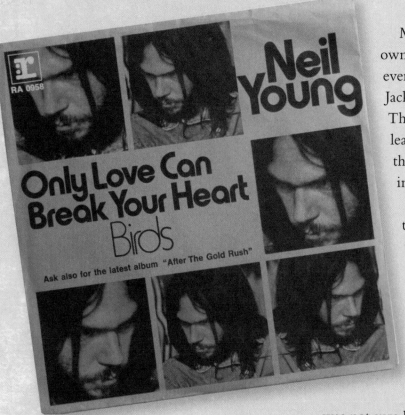

Much of the final recording took place in Young's own recording studio at his home in Topanga. He eventually brought in the rest of Crazy Horse and Jack Nitzsche to give a "family" feel to the lineup. Those last sessions were streamlined, to say the least, compared with the drawn-out process employed by CSNY in the studio.

"We would play through a song about four times to learn it with Neil doing all live vocals in the same room," Nils Lofgren would explain to Chris Briggs in the UK rock magazine *Zig Zag.* "In four days he had written six new songs. In fact the whole thing was on tape in under a week, allowing another week or two for mixing. Neil really liked it when it was finished. He liked the concept behind the songs, but it had been done so quick that he was not sure how the public would take to it. He was not sure if there was enough in it. Before it was not unusual to spend four months recording. It blew his mind that it was done so quick."

# "We would play the song about four times to learn it with Neil doing all live vocals in the same room"

**NILS LOFGREN**

The resulting album contained now-classic songs including the opener—the bittersweet "Tell Me Why" featuring precise harmonies between Lofgren and Young—"Only Love Can Break Your Heart," which gave Neil his first solo entry into the Top 40, and a riveting cover version of Don Gibson's country standard "Oh Lonesome Me."

And then there was the title track. The outstanding song from an outstanding album, "After the Gold Rush" painted a dream-like series of pictures of an apocalyptic past, present, and future, with a clear warning message about man's damage to the environment, long before green was cool—"Look at Mother Nature on the run in the 1970s" (later changed on stage to "the twentieth century," and subsequently "twenty-first century"). Recorded with just Neil Young on piano and a poignant flugelhorn accompaniment, the song has been covered by many artists since, most tellingly by Linda Ronstadt, Dolly Parton, and Emmylou Harris on their 1999 album *Trio II*.

The album wasn't greeted with universal acclaim first time round. *Rolling Stone* acidly stated, "None of the songs here rise above the uniformly dull surface" (though within five years the same magazine was declaring it to be a "masterpiece"), and many other reviewers were no more enthusiastic. Nevertheless, it gained a gold disc soon after release, chalking up half a million sales and reaching #8 on the U.S. album charts; it would go on to earn three platinum awards for multimillion sales over the years.

## Only Love Can Break Your Heart

**SINGLE**

**A-SIDE** Only Love Can Break Your Heart [Neil Young]

**B-SIDE** Birds [Neil Young]

**RECORDED** August 1969–June 1970

**RELEASED** September 19, 1970

**LABEL** Reprise

**PRODUCERS** David Briggs ✴ Neil Young ✴ Kendall Pacios

NEIL YOUNG
ONLY LOVE CAN BREAK YOUR HEART

birds

# After the Gold Rush

Combining his role of the singer-songwriter from his first solo album with the tough rocker of *Everybody Knows This Is Nowhere*, Neil initially dispensed with the services of Crazy Horse (who had helped make the latter album such a musical success) in favor of up-and-coming rock star Nils Lofgren, plus assorted names that included Jack Nitzsche and Stephen Stills. The album was finally completed with Crazy Horse back in the fold, adding their own rock 'n' roll gravitas to the proceedings, and with themes as diverse as politics, the environment, and matters of the heart—plus a nonoriginal country standard for good measure—the collection still stands as one of Neil Young's finest achievements.

## ⋆ SIDE ONE ⋆

Tell Me Why ⋆ After the Gold Rush ⋆ Only Love Can Break Your Heart ⋆ Southern Man ⋆ Till the Morning Comes

## ⋆ SIDE TWO ⋆

Oh, Lonesome Me [Don Gibson] ⋆ Don't Let It Bring You Down ⋆ Birds ⋆ When You Dance I Can Really Love ⋆ I Believe in You ⋆ Cripple Creek Ferry

All songs written by Neil Young except where indicated.

## ⋆ RECORDED ⋆

August 1969–June 1970, Sunset Sound, Los Angeles ⋆ Sound City, Los Angeles ⋆ Neil Young's home studio, Topanga, California

## ⋆ RELEASED ⋆

September 19, 1970

## ⋆ PERSONNEL ⋆

Neil Young (vocals, guitar, piano, harmonica, vibes) ⋆ Danny Whitten (vocals, guitar) ⋆ Billy Talbot (bass) ⋆ Ralph Molina (vocals, drums) Jack Nitzsche (piano) ⋆ Greg Reeves (bass) ⋆ Nils Lofgren (vocals, piano, guitar) ⋆ Stephen Stills (vocals) ⋆ Bill Peterson (flugelhorn)

## ⋆ LABEL ⋆

Reprise

## ⋆ PRODUCERS ⋆

David Briggs ⋆ Neil Young ⋆ Kendall Pacios

The inner gatefold inner sleeve of *After the Goldrush*, with Neil resplendent in patched jeans, courtesy of his wife, Susan (seen in the right of the picture).

The prime inspiration for the album was the screenplay for a projected movie of the same name, by the actor-filmmaker Dean Stockwell and Herb Berman, for which Neil offered to produce the soundtrack. The plot involved the aftereffects of a natural disaster in which Topanga Canyon (where Stockwell also lived) was engulfed by a tidal wave. The movie was never made, and the script apparently disappeared without a trace. Neil Young, luckily, made the album before the fate of the film project was in any doubt. It even gets a mention in the liner notes of *After the Gold Rush*, which cited it as inspiration for "most of the songs" on the album.

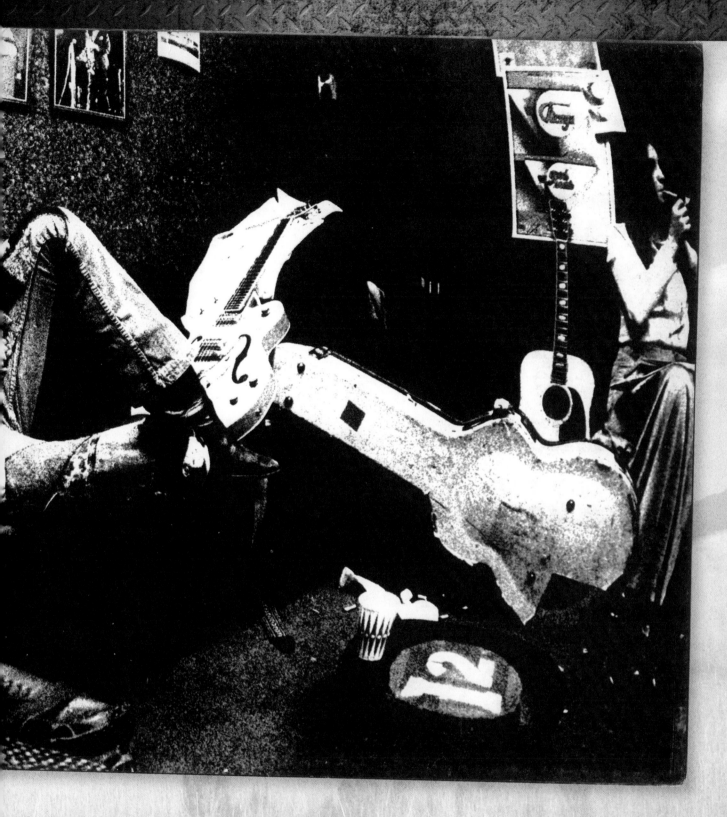

## Broken Arrow

Likewise mentioned in the sleeve notes was Neil's wife, Susan, a single line
reading "Patches: Susan Young," alluding to the singer's trademark repairs on his
well-worn jeans. Susan and Neil were also pictured together on an inner sleeve
photograph, implying that all was well in the Young marital household. But that
was far from the truth.

Susan Acevedo had been a feisty, independent woman raising a child, and
now she was merely the wife of a pop star. She had traded her previously hard
life for one of comparative luxury, but the price was her sense of security.

There was financial security, certainly, but all the time—especially when she accompanied her husband on the road—she was aware that there were other women, many of them, for whom he was the center of attention. By the time *After the Gold Rush* was released, in September 1970, Susan had reached the end of her tether.

When Neil bought a new place to live, a 140-acre $340,000 ranch in La Honda, California, his wife didn't make the move with him. He called his sprawling new abode Broken Arrow, but as someone observed, that wasn't the only thing broken in his life. Susan filed for divorce on October 9, 1970, Neil paying her a straight eighty thousand dollars—the sum she said needed to start a restaurant. According to Elliot Roberts, Neil's long-standing manager, she never came back to chase her millionaire ex-husband for a penny more.

## 4 Way Street

Back in July 1970, Crosby, Stills, Nash & Young had completed their on-again-off-again tour promoting *Déjà Vu*, which had been interrupted not just by Stephen Stills's car accident (and subsequent leg injury after being thrown from a horse) but also by further dissension in the ranks. Bass player Greg Reeves and drummer Dallas Taylor both got it into their heads that they deserved not just better billing (for a rhythm section, they had already been featured very prominently on *Déjà Vu*) but an upfront role, too, performing their own material during the shows. After increasing aggravation, onstage and off, both were fired in short order; Reeves was replaced by Calvin "Fuzzy" Samuels, and Taylor (following a huge bust-up with Neil Young) made way for Johnny Barbata soon after.

It was May 1970, with several weeks of the tour still to do. The rest of the dates were not without their dramas, with the quartet even announcing that they were splitting up for good the day before an appearance at the Chicago Auditorium. A week at New York's Fillmore East was also fraught, the members constantly arguing about set lists, who was playing for how long, and so on—wrangles, and even fights were conducted almost exclusively behind the scenes, it has to be said; their onstage persona was generally one of good-natured unity.

The tour finally wound up on July 9 at the Met Center Arena, Minneapolis. Despite the internecine friction, and even personnel changes midway, from the public's perception it was a huge success. They were simply one of the biggest (and most bankable) rock 'n' roll bands in the world, even lauded as "America's Beatles" by some overenthusiastic observers, and various concerts during June and July were recorded for a future live album. The recording was fortuitous, as it turned out, as a document of CSNY circa 1970—because the four superstars would not be touring together again for another four years.

The album of the tour, *4 Way Street*, finally appeared the following April. With CSNY going their separate ways immediately after the *Déjà Vu* tour, by the time it came out it was much in demand by their legions of followers, hungry for a new release. Spread over four sides, the double-disc album in its gatefold sleeve featured five songs by Neil Young—"On the Way Home," "Cowgirl in the Sand," "Don't Let It Bring You Down," "Southern Man," and the iconic "Ohio"—all familiar to his fans in their studio versions. A CD edition of the album released in 1992 had extra tracks that included a Neil Young medley comprising "The Loner," "Cinnamon Girl," and "Down by the River."

## Going Solo

The high-profile collaborations with Crosby, Stills, and Nash behind him (for the moment, at least), Neil spent the final months of 1970 settling into his new homestead ranch. Recently divorced, he had the time and freedom to consider his next move, concentrating on some solo acoustic gigs that were coming up at the end of the year. During the last week of November he played a few dates

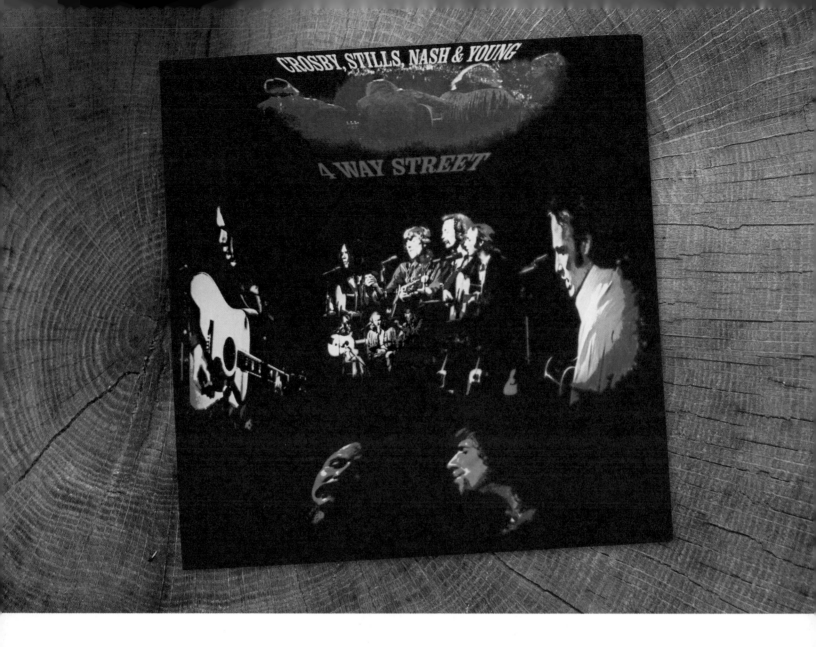

# 4 Way Street

ALBUM

### ⋆ SIDE ONE ⋆

Suite: Judy Blue Eyes [Stephen Stills] ⋆ On the Way Home [Neil Young] ⋆
Teach Your Children [Graham Nash] ⋆ Triad [David Crosby] ⋆
The Lee Shore [David Crosby] ⋆ Chicago

### ⋆ SIDE TWO ⋆

Right Between the Eyes ⋆ Cowgirl in the Sand [Neil Young] ⋆ Don't Let It
Bring You Down [Neil Young] ⋆ 49 Bye Byes/For What It's Worth/America's
Children [Stephen Stills] ⋆ Love the One You're With [Stephen Stills]

### ⋆ SIDE THREE ⋆

Pre-Road Downs ⋆ Long Time Gone [David Crosby] ⋆ Southern Man
[Neil Young]

### ⋆ SIDE FOUR ⋆

Ohio [Neil Young] ⋆ Carry On [Stephen Stills]
Find the Cost of Freedom [Stephen Stills]

### ⋆ RECORDED ⋆

June–July, 1970

### ⋆ RELEASED ⋆

April 7, 1971

### ⋆ LABEL ⋆

Atlantic

### ⋆ PRODUCERS ⋆

David Crosby ⋆ Stephen Stills ⋆ Graham Nash ⋆ Neil Young

at the Cellar Door club in Washington, D.C., something of a tryout for two all-important appearances at New York City's most prestigious venue, Carnegie Hall. Neil was well aware of the importance of a concert at Carnegie Hall, and approached the gigs, on December 4 and 5, with the seriousness he felt they deserved. He also thought his songs—particularly in the exposed context of a solo appearance—should be granted the same respect. When an overzealous fan punctuated his delivery with a noisy request for the next number, Neil admonished him before storming off the stage, later excusing himself in an interview with *Creem* magazine: "It was intermission, I just took it a little early."

The Carnegie Hall dates were a prelude to a full-blown tour that took Neil Young—with just his acoustic guitar and piano for backup—across the United States and Canada, and to England, through December 1970 and January 1971. Audiences were stunned by his minimized versions of formerly "electric" numbers like "Southern Man," "Cinnamon Girl," and "The Loner," while being introduced to a cornucopia of fresh material including such classics-to-be as "Journey through the Past," "Dance, Dance, Dance," and "Heart of Gold."

**Neil rehearsing a number backstage in 1971.**

For many fans, the highlights of the solo gigs were Neil's often-lengthy introductions to songs—colorful, almost intimate preambles that wouldn't have been appropriate in the context of an amplified rock concert. One such heartfelt intro was recorded during the tour, at Toronto's Massey Hall, when Neil spoke about the inspiration for his harrowing anti-heroin tract "The Needle and the Damage Done," written about the heroin addiction of ex–Crazy Horse guitarist Danny Whitten:

"Ever since I left Canada, about five years ago or so . . . and moved down south . . . I found out a lot of things that I didn't know when I left. Some of 'em are good, and some of 'em are bad. Got to see a lot of great musicians before they happened . . . before they became famous . . . y'know, when they were just gigging. Five and six sets a night . . . things like that. And I got to see a lot of, um, great musicians who nobody ever got to see. For one reason or another. But . . . strangely enough, the real good ones . . . that you never got to see was . . . 'cause of . . . heroin. An' that started happening over an' over. Then it happened to someone that everyone knew about. So I just wrote a little song."

## Carrie

Just as the acoustic tour had been about to begin, Neil hurt his back while hauling some heavy wood on the ranch. He'd already had a back problem for some time, and now it was serious. He was committed to a hospital, and for almost a year—starting with the two-month solo trek—he had to move around with the aid of a traction machine and metal back brace.

And it was while he was in the hospital that a new romantic partner entered his life, the up-and-coming actress Carrie Snodgress.

Snodgress was riding high on the success of her first major movie, *Diary of a Mad Housewife*, for which she had won a Golden Globe Award—and received an Oscar nomination—for Best Actress. Neil had seen the movie, and was immediately fascinated by the twenty-four-year-old screen star, to the extent that he had a note delivered to her dressing room while she was appearing in a stage play in LA. The brief message just read "Call Neil Young." Snodgress confessed to having never heard of the singer at the time—"I didn't know Neil Young from Neil Diamond"—but after a friend explained who it was, she was intrigued enough to make a date.

By the time they got to meet, Neil was in traction, and their initial rendezvous was at his sickbed, just like a scene from a romantic comedy. It was the beginning of a classic whirlwind romance, and before long Carrie Snodgress had moved into the Broken Arrow ranch.

## Harvest

Right after the end of the solo tour, during the first week of February 1971, Neil Young traveled to Nashville to appear on the *Johnny Cash Show*. The TV recording, shot at the Ryman Auditorium (original home of the Grand Ole Opry), featured Neil singing "The Needle and the Damage Done" and "Journey through the Past," backed by Carl Perkins and the Tennessee Three. Also on the program were James Taylor, Linda Ronstadt, and Tony Joe White, and the four stars were invited to dinner by record producer Elliot Mazer on the following Saturday, February 6.

With an impressive track record that included Janis Joplin, Joan Baez, and Linda Ronstadt, Mazer had moved to Nashville from New York to open the Quadrafonic Sound Studios. It turned out he and Neil had a mutual friend in Elliot Roberts, and over dinner they broached the idea of Young making some recordings while he was in town. Neil was particularly interested in a group of local players Mazer worked with, Area Code 615, some of whom had played on Bob Dylan's albums *Blonde on Blonde* and the more recent *Nashville Skyline*.

Neil Young enjoying life at a party.

# Harvest

**M**ainly drawn from sessions with the studio backing group who Neil dubbed the Stray Gators, *Harvest* was the release that put him firmly into the mega-selling rock mainstream, topping the album charts in America, the UK, and Australia, and becoming the U.S. best-selling record of 1972. Two hit singles—"Old Man" and the chart-topping "Heart of Gold"—certainly helped the album's sales potential, but there are other gems here that made the collection a classic. James Taylor and Linda Ronstadt, plus Crosby, Stills, and Nash make appearances on backing vocals, while two tracks—"There's a World" and "A Man Needs a Maid"—feature the full London Symphony Orchestra, in stark contrast to the country rockers elsewhere. One other riveting diversion is "The Needle and the Damage Done," recorded live in the shadow of Danny Whitten's death from a drug overdose.

### ✦ SIDE ONE ✦
Out on the Weekend ★ Harvest ★ A Man Needs a Maid* ★ Heart of Gold ★ Are You Ready for the Country?

### ✦ SIDE TWO ✦
Old Man ★ There's a World* ★ Alabama ★ The Needle and the Damage Done** ★ Words (Between the Lines of Age)

All songs written by Neil Young

### ✦ RECORDED ✦
January–September, 1971, Quadrafonic Sound Studios, Nashville Broken Arrow Studio #2, Woodside, California ★ *Barking Town Hall, London ★ **Royce Hall, UCLA, Westwood, California

### ✦ RELEASED ✦
February 1, 1972

### ✦ PERSONNEL ✦
Neil Young (with the Stray Gators) ★ Neil Young (vocals, guitar, piano, harmonica) ★ Ben Keith (pedal steel guitar) ★ Kenny Buttrey (drums) ★ Tim Drummond (bass) ★ Jack Nitzsche (piano, slide guitar)

### ✦ ADDITIONAL PERSONNEL ✦
John Harris (piano) ★ Teddy Irwin (guitar) ★ James McMahon (piano) James Taylor (vocals, banjo-guitar) ★ David Crosby (vocals) ★ Graham Nash (vocals) ★ Linda Ronstadt (vocals) ★ Stephen Stills (vocals) ★*London Symphony Orchestra, conducted by David Meecham

### ✦ LABEL ✦
Reprise

### ✦ PRODUCERS ✦
Elliot Mazer ★ Neil Young ★ *Jack Nitzsche ★ **Henry Lewy

Mazer hastily booked in studio time for the next evening, and set about contacting available musicians. Several of the Area Code lineup were unavailable—either already booked for sessions, or (as was common on a weekend) out of town on a fishing trip. In the event, they got the services of drummer Kenny Buttrey, who had appeared on both the Dylan albums, steel guitarist Ben Keith, and bass player Tim Drummond. That night they recorded the basic tracks for "Heart of Gold," "Old Man," "Harvest," and "Dance, Dance, Dance," the first three songs being the initial numbers laid down for Neil's next album, the hugely successful *Harvest*.

Linda Ronstadt and James Taylor, still in town fresh from the Johnny Cash program, added background vocals to "Heart of Gold" and "Old Man," while Taylor also played banjo guitar on the latter track. Session musicians Andy McMahon and John Harris were later brought in at Quadrafonic to play piano on "Old Man" and "Harvest" respectively, and Teddy Irwin added a second acoustic guitar to "Heart of Gold."

The essential spontaneity of that first session continued over the following days, and at later sessions at both Quadrafonic and Neil's own home studio back at the California ranch. For the home

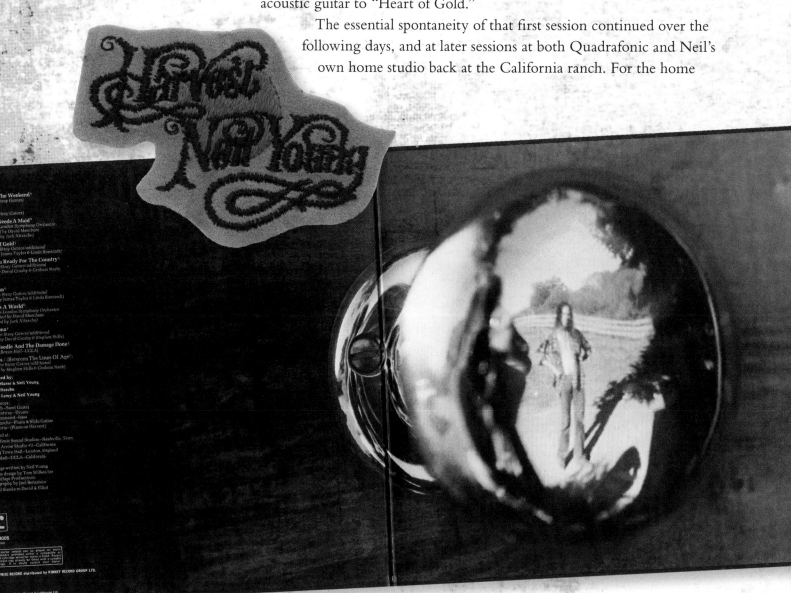

Out On The Weekend¹
(with the Stray Gators)

Harvest¹
(with the Stray Gators)

A Man Needs A Maid⁰
(with the London Symphony Orchestra
conducted by David Meecham
arranged by Jack Nitzsche)

Heart Of Gold¹
(with the Stray Gators/additional
vocals by James Taylor & Linda Ronstadt)

Are You Ready For The Country¹
(with the Stray Gators/additional
vocals by David Crosby & Graham Nash)

Side 2

Old Man¹
(with the Stray Gators/additional
vocals by James Taylor & Linda Ronstadt)

There's A World⁰
(with the London Symphony Orchestra
Conducted by David Meecham
Arranged by Jack Nitzsche)

Alabama¹
(with the Stray Gators/additional
vocals by David Crosby & Stephen Stills)

The Needle And The Damage Done³
(live at Royce Hall—UCLA)

Words¹ (Between The Lines Of Age)¹
(with the Stray Gators/additional
vocals by Stephen Stills & Graham Nash)

Produced by:
¹Elliot Mazer & Neil Young
⁰Jack Nitzsche
³Henry Lewy & Neil Young

Stray Gators:
Ben Keith—Steel Guitar
Kenny Buttrey—Drums
Tim Drummond—Bass
Jack Nitzsche—Piano & Slide Guitar
John Harris—(Piano on Harvest)

Recorded at:
Quadrafonic Sound Studios—Nashville, Tenn.
Broken Arrow Studio #2—California
Barking Town Hall—London, England
Royce Hall—UCLA—California

All songs written by Neil Young
Package design by Tom Wilkes for
Camouflage Productions.
Photography by Joel Bernstein
Special thanks to David & Elliot

K 54005
Stereo

A REPRISE RECORD distributed by KINNEY RECORD GROUP LTD.

Printed and made by Garrod & Lofthouse Ltd.

## Heart of Gold

### SINGLE

**A-SIDE** Heart of Gold* [Neil Young]

**B-SIDE** Sugar Mountain [Neil Young]

**RECORDED** February 8, 1971 [A-side]

**RELEASED** January 17, 1972

**LABEL** Reprise

**PRODUCERS** Elliot Mazer ✳ *Neil Young

sessions Mazer used a remote recording system, having speakers as monitors rather than the musicians wearing headphones. The resulting "leakage," when each microphone picked up the sound of other instruments, was just what Young and Mazer wanted; "Alabama," "Are You Ready for the Country," and "Words" were all recorded in this fashion, with additional "remote" backing vocals from Stephen Stills, David Crosby, and Graham Nash.

The basic band for these sessions, whom Neil decided to call the Stray Gators, appeared on seven tracks of *Harvest* when it was released in February 1972. Two more titles were recorded in far more extravagant circumstances, when Young and Jack Nitzsche shipped themselves to London to record "A Man Needs a Maid" and "There's a World" with the London Symphony Orchestra. And a tenth number was added to the track listing, a live recording of "The Needle and the Damage Done," taped near the end of Neil's solo tour at the Royce Hall, UCLA, in Los Angeles.

Throughout much of 1971, the progress of the album was continually interrupted by Neil's back condition, which wasn't getting any better. He finally went into the Cedars of Lebanon Hospital in Los Angeles to have discs in his back removed, an operation taking place on August 11. In the weeks that followed he was largely bedridden and only allowed to stay on his feet for four hours a day.

With the tracks completed in September, Reprise hoped for a Christmas release, but that was delayed when Neil rejected the cover artwork proposed for the album. The company wanted a straightforward picture of Neil Young for the sleeve, but Neil thought differently; he wanted no image of himself on it, just a

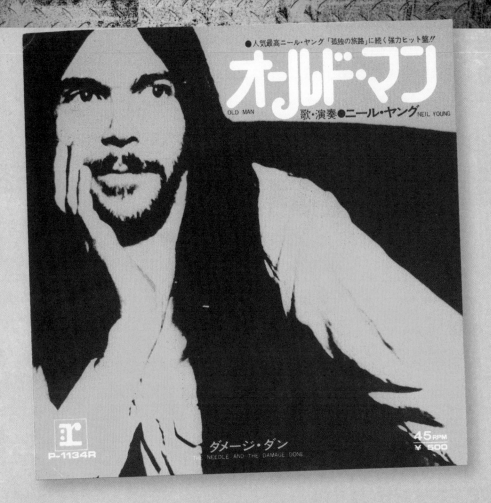

●人気最高ニール・ヤング「孤独の旅路」に続く強力ヒット盤!!

# オールド・マン
OLD MAN 歌・演奏●ニール・ヤング NEIL YOUNG

ダメージ・ダン
THE NEEDLE AND THE DAMAGE DONE

45 RPM
¥ 500

P-1134R

Japanese sleeve for the 1972 single "Old Man," backed with "The Needle and the Damage Done".

Far right: The "Heart of Gold" singer onstage in the early 1970s.

carefully crafted logo by graphics man Tom Wilkes on plain, high-quality paper. These final delays meant the release date of *Harvest* would now be postponed until February, although missing the lucrative holiday market was probably compensated for by the added anticipation for the first Neil Young album release since September 1970.

As with much of Neil Young's output both before and since, *Harvest* wasn't overwhelmingly praised by the critics on release, but its stock has risen dramatically over the years. Not for the first time, *Rolling Stone*'s assessment has been drastically revised, from John Mendelsohn's 1972 review calling it "A disappointing retread of earlier, superior efforts by Young," to the magazine naming it #78 among its "greatest albums of all time" in 2003.

Sales-wise it was a different story. Topping the charts in at least four major territories, and earning multiple platinum discs on either side of the Atlantic, it would be Neil Young's most successful album ever. And "Heart of Gold," seemingly tailor-made for the pop charts and released a couple of weeks ahead of the album, would be his best-selling single, and the only one to top the U.S. charts.

## Reluctant Superstar

To say that Neil Young wasn't the most obvious candidate for the role of top-of-the-chart pop star would be a gross understatement, and from the moment "Heart of Gold" broke big he seemed determined to keep the potential hype

and ballyhoo in perspective. In the liner notes to his *Decade* compilation of 1977, he referred to "Heart of Gold" as the song that "put me in the middle of the road. Traveling there soon became a bore, so I headed for the ditch. A rougher ride but I saw more interesting people there."

"I guess at that point I'd attained a lot of fame and everything that you dream about when you're a teenager," he would reflect in a 1985 *Melody Maker* interview. "I was still only twenty-three or twenty-four, and I realized I had a long way to go and this wasn't going to be the most satisfying thing, just sittin' around basking in the glory of having a hit record. It's really a very shallow experience, it's actually a very *empty* experience. It's nothing concrete except ego gratification, which is an empty unnerving kind of feeling. So I think I subconsciously set out to destroy that and rip it down, before it surrounded me. I could feel a wall building up around me."

With his health problems not completely resolved, the easiest way to avoid the limelight was to live the life of a semi-recluse. Young spent most of his time at the La Honda ranch amid rock-gossip speculation that there might be a reunion with Crosby, Stills and Nash in the cards. The rumors had been initially fueled a few months earlier, when Neil appeared as a guest at a Crosby and Nash show in Boston on October 3, 1971—and Stephen Stills turned up onstage as well. They repeated the exercise at Carnegie Hall the following evening, and then again (this time without Stills) in Berkeley, California. In March 1972, Neil once again guested with Crosby and Nash, at a benefit for prison inmates staged at the Winterland Ballroom in San Francisco.

Any kind of an official get-together was a long way off, however. Stephen Stills had recently launched his band Manassas, with a debut double album scheduled for May 1972, and Neil's health was certainly not up to the rigors of a full tour, with or without former colleagues.

## Journey through the Past

As his health and mobility gradually improved through the summer months of 1972, Neil Young embarked on a typically idiosyncratic project—a full-length movie, with soundtrack album to match, titled *Journey through the Past*. As the name suggested, ostensibly the subject would be a comprehensive trawl through Neil's musical history via archive film clips, studio outtakes, and so on. With the promise that the film would include never-before-seen concert footage of Crosby, Stills, Nash & Young, Warner Bros. liked the idea enough to fund the production, on the understanding that there would be a highly marketable album to go with it. But what transpired would be very, very different.

Initially, the movie seemed to be panning out as planned; Neil acquired the rights to the unseen CSNY footage, plus film of Buffalo Springfield via various New York TV companies, and to Warner managers it looked like they were getting what they expected. Neil, however, had other ideas, and began sourcing a bizarre collection of unrelated material, including Richard Nixon speaking at a

# Journey through the Past

ALBUM

Kings [Miklós Rózsa]**  ★  Soldier  ★  Let's Go Away for Awhile [Brian Wilson] *

All songs written by Neil Young except where indicated.

**RECORDED**

January–September, 1971

**RELEASED**

February 1, 1972

**LABEL**

Reprise

**PRODUCERS**

Elliot Mazer  ★  Neil Young  ★  *Jack Nitzsche  ★  **Henry Lewy

religious revival rally and shots of the Ku Klux Klan. He recruited an assortment of neighbors from Topanga Canyon to play out the roles in a loose plot he contrived, involving a central character called the Graduate who would aimlessly roam around in the desert for most of the film. As it became apparent that the movie was taking on a whole new surreal flavor, far removed from a straight documentary about Neil Young, Warner withdrew funding for the project, but still demanded a soundtrack album be ready in time for the Christmas market at the end of the year.

Appearing on November 7, 1972, the double album consisted mainly of live recordings that Young had made with Buffalo Springfield, CSNY, Crazy Horse, and the Stray Gators, plus snippets reflecting the "experimental" film to come—outtakes from recording sessions, studio conversations among Young, Crosby, and Stills, excerpts from Handel's *Messiah* and the theme music from the religious cinema epic *King of Kings*.

It was all a bit bewildering, both to longtime devotees expecting a musical compilation covering Neil's career to date, and to newfound fans who had discovered Neil through his chart-topping album and single earlier in the year. The music press was similarly dumfounded, a scathing review by Alan Lewis in *Melody Maker* being typical. Lewis called it "A rag-bag collection . . . seemingly salvaged from the cutting-room floor," adding, "Personally, I think it smacks of self-indulgence and laziness." As a follow-up to the phenomenally successful

REP 14 167
(1084)

Neil Young

Old Man
The Needle And
The Damage Done

From The
New Album
Harvest · Neil Young
REP 44 131

Product of Kinney Music GmbH · 2000 Hamburg 76 · Postbox 8754

## Old Man

SINGLE

**A-SIDE** Old Man* [Neil Young]
**B-SIDE** The Needle and the Damage Done** [Neil Young]
**RECORDED** January—September, 1971 [A-side]
**RELEASED** April 17, 1972
**LABEL** Reprise
**PRODUCERS** Elliot Mazer *
Neil Young* * Henry Lewy**

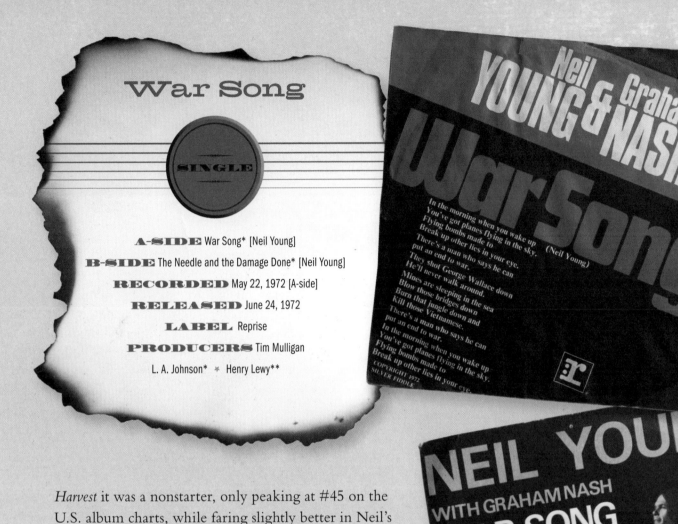

## War Song

**A-SIDE** War Song* [Neil Young]

**B-SIDE** The Needle and the Damage Done* [Neil Young]

**RECORDED** May 22, 1972 [A-side]

**RELEASED** June 24, 1972

**LABEL** Reprise

**PRODUCERS** Tim Mulligan

L. A. Johnson*  ✳  Henry Lewy**

*Harvest* it was a nonstarter, only peaking at #45 on the U.S. album charts, while faring slightly better in Neil's native Canada, where it reached #19.

The film did no better, opening at the U.S. Film Festival in Dallas on April 8, 1973, then playing at a handful of art houses before disappearing almost without a trace. Talking to *Rolling Stone* in 1975, Neil defended the movie as a worthwhile experiment, but admitted to its self-indulgence: "I made it for me . . . I never even had a script."

In addition to "Heart of Gold," two other singles appeared during Neil's convalescence over the first half of 1972. The first was "Old Man" from *Harvest*, released in April; the second was "War Song," recorded with Graham Nash and released on June 2. Credited on some single sleeves as "Neil Young–Graham Nash–Stray Gators," the song was a comment on the Vietnam War inspired by the shooting of the racist governor George Wallace of Alabama. Unlike Neil's blockbuster single at the beginning of the year, neither sold spectacularly, either at home or abroad. But over the months of post-invalid recovery, one event did highlight Neil Young's life more than any chart triumph could: On September 8, 1972, Carrie Snodgress gave birth to his first son, Zeke.

# Maverick

**F**OLLOWING the Kent State shootings of 1970, the deaths of Jimi Hendrix and Janis Joplin that same year, and that of the Doors' Jim Morrison in 1971, the early 1970s seemed to mark the death of the hippie dream and the idealism of the counterculture. There was enormous pressure on big-selling acts like Crosby, Stills & Nash—and the post-*Harvest* Neil Young—to play the game with the big record corporations, which were helping create the acts' vast, conspicuous wealth. But as ever the maverick, Neil Young would react against the presumed rock star formula again and again, with a series of stylistic changes that often bewildered the critics, and even the most faithful of his fans.

## Tragedy

During the fall of 1972, Neil Young felt well enough to think about touring again, and this time decided on working with an instrumental backup rather than taking on another solo trek. His thoughts automatically turned to his most recent compatriots the Stray Gators, who had served him well on he record-breaking *Harvest*. And despite Danny Whitten's well-known problems with heroin, Neil also contacted the musician—now an *ex*-member of Crazy Horse.

After their appearance on just three tracks of *After the Gold Rush* in 1970, Crazy Horse had decided to strike out on their own while Neil pursued his solo projects. They negotiated a deal with Reprise, and February 1971 saw the release of their Jack Nitzsche–produced debut album as a separate unit, titled simply *Crazy Horse*.

Danny Whitten, already fired from the *Gold Rush* sessions partway through, had continued with Crazy Horse, but with no sign of his heroin problem getting any better. Though sometimes playing brilliantly, he struggled through many of the *Crazy Horse* recordings, and when it came time to tour in support of the album,

he could hardly keep it together sufficiently to rehearse, let alone perform live. Eventually the others couldn't tolerate his debilitated state any longer; they dismissed Whitten prior to making their next album, *Loose*, released in January 1972. From there Danny Whitten continued on a downward spiral, with all the hallmarks of a committed junkie, interested in little but his next fix.

Nevertheless, having heard a rumor that Whitten was kicking his habit, Neil decided to give the guitarist a chance. But however the gossip had started, it was certainly ill founded. Whitten accepted Young's invitation eagerly, and arrived at Broken Arrow for rehearsals; seeking to help his errant friend, Neil had arranged for Danny to receive a five-hundred-dollar weekly retainer—probably not the best idea in the case of someone with a serious addiction problem. The sessions were chaotic as far as Whitten's participation was concerned, the guitarist sometimes falling asleep while standing ready to play. Neil remembered one occasion when Danny moved from one song to another midtune without even realizing he was doing it. After agonizing over the decision—he even tried to teach Whitten the new songs chord-by-chord prior to the actual rehearsals— Neil knew he had to fire Danny, once again. They put him on the next flight back to Los Angeles with fifty dollars in his pocket as compensation; that was the last Neil would see of Danny Whitten, who was found dead from an overdose the following morning, November 18, 1972.

The members of Crazy Horse were on tour, playing a gig in Detroit, when they heard the news; although shocked and saddened, unfortunately they knew it had been a tragedy waiting to happen. Neil likewise took it badly—especially as they had not parted on the best of terms—imagining how Whitten might have survived had he kept him in the lineup.

*"He couldn't remember anything. He was too out of it. Too far gone. I had to tell him to go back to L.A."*

## Time Fades Away

After Danny Whitten's death, an atmosphere of gloom pervaded proceedings as Neil and the band prepared for their tour, scheduled for sixty-plus dates starting on January 5, 1973, in Milwaukee. Many of the gigs were in large stadiums, not best suited for the acoustic set with which Neil opened each show. In the wake of his chart-storming *Harvest* and "Heart of Gold," Young's audiences were noisier and rowdier than before; when he couldn't get the kind of attention he wished for during the solo set, he would perversely crank up the volume when the Gators came on, to the extent that neither audience nor musicians could clearly hear what was going on. Producer Elliot Mazer, struggling to make a live recording under increasingly fraught conditions, would call it "the anti-*Harvest* tour."

Tensions within the band rose as the thorny question of money came up. A top session man, drummer Kenny Buttrey had demanded one hundred thousand dollars for the tour; when news leaked to the others, they wanted a similar slice of the action. Buttrey also had ongoing issues with the bass player Tim Drummond, which surfaced in arguments and fights, both onstage and off. About a month into the tour, Buttrey quit; Neil brought in Johnny Barbata (from the CSNY lineup) in his place.

Meanwhile as the tour wore on, Neil's voice began to give out. Straining to be heard during the overly loud electric sets hadn't helped, and now he was simply screaming the lyrics as best he could. In need of some vocal assistance (and moral backup no doubt), Neil brought in David Crosby and Graham Nash to help out. The addition of the two CSNY men smoothed things over to a degree, both sound-wise and in tempering the inter-band tensions—not least

Neil honing his guitar skills during the 1970s, by which time he was a huge star.

45-1017

**NEIL YOUNG**
**El tiempo se esfuma**
El último viaje a Tulsa reprise

A foreign version of *Time Fades Away*.

Crosby, Stills, Nash & Young featured on the cover of a 1974 *Rolling Stone* magazine.

those between Neil and Jack Nitzsche—that had continually bugged the tour.

Despite the sometimes near-impossible conditions, Elliot Mazer managed to record significant samples of the tour, aiming at a live album release later in the year. The result was *Time Fades Away*, which, considering the situation it came out of, was a moderate commercial success—certainly a better result than anyone involved could have hope for.

When deciding which of Mazer's usable recordings to use on the album, Neil made the typically unexpected decision to feature only songs that had never been released before in any form—a full album of originals unfamiliar to the fans. That of course is what was expected of a new studio release, but live albums were usually balanced with crowd-pleasing favorites that listeners were happy to hear again in the context of an in-concert performance.

Although Young himself would later declare that it was his "least favorite" album, it certainly achieved the expression of naked emotions, which at the time he said was the intention of the choice of numbers. With songs addressing deeply emotive subjects including organized religion ("Yonder Stands the Sinner"), the urban apocalypse he'd only hinted at in "After the Gold Rush" ("L.A."), and the futile lives of a city's desperate underclass ("Time Fades Away"), the overall feel of the collection was one of stark passions directly addressed. And of course there was the openly autobiographical "Don't Be Denied," tracing his life from a Winnipeg childhood to Los Angeles superstardom in six compact verses.

By the time the album appeared in October 1973, Neil Young had moved on yet again—via a brief flirtation with Crosby, Stills and Nash—to a full-blown reconciliation with Crazy Horse.

## Hawaii

Near the end of May 1973, there was once again movement toward a reassembling of CSNY. With Stephen Stills having just disbanded his group Manassas, he was raring to go, and Nash and Crosby persuaded Neil to join them on the Hawaiian island of Maui. There, away from the usual pressures of California (or almost anywhere on mainland North America for that matter), they worked on new songs that each of the quartet had been stockpiling. Neil Young also brought material he wrote while there, including "Hawaiian Sunrise" and "Sailboat Song" (which would eventually become "Through My Sails"). The idea was to take the preliminary tapes made on Maui back to Neil's Broken Arrow ranch studio for completion. They even had a working title for the album, *Human Highway*, named for one of Neil's new songs.

Nixon's New Defenders & Their Strange Pasts

# ROLLING STONE

ISSUE NO. 168 · AUGUST 29, 1974 · 75¢ UK25p

The United States
of America
vs. John Lennon

The Private
Thought
of Raquel
Welch

Mama Cass
(1941-1974)

Crosby,
Stills, Nash
& Young
Anatomy of a Reunion
By Ben Fong-Torres

SM14170

# Time Fades Away

ALBUM

A collection of live recordings made during Neil's grueling U.S. tour in early 1973, the album captures the often-frustrating challenge of playing a meaningful set in front of an audience of 20,000 or more. What it lacks in finesse, however, is more than compensated for by the sheer emotion that Neil Young pours into the performances. At Neil's insistence no "old favorites" were included, contrary to common practice with live albums. The songs tackle intensely emotive issues, including the desperate lives of the L.A. underclass, the hypocrisy of formal religion, and impending environmental catastrophe. The high point for many, however, remains the track that opens Side Two in the vinyl version, "Don't Be Denied," in which Neil sums up his life story in just six typically economic verses.

### SIDE ONE

Time Fades Away ★ Journey through the Past
Yonder Stands the Sinner ★ L.A. ★ Love in Mind

### SIDE TWO

Don't Be Denied ★ The Bridge ★ Last Dance
All songs written by Neil Young

### RELEASED

October 15, 1973

### RECORDED

Royce Hall, UCLA, Westwood, California, January 30, 1971
Public Hall, Cleveland, February 11, 1973 ★ Myriad, Oklahoma City,
March 1, 1973 ★ Coliseum, Seattle, March 17, 1973; Sports Arena,
San Diego, March 19, 1973 ★ Coliseum, Phoenix,
March 28, 1973 ★ Memorial Auditorium, Sacramento, April 1, 1973

### PERSONNEL

Neil Young (guitar, piano, harmonica, vocals) ★ Ben Keith (pedal
steel guitar, vocals) ★ Johnny Barbata (drums) ★ Tim Drummond
(bass) ★ Joe Yankee (bass) ★ Jack Nitzsche (piano, vocals)

### ADDITIONAL PERSONNEL

David Crosby (guitar, vocals) ★ Graham Nash (guitar, vocals)

### LABEL

Reprise

### PRODUCERS

Elliot Mazer ★ Neil Young

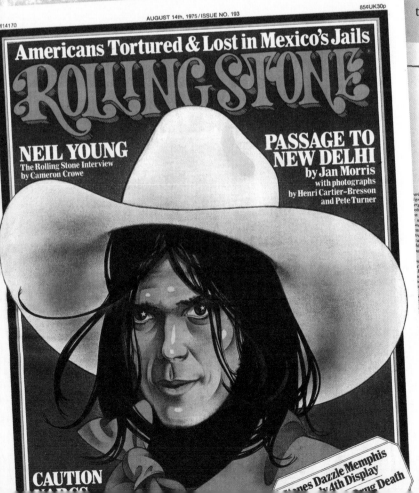

Neil featured in an extensive interview with Cameron Crowe in the August 14, 1975 edition of *Rolling Stone*, including an illustration by Joni Mitchell (opposite).

Neil contacted Elliot Mazer, in England at the time, and as soon as the producer arrived at La Honda recording got underway. But things were difficult from the start. Mazer would recall how Graham Nash and David Crosby tried to move things along in their own, often earnest, way while Stephen Stills was happy to get high all night, then drag himself to the studio in an often-confused attempt at recording. "We tried to do an album and it fell apart," Stills later confessed, implying that he was not the only culprit. Neil meanwhile kept all three at a distance, as it quickly became apparent that there was not going to be a new CSNY album in the offing—at least not in the immediate future.

## Tonight's the Night

While the latest CSNY project was still crumbling, news broke of the death of Bruce Berry, a well-liked roadie whom they had all worked with. Berry had worked in his brother's business, the Los Angeles–based Studio Instrument Rentals, and through that connection started operating as a roadie. He was soon working for some of the biggest names around, including CSNY and their various individual projects, and with the high life in the upper echelons of the rock scene came the inevitable exposure to drugs—in Bruce's case, lots of them.

Allegedly turned on to heroin by the ill-fated Danny Whitten, Berry had by now reached the stage in his dependence where he was selling the business stock (or even musicians' instruments he had access to as a roadie) to buy his next fix. When Berry was found dead from an overdose, early in June 1973, it hit Neil Young—still coming to terms with Whitten's passing—particularly hard.

With the bleak vision of these two close-to-home fatalities very much in mind, before long Neil had reconvened Crazy Horse to start work on a new batch of songs, assembling, appropriately, at Ken Berry's Studio Instrumental Rentals rehearsal space.

With Nils Lofgren and Ben Keith added to the Crazy Horse lineup, and old partner David Briggs on the production desk, in early August recording began for *Tonight's the Night* with a mobile studio rigged up at the back of the SIR building. Because the title track mentioned Bruce Berry by name, the sessions were regarded as a wake for Berry and Danny Whitten, with large quantities of alcohol to match. The final release also included "Come On Baby Let's Go Downtown," featuring a live recording made with Danny Whitten in 1970.

Not a concert album as such, the sessions were nevertheless recorded as live, straight from a small stage set up in the rehearsal room. Even when a performance was off-key, there was no re-recording or overdubbing; everything was preserved as live, and from this the chosen tracks emerged. The spontaneous, rough-at-the-edges quality thus achieved was further enhanced by snatches of conversation between tracks: "They were intros to the songs," Neil would explain in a 1985 *Melody Maker* interview. "Not counts but little discussions, three- and four-word conversations between songs, and it left it with a very spooky feeling."

These preambles to songs were excluded from the final album before Neil submitted it to Warner Bros. Even then, record company executives were apprehensive about the ragged quality of the entire recording: "They couldn't believe how sloppy it was, they couldn't believe that I really wanted to put it out. I said, 'That's it, that's the way it's going out.'"

Challenging, to say the least, *Tonight's the Night* nevertheless garnered sympathetic reviews when it was eventually released nearly two years later, in June 1975. *Rolling Stone* acknowledged that "The jitteriness of the music, its sloppy, unarranged (but decidedly structured) feeling is clearly calculated," while *Creem* magazine's Wayne Robbins colorfully summed up: "This is not the work of a detached, millionaire pop star. Young has assimilated the collective unconscious of the knife-wielding, gun-toting, dope-burning street people who populate western towns like Boulder or Santa Fe, the acid casualties of the counter-culture who'll call you brother but kill you for some spare change."

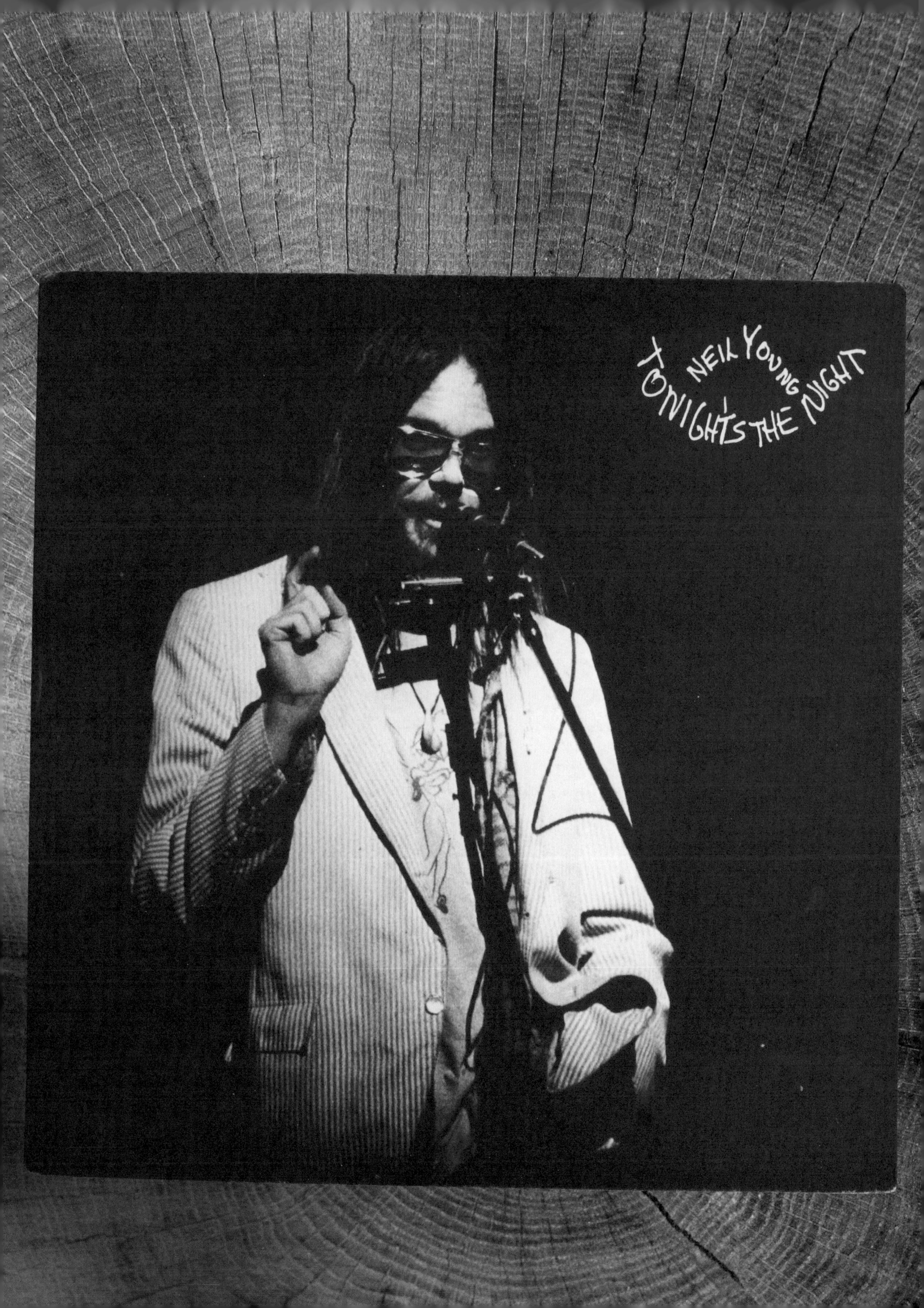
NEIL YOUNG
TONIGHT'S THE NIGHT

# Tonight's the Night

**R**ecorded in a mobile studio but "as live," with no overdubbing or editing involved, the entire album has a spontaneous, off-the-cuff quality that some (particularly the record company) found disconcerting at the time, while others applauded its raw, natural ambience. Made as a "wake" for deceased colleagues guitarist Danny Whitten and roadie Bruce Berry, although two added songs ("Lookout Joe" and "Borrowed Tune") soften the blow somewhat, the album retains its uncompromising feel throughout. For Neil, one suspects it was a means of purging some of the guilt and sense of responsibility he clearly felt over the deaths, confirmed by the inclusion of a live track, "Come on Baby Let's Go Downtown," recorded with Whitten in 1970.

## SIDE ONE

Tonight's the Night ★ Speakin' Out ★ World on a String ★ Borrowed Tune [based on "Lady Jane" by the Rolling Stones] ★ Come on Baby, Let's Go Downtown [Danny Whitten, Neil Young] ★ Mellow My Mind

## SIDE TWO

Roll Another Number (for the Road) ★ Albuquerque ★ New Mama ★ Lookout Joe ★ Tired Eyes ★ Tonight's the Night—Part II

All songs written by Neil Young except where indicated.

## RECORDED

August–September 1973, Studio Instrumental Rentals, Los Angeles ★ March 1970, Fillmore East, New York ★ December 1972, Broken Arrow Ranch, La Honda, California ★ December 1973, Broken Arrow Ranch, La Honda

## RELEASED

June 20, 1975

## PERSONNEL

Neil Young (guitar, piano, harmonica, vibes, vocals) ★ Ben Keith (pedal steel guitar, slide guitar, vocals) ★ Nils Lofgren (guitar, piano, vocals) ★ Danny Whitten (guitar, vocals) ★ Jack Nitzsche (electric piano, vocals) ★ Tim Drummond (bass) ★ Billy Talbot (bass) ★ Ralph Molina (drums) ★ Kenny Buttrey (drums) ★ George Whitsell (vocals)

## LABEL

Reprise

## PRODUCERS

David Briggs ★ Tim Mulligan ★ Neil Young ★ Elliot Mazer

Neil Young &
Santa Monica Flyers

Zueens College
New York City,
November 15, 1973

Don't Be Denied
When You Dance I Can Really Love
World On A String        ROCK RARE
New Mama                 COLLECTION
Roll Another Number      FETISH
Tired Eyes
The Needle And The Damage Done
Flying On The Ground Is Wrong
Human Highway
Helpless
I Believe In You
Cinnamon Girl
Cowgirl In The Sand        Neil Young &
Tonight's The Night        Santa Monica Flyers
                           November 15, 1973
                           Zueens College
                           New York City, New York
                           November 15, 1973

**A poster for the Santa Monica Flyers tour of England and Scotland in 1975.**

## Santa Monica Flyers

Almost immediately after the recording sessions for *Tonight's the Night* were over, Neil and the remodeled Crazy Horse embarked on a promotional tour. A series of North American dates in cities across the United States and Canada was followed by a week of appearances in the United Kingdom. Even when staged primarily to promote a new album, the usual practice on tours was to balance the old with the new, giving the audience a mix of the familiar and the fresh. Neil, however, had other ideas.

On the American dates he played almost all new material, restricting oldies to just the encore. And although as far as the record company was concerned it was *Time Fades Away*—due out in October—that he should have been plugging, Neil went ahead and played entire concerts of just *Tonight's the Night* material.

From the start of the tour the performances took on the drunken character of the wake-like recording sessions, in front of nonplussed audiences who did not know the circumstances referred to in the songs. Vast amounts of tequila were consumed onstage every night, and Neil introduced each number with long, often incoherent ramblings that meant nothing to the crowd.

The dates in England and Scotland (for which Neil renamed the band the Santa Monica Flyers), where fans had not seen him playing live for a couple of years, were particularly problematic. Neil would open with "Tonight's the Night," devote the whole hour-plus set to the SIR material, then close with "Tonight's the Night." When the crowd howled for an encore, hoping for at least a snatch of a well-known classic, on more than one occasion Neil returned to the stage, said he'd like to play something they were familiar with, then launched into yet another take on "Tonight's the Night." The slick opening sets of the soon-to-be megastar band the Eagles set a stark contrast with the shambling delivery of the headliner. And at every venue, the record company had a display of *Time Fades Away* posters and album sleeves on show, plugging Neil Young's current release.

Returning to the States, Neil—perhaps wary of home-ground reactions after the reception he'd suffered in Britain—concluded the tour with more considered concessions to the crowd. The bigger venues made his "intimate" ramblings about Miami Beach, which preceded every performance, even more meaningless, so he cut down on the intros and slipped a few more oldies-but-goldies into the set list. For the *Tonight's the Night* album itself, a release date was a long way off. While the live-concert *Time Fades Away* sold steadily, Warner and Neil Young had a rare moment of total agreement when both parties decided that a lot more work was needed before the SIR sessions could be considered fit for the marketplace.

## On the Beach

As always impatient to get into new areas, Neil postponed further work on *Tonight's the Night* while he prepared his next project. Pedal steel player Ben Keith was there from the start, along with Greg Reeves on bass, at some Broken Arrow sessions supervised by David Briggs during February and March 1974. When Briggs was forced to drop out due to illness, the focus shifted to the Sunset Sound studios in LA where Keith, Ralph Molina, and Tim Drummond provided the backbone to *On the Beach*.

Neil looking somewhwat dishevelled during the controversial "Time Fades Away" tour in which he just plugged songs from *Tonight's the Night*.

# "One of the most depressing records I've ever made.

## NEIL ON "ON THE BEACH"

Finally concluding the first week in April, the sessions involved a powerful mixed bag of musicians, including Rick Danko and Levon Helm from the Band, David Crosby and Graham Nash, the virtuoso Nashville fiddle and slide guitar player Rusty Kershaw, and the guitar player from the embryo Crazy Horse group the Rockets, George Whitsell.

The recording of *On the Beach* was chaotic to say the least, with the veteran and much-respected producer Al Schmidt dropping out of the project after finding it impossible to work with the stoned assembly of musicians. In his place Neil brought in Mark Harmon, and somehow the sessions lurched to a seemingly befuddled, ultra-laid-back completion. The result, however, despite being cited by Young as "one of the most depressing records I've ever made," was one of his strongest collection of songs to date.

Apart from a perhaps unnecessary remake of 1971's "See the Sky About to Rain," the album was replete with memorable—if consistently doom-laden—imagery, in numbers like "Ambulance Blues," "Walk On," his dedication to Carrie Snodgress, "Motion Pictures," and the surprisingly topical "Revolution Blues." Not normally given to pontificating on "issues" in his songs, "Revolution Blues"—inspired by his brief association with Charles Manson—has Neil satirizing not just the capitalist establishment but also contemporary radicals epitomized by the heiress-turned-revolutionary Patty Hearst.

"Ambulance Blues" is of particular interest to fans of the British acoustic guitarist Bert Jansch, whose "Needle of Death" was (apparently "unintentionally") quoted in the melody. "As for acoustic guitar, Bert Jansch is on the same level as Jimi [Hendrix]," Young told the French *Guitare & Claviers* magazine in 1992. "That first record of his is epic. It came from England, and I was especially taken by 'Needle of Death,' such a beautiful and angry song. That guy was so good. . . ."

The cover illustration, with a surreal beachscape conceived by Neil, has him with his back to us, staring out to sea, while in the foreground a bizarre collection of items includes beach furniture, a can of Coors beer, a fender off a

Neil Young and Stephen Stills on stage at Oakland Stadium, July 14, 1974, during the concert by CSNY.

ON THE BEACH

# On the Beach

**B**y Young's own admission, this is certainly a depressing album—not by virtue of any musical shortcomings, but by the overriding atmosphere of gloom that pervades the collection. That's not to say the songs are lackluster by any means, in fact at the time of its first release the 1974 album proved to be one of Neil Young's strongest offerings to date. His concerns in these lyrics are, on the one hand, deeply personal, but at the same time recognizable to all. He voices his increasing disenchantment with the superstar lifestyle, which he unwittingly embraces, and the sad realization that the optimism of the 1960s was, in the main, a naïve pipe dream. And in "Revolution Blues" he addresses his doom-laden angst to not just the predictable target of the consumer society, but also the trendy revolutionaries who had inherited the post-hippie mantle of protest by the mid–1970s.

### SIDE ONE

Walk On ★ See the Sky About to Rain ★ Revolution Blues ★ For the Turnstiles ★ Vampire Blues

### SIDE TWO

On the Beach ★ Motion Pictures (For Carrie) ★ Ambulance Blues

All songs written by Neil Young

### RECORDED

November 30, 1973–April 7, 1974, Broken Arrow Ranch, La Honda, California ★ Sunset Sound, Los Angeles

### RELEASED

July 19, 1974

### PERSONNEL

Neil Young (guitar, banjo-guitar, harmonica, piano, vocals) ★ Ben Keith (pedal steel guitar, slide guitar, piano, organ, percussion, bass, vocals) ★ Tim Drummond (bass, percussion) ★ Ralph Molina (drums, vocals)

### ADDITIONAL PERSONNEL

David Crosby: (guitar) ★ Rick Danko (bass) ★ Levon Helm (drums) ★ Rusty Kershaw (slide guitar, fiddle) ★ Graham Nash (electric piano) ★ Billy Talbot (bass) ★ Joe Yankee (harp, electric tambourine) ★ George Whitsell (guitar)

### LABEL

Reprise

### PRODUCERS

Neil Young ★ David Briggs ★ Neil Young, Mark Harman ★ Al Schmidt

Cadillac, and that day's newspaper announcing the desire for President Richard Nixon's resignation.

Reviews of the album were mixed, particularly in the UK, although the influential *New Musical Express* revised an initially downbeat assessment with a slightly surprising comparison to Bob Dylan. "There's scattered evidence for a Dylan Experience in many tracks from *On the Beach*," wrote Ian MacDonald, "but the more important thing is that, though Dylan and Young may have taken a parallel path recently, Young now sounds actively dangerous, whereas Dylan's just singing his own peculiar gospel." *Rolling Stone* likewise at the time called it "One of the most despairing albums of the decade," but has similarly changed its assessment over the years.

## The Doom Tour

On July 9, 1974, just ten days prior to the release of *On the Beach*, a reconvened Crosby, Stills, Nash & Young embarked on their most ambitious tour yet. After months of rumor, the long-awaited get-together had finally been announced to the press in March, while Neil was still finishing the album. What was to be the biggest rock tour ever staged was the brainchild of a triumvirate of industry heavyweights, namely Elliot Roberts, record boss David Geffen, and Fillmore promoter Bill Graham. The plan was to present CSNY in a string of mainly outdoor stadiums, each with a fifty-thousand-plus capacity, the tour comprising thirty-one concerts staged in twenty-four cities in just over two months. The sheer audacity of the idea was capped by the level of support acts enrolled for the trek, with superstars Joni Mitchell, Santana, the Beach Boys, and the Band opening for the quartet. Confirming the previous formula of CSNY being not so much a group as four individual artists, the trek was characterized by each having his own on-tour arrangements, to the extent that there were four separate sets of road managers serving their personal needs. Neil in particular kept his distance from the others, although his well-remembered feuding with Stephen Stills was not as apparent as on previous occasions, and while CSN—especially Crosby and Stills—wallowed in various levels of rock star excess, Young actually traveled from city to city in his own private motor home. All four did plenty of drugs on the road, as usual, but again CSN were out there in a world of their own when it came to cocaine abuse, not a favorite kick as far as Neil was concerned.

From the earliest days of planning, there was a general consensus that as far as the motives for the tour were concerned, all four were mainly in it for the money. It was being driven by record company managers and their respective accounting departments rather than any artistic ambition on the musicians' part. David Crosby even came up with an apt name for it, dubbing it "the Doom Tour." The trek wound up in spectacular fashion in England, in front of a

*So Far*, a compilation of Crosby, Stills, Nash & Young tracks released in August 1974 to coincide with the mammoth tour. Cover art by Joni Mitchell.

Previous pages: CSNY playing to huge crowds during the 1974 trek that became known as the "Doom Tour."

Below: The members of Crazy Horse: Ralph Molina, Billy Talbot, Frank "Poncho" Sampedro, and Neil Young.

capacity audience of seventy-two thousand at London's Wembley Stadium, at a gig hailed by the British music press as "the concert of the century."

## Homegrown

With the Doom Tour finally completed, and *On the Beach* in the record stores—climbing to a healthy #16 among the U.S. best-sellers and earning a gold disc in the process—Neil was ready for another foray into the recording studio, this time with his producer from the triumphant *Harvest* sessions, Elliot Mazer. With an impressive lineup of participants, including the Band's Robbie Robertson and Levon Helm, and the then-rising country star Emmylou Harris, the sessions took place between November 1974 and January 1975, not long after Neil's separation from Carrie Snodgress. The relationship between the singer and actress had been troubled for some time, and a reported infidelity on the

part of Snodgress was the last straw for Young. Added to this was the shared trauma surrounding their two-year-old son Zeke, who had been diagnosed with cerebral palsy not long before.

Never actually released, the material for the album (called *Homegrown*) remained a lost archive much discussed by Neil Young fans for many years. There was an overriding darkness to most of the songs—according to Neil, the main reason for shelving the project—and although a complete track listing has never been revealed, the titles of some of the numbers from the sessions ("Separate Ways," "Vacancy," and so on) suggested the general feeling of lost love and hopelessness. The recording was actually completed, and a cover even designed ready for release, when Neil decided to put out a finalized version of *Tonight's the Night* instead, in June 1975. Of *Homegrown*, he has since been quoted, "It was just a very down album."

## Zuma

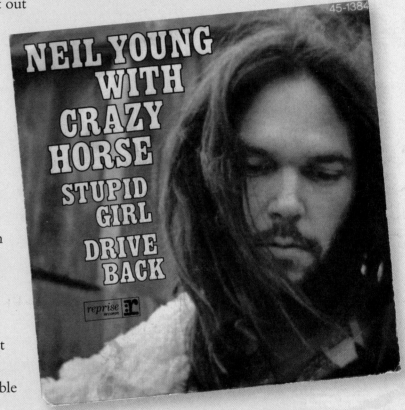

Before he began recording the *Homegrown* songs—some of which would appear in later album contexts over the years—Neil's other project was to get together a refreshed lineup of Crazy Horse. He'd done the marathon CSNY gigs, and now he felt the need to work with a regular band of his own once more. He had already contacted Billy Talbot and Ralph Molina, who told him they had a new guitarist in line to replace the late Danny Whitten, a larger-than-life character from Detroit by the name of Frank "Poncho" Sampedro. After an almost abortive first meeting at Chicago's Chess Studios, Neil got together with the new Crazy Horse ensemble and began recording *Zuma* in the summer of 1974.

His first album after the so-called Ditch Trilogy of *Time Fades Away*, *Tonight's the Night*, and *On the Beach*, *Zuma* marked a move from the dark moods of those works to a more upbeat atmosphere with a country-rock feel, harking back to his previous album with Crazy Horse, 1969's *Everybody Knows This Is Nowhere*. The title was almost certainly taken from Zuma Beach in Malibu, where Neil had a place and Crazy Horse and their entourage hung out at the time, although another school of thought places it in the context of the Aztec leader Montezuma, who features in the song "Cortez the Killer."

Although delivered in a tough, gritty style, many of the songs on *Zuma* (such as "Stupid Girl," "Don't Cry No Tears," and "Lookin' for a Love") address the theme of unrequited love and failed relationships—even "Cortez the Killer," ostensibly about the Spanish conquest of Mexico from the viewpoint of the

# Zuma

**R**eunited with Crazy Horse, with a new guitarist Frank Sampedro in place of the late Danny Whitten, this marks a move away from the rather difficult trilogy of *Time Fades Away*, *On the Beach*, and *Tonight's the Night*, to the more upbeat territory of Neil's earlier excursions with the band. Certainly more listener-friendly, tracks like "Don't Cry No Tears" and "Lookin' for a Love"—both paeans to unrequited love—exude a commercial appeal that many fans thought Young had abandoned forever. But the highlight is "Cortez the Killer," the seven-and-a-half minute epic about the Spanish conquest and destruction of the Aztec civilization, with an instrumental break by Neil, which has been ranked among the greatest rock guitar solos of all time.

## SIDE ONE

Don't Cry No Tears ★ Dangerbird ★ Pardon My Heart ★ Lookin' for a Love* ★ Barstool Blues*

## SIDE TWO

Stupid Girl ★ Drive Back ★ Cortez the Killer ★ Through My Sails*

All songs written by Neil Young

## RECORDED

June 16, 1974–August 29, 1975, Broken Arrow Ranch, La Honda, California ★ Point Dume, California

## RELEASED

November 10, 1975

## PERSONNEL

Neil Young & Crazy Horse:

Neil Young (guitar, vocals) ★ Frank Sampedro (guitar) ★ Billy Talbot (bass, vocals) ★ Ralph Molina (drums, vocals) ★ Tim Drummond (bass) ★ Crosby, Stills, Nash & Young ("Through My Sails" only): David Crosby (vocals) ★ Stephen Stills (bass, vocals) ★ Graham Nash (vocals) ★ Neil Young (guitar, vocals) ★ Russ Kunkel (congas)

## LABEL

Reprise

## PRODUCERS

Neil Young ★ David Briggs ★ *Neil Young & Tim Mulligan

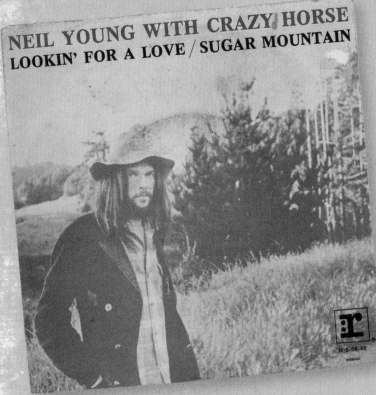

NEIL YOUNG WITH CRAZY HORSE
LOOKIN' FOR A LOVE / SUGAR MOUNTAIN

Aztecs, and one of Neil Young's greatest-ever compositions, can be interpreted as being symbolic of a lost love.

Released in November 1975, the album was well received by the critics, seen as a return to accessible rock 'n' roll after what many considered the deliberately obscure self-indulgence of the Ditch albums, but it failed to sell in spectacular numbers, only reaching the #25 position on the U.S. long-player charts.

To promote the album, rather than a major record-company-financed tour, Neil took his inspiration from Bob Dylan's Rolling Thunder Revue, which from October that year had been playing modest venues virtually unannounced, with a collection of fellow performers including Joan Baez, Joni Mitchell, and Roger McGuinn among others. In what was subsequently dubbed the "Rolling Zuma Revue," Young booked himself and Crazy Horse into a series of low-key venues across Northern California—mostly music bars and local clubs—the last-minute arrangements allowing for a degree of anonymity impossible on the regular rock circuit. Around the same time there were, however, a clutch of informal appearances that did draw the rock media's attention, when Neil Young got up on stage with his old Buffalo Springfield and CSNY sparring partner Stephen Stills.

## Long May You Run

The final track on *Zuma*, "Through My Sails" (originally titled "The Sailboat Song"), was by Crosby, Stills, Nash & Young, the only track to be released from the quartet's abortive recording sessions from late 1974 in Hawaii. Less than three weeks after the album's November 10 release, Neil was back onstage with Stills at a Stanford University date, followed by another impromptu appearance at Stills's gig at UCLA Westwood. Further fueling speculation that the two compatriots were up to something, on New Year's Eve Young again sat in on a Stills set, this time at Alex's, a bar near his ranch at La Honda.

Beginning February 16, 1976, Young and Stills began recording at the Criteria Studios in Miami, with Stephen's backing musicians. The sessions, engineered by Atlantic Record's legendary Tom Dowd, progressed through the next few weeks until Neil was obliged to call a halt due to a world tour booked with Crazy Horse. With dates in Japan, Norway, Denmark, Germany, France, Holland, Belgium, and the UK, the tour concluded with four nights in London followed by one in Scotland, at Glasgow's Apollo Theatre. The reception was

# Long May You Run

## "The greatest rock band in the world"

Opposite: Neil in action during
the Spring 1976 world tour
with Crazy Horse.

ecstatic, especially in England, where some critics hailed Crazy Horse as the
"greatest rock band in the world."

As soon as the trek was over, Neil was back in the studio, anxious to finish
off the Stills/Young album that was now being followed by a summer tour. At
one point soon after the recording resumed, the entire exercise looked to be
turning into a full-blown CSNY project when David Crosby and Graham Nash
were briefly involved, before the almost inevitable verbal fireworks turned into
a full-scale conflagration of rival egos and interests. Much to Crosby and Nash's
annoyance, Young and Stills opted to discard any joint efforts recorded with
their two former buddies, and returned to the original Stills/Young concept.
And just as Crosby and Nash's participation was aborted seemingly on a whim,
so was the Stills/Young tour when Neil Young abandoned it halfway through—
jumping ship without warning on their way to Atlanta, Georgia, leaving just
a telegram message reading, "Dear Stephen, Funny how some things that start
spontaneously end that way. Eat a peach, Neil."

Credited to the Stills/Young Band, the album *Long May You Run* was
released on September 26, 1976. It made only a modest impression in the

Top 40, with one song—the title-track opener, dedicated to Neil's old hearse Mort—getting significant airplay on FM radio.

## The Last Waltz

With the Stills/Young tour still fresh in people's minds, Neil took to the road again in November 1976 for a three-week trek with Crazy Horse, after which he made what can only be described as an embarrassing appearance on the Band's farewell concert at San Francisco's Winterland Ballroom.

Featuring a galaxy of rock and blues stars including Bob Dylan, Muddy Waters, Van Morrison, Eric Clapton, Emmylou Harris, Joni Mitchell, Ringo Starr, and many more, the concert on November 25 was famously filmed by director Martin Scorsese as *The Last Waltz*. Backed by the Band, Neil's short two-number appearance (singing "Helpless" and "Four Strong Winds") was a lackluster performance, significant in retrospect by virtue of the trouble it subsequently caused Scorsese: A large lump of cocaine could clearly be seen

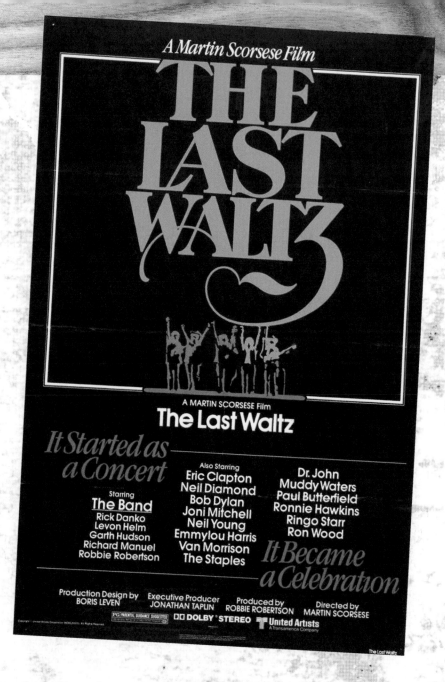

hanging from Young's nose, which the director was obliged to have edited out at the cost of several thousand dollars, which caused a delay in the film's release into the bargain.

## American Stars 'n Bars

Through the end of 1976, between gigging commitments Neil had also been preparing his next album, tentatively called *Chrome Dreams*. Songs had been accumulated from various sessions with Crazy Horse, as well as tracks from the abandoned *Homegrown* sessions of eighteen months earlier, and by early 1977 things looked ready for a springtime release.

As often was the case with Neil Young, however, things wouldn't be that simple or predictable. Just when the record company anticipated a soon-to-be-delivered firm track list of already recorded material, Neil announced a last-minute adjustment that would radically change the nature of the projected album.

With the title changed from *Chrome Dreams* to *American Stars 'n Bars*, there was an entire side comprising a country-flavored session yet to be recorded. Neil

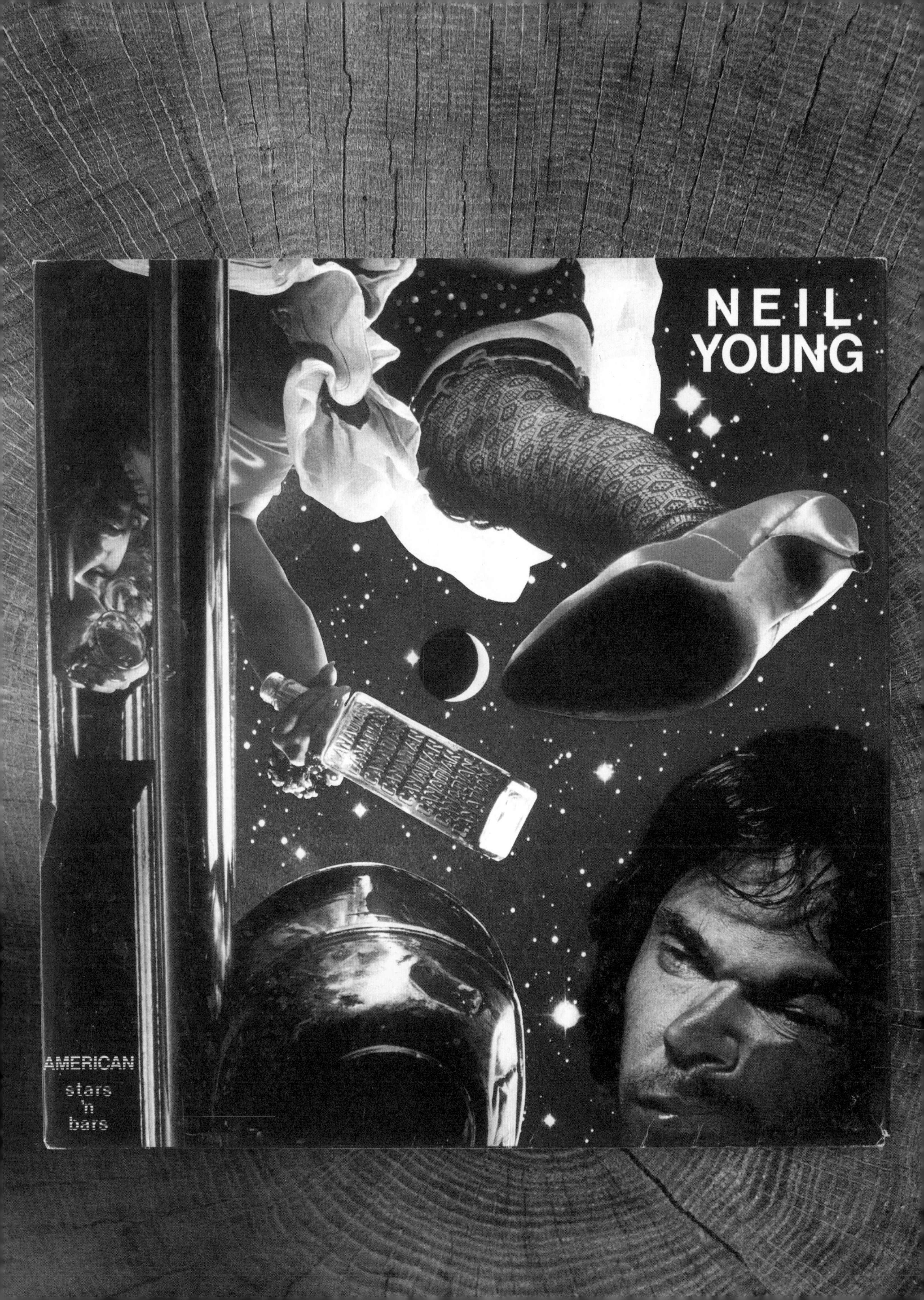
NEIL
YOUNG
CANADIAN
AMERICAN
stars
'n
bars

# American Stars 'n Bars

ALBUM

**S**omething of an oddity in its range of material, the vinyl album was released with one side entirely devoted to country-flavored songs, the other a mixed bag of tracks recorded at various earlier sessions. With female back-up singers Linda Ronstadt and Nicolette Larson, the five tracks of country material sound as fresh as when they were recorded (all in one single session) in 1977—leaving the listener wanting more of the same, rather than the abrupt change of musical gear that constitutes the album's major flaw. There is an added bonus in the Side Two songs, however, in "Like a Hurricane," a studio version of Neil's guitar extravaganza, which has been a major feature of live shows before and since.

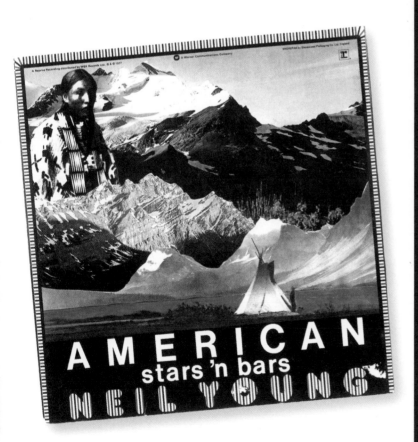

### SIDE ONE

The Old Country Waltz ★ Saddle Up the Palomino [Neil Young, Tim Drummond, Bobby Charles] ★ Hey Babe ★ Hold Back the Tears ★ Bite the Bullet

### SIDE TWO

Star of Bethlehem* ★ Will to Love** ★ Like a Hurricane ★ Homegrown

All songs written by Neil Young except where indicated.

### RECORDED

December 13, 1974–April 4, 1977, Quadrafonic, Nashville ★ Wally Heider Recoding Studios, Los Angeles ★ Broken Arrow Ranch, La Honda, California ★ Indigo Recording Studio, Malibu

### RELEASED

May 27, 1977

### PERSONNEL

Neil Young (guitar, harmonica, vocals, plus all instruments and vocals on **) ★ Billy Talbot (bass) ★ Ralph Molina (drums) ★ Frank "Poncho" Sampedro (guitar, stringman) ★ Linda Ronstadt (vocals) ★ Nicolette Larson (vocals) ★ Carole Mayedo (violin) ★ Ben Keith (steel guitar, Ddobro, vocals) ★ Tim Drummond (bass) ★ Karl T. Himmel (drums) ★ Emmylou Harris (vocals)

### LABEL

Warner Bros.

### PRODUCERS

Neil Young ★ David Briggs with Tim Mulligan ★ *Elliot Maze

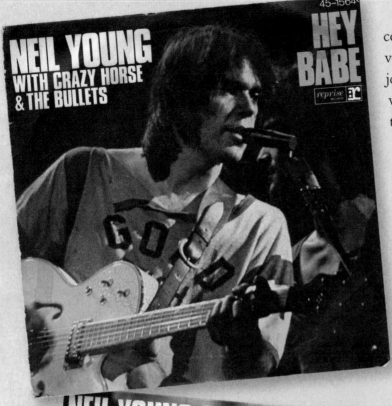

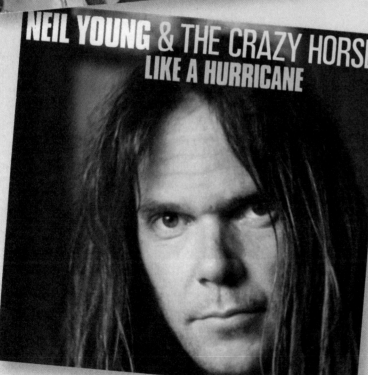

contacted Linda Ronstadt to contribute backing vocals, asking if she knew another female singer to join her. Ronstadt recommended Nicolette Larson, who had worked with some of the best, including the hot country-rock outfit Commander Cody and the Lost Planet Airmen. Neil soon had a name for the dynamic female duo: "the Saddlebags."

Sessions were set for the first few days of April 1977 at the Broken Arrow Ranch, where Neil and the girls were joined by Crazy Horse, plus Ben Keith on steel guitar and Carole Mayedo on fiddle. The recording was sensational, everything being cut in one single session, with the girls not even realizing it wasn't still a run-through when the tapes were rolling. Almost a pastiche of country music clichés, the five songs on the top side of the album ranged from the opener "Saddle Up the Palomino," in which Neil describes his horse Melody, to the closing hoedown "Bite the Bullet," satirizing the stereotypical Nashville macho man.

The main problem with *American Stars 'n Bars* was the contrast between the country side—a solid, self-contained concept—and the mixed bag of tracks from various sessions that constituted Side Two, including "Star of Bethlehem" from the *Homegrown* recordings, and a studio version of Young's in-concert guitar tour de force "Like a Hurricane."

## The Ducks

While *American Stars 'n Bars* was struggling in vain to make the *Billboard* Top 20 album list (it stalled at #21) following its release at the end of May 1977, Neil Young was getting involved in yet another journey way off the route of the conventional rock star. With one of his roadies, Jim Mazzeo, he had begun spending time in the sleepy California college town of Santa Cruz, not far from his ranch at La Honda. He hooked up with some local musicians—guitarist Jeff Blackburn, bass player Bob Mosley, and drummer Johnny "C" Craviotto, all former members of the West Coast band Moby Grape, whom he'd encountered when they supported Buffalo Springfield.

In what was another attempt to avoid the limelight and just spend some time gigging as "ordinary" musicians, the band—calling themselves the Ducks—played a couple of dozen gigs around Santa Cruz bars and clubs through July and August 1977. Although Neil recorded several of the dates, and even hinted at a live album, nothing has ever surfaced from the archive. When they played their final gig, at the Santa Monica Auditorium on September 2, 1977, word had gotten around and the place was packed with fans and journalists—but by the time the Ducks story broke over the next weeks, the band was already the stuff of rock 'n' roll legend.

Neil back stage at the Catalyst Club, Santa Cruz in 1977 with the Ducks (left to right): Bob Mosley, Johnny Craviotto, Jeff Blackburn, and Neil Young.

# Decade

BOXSET

escribed by one writer as "a yardstick by which all other greatest hits compilations should be measured," the three-disc 1977 release assembled by Neil himself features the majority of his various musical phases and lineups from the days of Buffalo Springfield up to 1976. Five then-previously unheard songs include "Down the Wire," a Buffalo Springfield track featuring the great Dr. John from their shelved *Stampede* album, "Winterlong" (covered by the Pixies in 1989), and the 1975 Linda Ronstadt country hit "Love Is a Rose," written by Neil for his unreleased *Homegrown* in 1974. Most intriguing, however, is "Campaigner," a diatribe against ex-president Richard Nixon, whose policies had contributed to Neil writing "Ohio" in 1970. After its release, *Decade* would be the only full Neil Young compilation for many years, until *Greatest Hits* in 2004.

### SIDE ONE
Down to the Wire* ★ Burned ★ Mr. Soul ★ Broken Arrow
Expecting to Fly ★ Sugar Mountain**

### SIDE TWO
I Am a Child ★ The Loner ★ The Old Laughing Lady ★ Cinnamon Girl
Down by the River

### SIDE THREE
Cowgirl in the Sand ★ I Believe in You ★ After the Gold Rush
Southern Man ★ Helpless

### SIDE FOUR
Ohio ★ Soldier ★ Old Man ★ A Man Needs a Maid ★ Harvest
Heart of Gold ★ Star of Bethlehem

### SIDE FIVE
The Needle and the Damage Done ★ Tonight's the Night (Part 1) ★
Tired Eyes ★ Walk On ★ For the Turnstiles ★ Winterlong*
Deep Forbidden Lake*

### SIDE SIX
Like a Hurricane ★ Love Is A Rose* ★ Cortez the Killer ★ Campaigner*
Long May You Run
*Previously unreleased ★ **Previously unreleased on album.

### RECORDED
Various

### RELEASED
October 28, 1977

### LABEL
Reprise

### PRODUCERS
Various

## Decade

Neil Young enjoying a moment
onstage with David Crosby
at the Santa Cruz Civic
Auditorium in 1977.

October 1977 saw the long-anticipated release of what was then a novel concept, a three-disc anthology of Neil Young's career up to that point. The package would set the industry's template for similar box sets by innumerable artists, both in the closing days of the vinyl era and in the CD age just dawning.

Neil had been closely involved in the project, with each song accompanied by handwritten liner notes he had prepared himself. Given his track record for unpredictable and often anti-commercial decision making, Warner executives were understandably nervous that Neil's choice of tracks—in which he had the final say—might have undermined the costly release's sales potential. But they needn't have worried. Neil came up with a classic "greatest hits" compilation, plus a few nuggets of previously unreleased material to at least partly satisfy the archivists among his fans. The box set was a resounding success with the critics

and over the sales counter, with rave reviews followed by huge sales—by 1979 the set had earned a gold disc for over half a million sales in the United States, and by 1986 it had tipped the platinum million–plus mark.

## Comes a Time

As the fall of 1977 saw *Decade* retrospecting Neil Young's career, the singer was already preparing his most ambitious studio outing yet, the result of which would be his most commercially accessible album since *Harvest* in 1972.

Now "officially" separated—although their relationship was never legally bound by marriage in the first place—Neil Young and Carrie Snodgress continued to have a good personal bond, especially with regard to the welfare of their son Zeke. So through the late summer, Neil embarked on a bus tour of the States with his young son, breaking off the trip when they hit Nashville, where he organized some sessions for his latest project.

As well as recruiting some key session players including ace keyboard man "Spooner" Oldham, guitarist J. J. Cale, and the New Orleans drummer Carl Himmel, he put together a huge ensemble of rhythm guitarists and string players—a total of thirty-five musicians, whom he dubbed the Gone with the Wind Orchestra. And crucial to much of the recording was his choice of Nicolette Larson, who had teamed with Linda Ronstadt so successfully on the *American Stars 'n Bars* recordings, to join him on the vocals.

The process for much of the recording involved the mammoth orchestra overdubbing backings to Neil's previously recorded solo demos, with Young and Larson then adding a fresh vocal input. Highlights included "Human Highway," long a favorite of Neil Young concert audiences; the emotionally charged "Lotta Love"—one of two tracks with Crazy Horse, a demo tape of which Larson had literally picked up off Neil's floor, and would make a Top 10 hit of her own in 1978—and the strident opener "Goin' Back," bringing in the strings dramatically for the first time after a stark acoustic intro.

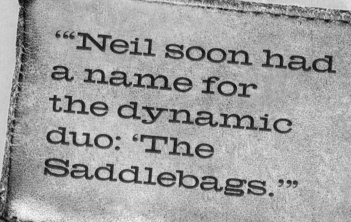

"Neil soon had a name for the dynamic duo: 'The Saddlebags.'"

When it was released nearly a year after the Nashville sessions, *Comes a Time*—making the Top 10 in the United States as well as several other major territories worldwide, and outselling all six albums since *Harvest*—proved a vital boost to Neil Young's standing as a major figure in rock's commercial mainstream, not just a well-respected but maverick outsider. But in the months between the record's completion and its release, crucial changes were also occurring in Neil's personal life.

Neil Young - Comes A Time

# Comes a Time

ALBUM

**A** predominantly melodic collection, *Comes a Time* put Neil Young firmly back in the commercial mainstream, outselling all six of his albums since *Harvest*, and reestablishing him as a musical force to be reckoned with. Backed by an enormous lineup of thirty-five musicians (dubbed the Gone With the Wind Orchestra), a mellow feel dominates throughout, with the trademark laid-back approach of guitarist J.J. Cale contributing significantly to the mood. Neil teams with Nicolette Larson for many of the vocals, including the emotive "Lotta Love," one of a pair of tracks with Crazy Horse. The feel-good textures that characterize the set are conspicuous by their absence on just one song, the gritty, fuzz guitar blues piece "Motorcycle Mama."

### SIDE ONE

Goin' Back ★ Comes a Time ★ Look Out for My Love ★ Lotta Love ★ Peace of Mind

### SIDE TWO

Human Highway ★ Already One ★ Field of Opportunity

Motorcycle Mama ★ Four Strong Winds [Ian Tyson]

All songs written by Neil Young except where indicated.

### RECORDED

November 28, 1975–November 21, 1977, Triad Recording, Fort Lauderdale, Florida ★ Columbia Recording Studio, London ★ Wally Heider Recording Studio, Los Angeles ★ Woodland Sound Studios, Nashville ★ Sound Shop, Nashville ★ Broken Arrow Ranch, La Honda, California

### RELEASED

October 21, 1978

### PERSONNEL

Neil Young (guitar, harmonica, vocals) ★ Gone With the Wind Orchestra: Nicolette Larson (vocals), Ben Keith (pedal steel guitar), Carl Himmel (drums), Tim Drummond (bass), Spooner Oldham (piano), Rufus Thibodeaux (fiddle), Joe Osborne (bass), Larrie Londin (drums), J. J. Cale (electric guitar), Farrel Morris (percussion), Grant Boatright (guitar), Bucky Barret (guitar), John Christopher (guitar), Jerry Shook (guitar), Vic Jordan (guitar), Steve Gibson (guitar), Dale Sellers (guitar), Ray Edenton (guitar), Rita Fey (autoharp), Shelly Kurland (strings), Stephanie Woolf (strings), Marvin Chantry (strings), Roy Christensen (strings), Gary Vanosdale (strings), Carl Goroditzby (strings), George Binkley (strings), Steve Smith (strings), Larry Harvin (strings), Larry Lasson (strings), Carol Walker (strings), Rebecca Lynch (strings), Virginia Christensen (strings), Maryanna Harvin (strings), George Kosmola (strings), Martha McCrory (strings) ★ *Neil Young & Crazy Horse: Neil Young (guitar, vocals), Frank Sampedro (guitar, vocals), Billy Talbot (bass, vocals), Ralph Molina (drums, vocals), plus guest Tim Mulligan (saxophone)

### LABEL

Reprise

### PRODUCERS

Neil Young ★ Ben Keith ★ Tim Mulligan ★ David Briggs

# NEIL YOUNG, ACTIVIST

Ever since he wrote the powerful "Ohio" in 1970, in response to the killing of the Kent State University students protesting the war in Vietnam, Neil Young—though certainly not a "protest singer" as such—has been no stranger to social and political commentary.

While his involvement in specific causes— particularly the continuing Farm Aid campaign and the even closer-to-home Bridge School project—has reached far beyond the musical arena, he has worn his heart on his sleeve through his songwriting on various occasions, and more so in recent years.

Of central concern to Neil has been the environment and our attitude toward it. In his 2003 "audio-novel" album *Greendale* (and the movie and graphic novel that spun off it), his exploration of life in small–town U.S.A. addressed themes as diverse as

Neil at the Live 8 concert (in aid of third world poverty relief) in Barrie, Toronto, July 2, 2005, with Bruce Cockburn and Josh Todd singing the finale "Rockin' in the Free World."

political corruption, the state of post-9/11 America, and environmentalism. In this latter respect, when he took the album on tour in 2004, he powered all the trucks and buses with biodeisel fuel, declaring the trek "ozone friendly," and raising the profile of the whole fossil fuel debate in the process.

Then in 2008 he announced the Lincvolt project, in which he converted a 1959 Lincoln Continental to a hybrid vehicle combining a conventional engine with an electric system. Along with Wichita mechanic Johnathan Goodwin, the aim was for the Lincvolt to provide a model for the world's first affordable mass- produced electric-powered automobile. "Johnathan and this car are going to make history," Young told the press. "We're going to change the world; we're going to create a car that will allow us to stop giving our wealth to other countries for petroleum." Although the project suffered a setback in 2010 when the car was damaged in a fire, Neil has continued with the

'development of his dream eco-friendly vehicle. His 2009 album *Fork in the Road* was loosely based on the Lincvolt project, with songs dedicated to the car, alongside tracks commenting on the economic crisis and the Wall Street bailouts of 2008.

Prior to the last decade, Neil Young's most overtly political song since "Ohio" was undoubtedly "Rockin' in the Free World" from his 1989 album *Freedom*. Casting a critical eye on the last days of the Reagan era and early phase of George H. W. Bush's presidency, the song lambasted the government's attitude toward urban homelessness, the environment, and most of all its foreign policy (in lines like a "kinder, gentler, machine gun hand").

But the gloves were really off fifteen years later, when Neil released the highly provocative *Living with War*. Triggered during a visit to his daughter at her college in Ohio, when he noticed a newspaper photo of wounded U.S. soldiers on their way from Iraq, the album castigated George W. Bush's war policy by examining the human cost of the conflict to soldiers, their families, and Americans generally—many of whom, like himself, were not directly affected. Most controversially, in "Let's Impeach the President," he suggested that Bush had lied to lead the country into war—an impeachable offence.

Prophetically, one track on *Living with War*, "Lookin' for a Leader," seems to have predicted the tussle for the Democratic presidential nomination between Hillary Clinton and Barack Obama—"And maybe it's a woman, or a black man after all"—two years before it happened. At the time Obama said he had no intention of running for president, but conceded he was a "big Neil Young fan." He had met Neil at a Farm Aid concert the previous year, sitting in a trailer while the singer rehearsed "Southern Man." "The acoustics in a trailer are terrific" commented the future leader of the United States. "It was unbelievable. . . . It was one of the best times that we've had since I was a senator."

Top: The DVD of Neil's radical movie *Greendale*.

Bottom: The "Tribute to Heroes" concert, September 21, 2001, in the aftermath of the 9/11 attacks, at which Neil sang John Lennon's "Imagine".

# Ready for the Country?

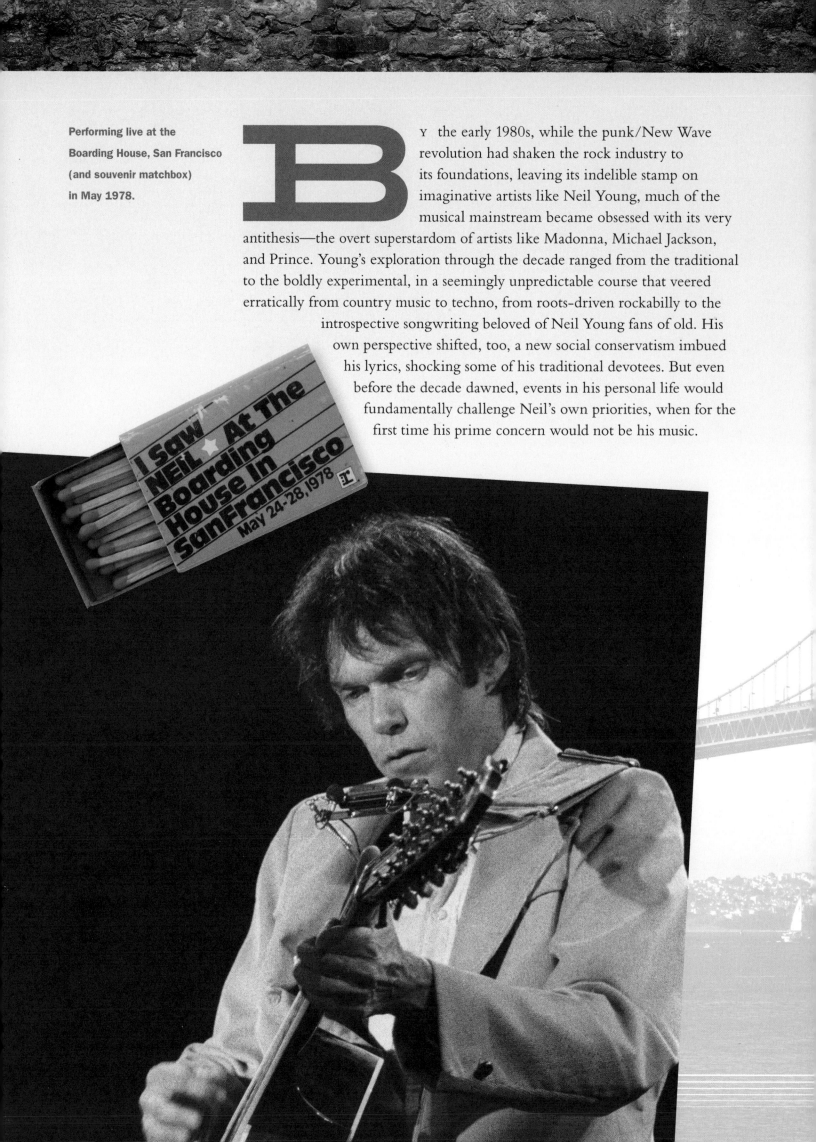

Performing live at the
Boarding House, San Francisco
(and souvenir matchbox)
in May 1978.

**I Saw NEiL At The Boarding House In SanFrancisco May 24-28, 1978**

B
Y the early 1980s, while the punk/New Wave revolution had shaken the rock industry to its foundations, leaving its indelible stamp on imaginative artists like Neil Young, much of the musical mainstream became obsessed with its very antithesis—the overt superstardom of artists like Madonna, Michael Jackson, and Prince. Young's exploration through the decade ranged from the traditional to the boldly experimental, in a seemingly unpredictable course that veered erratically from country music to techno, from roots-driven rockabilly to the introspective songwriting beloved of Neil Young fans of old. His own perspective shifted, too, a new social conservatism imbued his lyrics, shocking some of his traditional devotees. But even before the decade dawned, events in his personal life would fundamentally challenge Neil's own priorities, when for the first time his prime concern would not be his music.

## Pegi

Toward the end of the work in Nashville, Neil had a brief affair with the undeniably attractive Nicolette Larson. With the music drawing them together—"We sang on the same mike. I could look in his eyes and keep up with him," she would tell Young's biographer Jimmy McDonough—it was probably not meant to last much longer than the sessions, and it didn't. By the end of the year, the relationship was over, but early in 1978 Neil embarked on a romantic course with far more permanent consequences.

He had first met Pegi Morton three years earlier, initially setting eyes on her when she was working as a waitress not far from his La Honda ranch. They'd struck up a casual friendship that went no farther and continued until February 1978 when, on Valentine's Day, they had their first serious date together. From then on, it was a whirlwind romance, with the couple marrying on August 2, 1978, and their son Ben being born on November 28 of that same year. In what became a genuinely lifelong commitment, they have remained together ever since.

## We Are Not Men

During the spring of 1978, Neil Young cultivated an unlikely collaboration of sorts, with the post-punk New Wave group Devo. From Akron, Ohio—its two founding members were both at nearby Kent State University when the 1970 shootings occurred—Devo was a bizarre outfit, even by the standards of punk.

Since early 1976, first in New York City and then in the UK, punk had taken over as the cutting-edge music of youth, condemning artists of Neil's generation as "rock dinosaurs"—particularly the superstars of post-hippie stadium rock personified by the likes of Fleetwood Mac, the Eagles, and of course Crosby, Stills & Nash. In the wake of punk proper came a clutch of left-field bands, loosely described as "new wave" by a music press eager to pin labels on everything, but Devo proved to be farther out than most, by their own admission developed "as an art concept, not as music."

Their stage act consisted of their assuming the role of bizarre characters, often dressed in rubber industrial overalls and weird masks, chanting rather than singing songs full of surreal imagery and gobbledegook nonsense images, over a backing of science-fiction electronic music. In their collective persona, the five-piece did everything to live up to their catchphrase "We are not men, we are Devo."

Neil Young, meanwhile, was preparing for the filming of his second movie, *Human Highway*, the production of which involved, among others, his old friend from the Topanga Canyon days, actor Dean Stockwell. And it was Stockwell who would take Neil to see a Devo performance, where the singer was so taken by the Ohio oddballs that he immediately offered them parts in his film.

Although it would develop into something altogether more eccentric (and financially disastrous), the original plan for *Human Highway* was to use concert footage and semi-documentary sequences to evoke the feeling of life on the rock 'n' roll road. With that in mind, in May 1978, Neil staged some concerts at the Boarding House venue in San Francisco, in which he appeared before an astonished crowd with short hair, a neat white jacket, and a shoestring necktie; the only other figures onstage were those of three wooden Indians, the kind that used to stand outside American cigar stores.

The entire sixteen-song performance was filmed, as was a private follow-up show on May 27 starring Devo at the Mabuhay Gardens, a noted punk venue. The new wave avant-gardists mimed through the set of their own numbers before launching into a parody of "After the Gold Rush" as Neil lurched onto the stage, only to be thrown into the audience of eager hippie-hating punks. More fun and games ensued the next evening at the Different Fur recording studios, all being filmed for *Human Highway*, when Devo and Neil collaborated on the latter's new song "My My, Hey Hey (Out of the Blue)"—with its reference to British punk star Johnny Rotten—in a revised Devo version titled "Hey Hey, My My (Into the Black)" in which Johnny Rotten becomes Johnny Spud. And it was in that performance that a new line inserted by Devo caught Neil Young's ear. Based on a slogan culled from a rust-proofing advertisement when two members of the Akron band were in graphic design, "Rust Never Sleeps" would be the title of the next phase in Neil Young's performing career.

## Rust Never Sleeps

Clearly heavily influenced by Devo's off-the-wall stage persona, Neil mounted an ambitious presentation for his next tour, which opened on September 16, 1978. The main features of the stage set were giant-sized imitation amps and speaker columns, plus a microphone that dwarfed the performers. The roadies who normally busied themselves onstage prior to a concert were now "Road-eyes," dressed in long robes with piercing red eyes like

the Jawas in the *Star Wars* movie. Devo-style, the sound crew were dressed as Coneheads. Leaping down from the top of one of the huge speakers, Neil would launch into a delicate acoustic set before the onslaught with Crazy Horse. Clips from the soundtrack at Woodstock were played over the intermission between the sets, while the show was introduced and concluded with excerpts from rock classics played over the PA, including Jimi Hendrix's "Star Spangled Banner" and the Beatles' "A Day in the Life."

Reaction to the monthlong tour was mixed. The show went down sensationally with most of the audience at every concert, although some critics felt Young was "cheapening" himself with all the theatrics. Of course, he couldn't win with everybody—when he toured as a bejeaned old-school rocker, he was accused of being out of touch with the current dynamic of punk.

Neil surrounded by the "Road-eyes" roadies during one of the *Rust Never Sleeps* concerts in 1978.

# Rust Never Sleeps

**ALBUM**

A semi-live album, *Rust Never Sleeps* was produced from overdubbed performances from concerts, plus two takes from a solo gig at the Boarding House, San Francisco. Aware that many of his rock contemporaries were being swept aside in the face of the punk revolution, on these tracks we can hear Neil Young taking the challenge on board—with "My My Hey Hey (Out of the Blue)," for instance, contemplating the impermanence of rock 'n' roll success whatever its guise. The sheer power of his performances with the ever-reliable Crazy Horse—on an album that was greeted with almost universal approval—confirm that this old-school rocker, at least, was not giving in that easily.

### SIDE ONE

My My, Hey Hey (Out of the Blue) [Neil Young, Jeff Blackburn] ★ Thrasher
Ride My Llama ★ Pocahontas* ★ Sail Away**

### SIDE TWO

Powderfinger (October 19) ★ Welfare Mothers ★
Sedan Delivery ★ Hey Hey, My My (Into the Black) (October 22)
All songs written by Neil Young except where indicated.

### RECORDED

May 24–26, 1978, Boarding House, San Francisco ★ October 15, 1978, Civic Center, St. Paul ★ October 19, 1978, McNichols Arena, Denver ★ October 22, Cow Palace, San Francisco; all with later overdubs at Broken Arrow Studio / August 11, 1976, Indigo Recording Studio, Malibu ★ later at Triad Recording, Fort Lauderdale, Florida ★ Broken Arrow Studio, La Honda, California ★ **September 12, 1977, Triad Recording, Fort Lauderdale, Florida ★ later at Woodland Sound Studios, Nashville

### RELEASED

June 22, 1979

### PERSONNEL

Neil Young and Crazy Horse: Neil Young (guitar, vocals), Frank Sampedro (guitar, stringman, vocal), Billy Talbot (bass, vocals), Ralph Molina (drums, vocals) ★ **Neil Young and the Gone with the Wind Orchestra: Neil Young (guitar, vocals), Nicolette Larson (vocals), plus ensemble

### LABEL

Reprise

### PRODUCERS

Neil Young ★ David Briggs ★ Tim Mulligan

The whole joyful noise of the tour was captured on the semi-live album *Rust Never Sleeps*, produced from overdubbed live performances and two tracks from the solo gig at the Boarding House, and released in June 1979 to almost unanimous acclaim. It was followed by the double album *Live Rust*, another document of Neil Young in concert at this crucial stage in his continuing development as a rock 'n' roll performer.

The movie, *Rust Never Sleeps*, which Neil shot under the pseudonym Bernard Shakey at the San Francisco Cow Palace on October 22, 1978, premiered in Hollywood at the same time *Live Rust* was released. Armed with special cardboard "Rust-O-Vision" glasses, reminiscent of the cheapo specs used for 3-D films in the 1950s, the audience was told they could "see the rust falling off" during the filmed concert. What difference the glasses *actually* made, apart from adding a brownish tint to the proceedings on screen, is another matter.

Never taking himself too seriously in his extracurricular activities, Neil had a circumspect attitude to filmmaking. Talking about *Rust Never Sleeps*, he admitted to Richard Cook in the *New Musical Express*, "It didn't take much money. Film isn't something that comes naturally to me. I tried to paint but I can't do that. I know I'm not a great filmmaker but I have a lot of fun trying. The concept was like a daydream. You know the way dreams jumble up things that you've seen

Neil in action on the
*Rust Never Sleeps* tour,
Opposite: Sheet
music from the album.

that day, maybe with people you knew five or ten years ago at some place you think, you sort of know? That's how *Rust Never Sleeps* came out. It put the music in a different perspective."

Whatever detractors may have said following the extravaganza of the *Rust Never Sleeps* tour, the album release in 1979 was a triumph, making the U.S. Top 10 at #8 and being voted Album of the Year by both readers and critics in *Rolling Stone*. Neil Young was also voted Male Vocalist of the Year in the same magazine, while New York's influential *Village Voice* named him Artist of the Decade at the end of 1979.

# HEY HEY, MY MY

(INTO THE BLACK)

Words and Music by NEIL YOUNG

Recorded by NEIL YOUNG on Re[

# Live Rust

**ALBUM**

The soundtrack album to the *Rust Never Sleeps* movie is a straightforward live recording of just one concert from the tour of the same name. There are no new songs here, the original double album offering one acoustic and three electric sides of already well-known material in sometimes unfamiliar—and, it has to be said, uncomfortable—musical settings; a stark example being the reggae treatment of the otherwise wonderful "Cortez the Killer." Nevertheless, the album now stands as yet another manifestation of Neil Young's continuing evolution as a rock performer, at a stage when many at that point in their career were content to sit on the laurels of past triumphs.

### SIDE ONE

Sugar Mountain ★ I Am a Child ★ Comes a Time
After the Gold Rush ★ My My, Hey Hey (Out of the Blue)

### SIDE TWO

When You Dance I Can Really Love ★ The Loner ★ The Needle
and the Damage Done ★ Lotta Love ★ Sedan Delivery

### SIDE THREE

Powderfinger ★ Cortez the Killer ★ Cinnamon Girl

### SIDE FOUR

Like a Hurricane ★ Hey Hey, My My (Into the Black) ★ Tonight's the Night

### RECORDED

October 4–22, 1978, Boston Gardens ★ Chicago Stadium ★ Civic
Center, St. Paul ★ McNichols Arena, Denver ★ Cow Palace, San Francisco

### RELEASED

November 14, 1979

### PERSONNEL

Neil Young and Crazy Horse: Neil Young (guitar, piano, vocals), Frank Sampedro (guitar, stringman, vocals), Billy Talbot (bass, vocals), Ralph Molina (drums, vocals)

### LABEL

Reprise

### PRODUCERS

David Briggs ★ Tim Mulligan ★ Bernard Shakey

## Ben

The front cover and inner
pages of an interview with Neil
in *Rolling Stone*, 1979.

Just a month after the end of the *Rust Never Sleeps* tour, on November 29, 1978, Neil's wife of less than four months, Pegi, gave birth to his second son, Ben. What should have been a joyous time for the couple would soon turn to Neil's worst nightmare, however, when by the spring of 1979 doctors diagnosed that the child had cerebral palsy. His first son, Zeke, also suffered from the condition, but in Ben's case the prognosis was far worse; whereas Zeke—by this time six years old—had been growing up with learning and behavioral difficulties, Ben would be confined to a wheelchair for the rest of his life, unable to speak, let alone move or walk normally.

Pegi and Neil were devastated, and for Neil, the trauma—if anything—was greater, given his elder son's history. As the singer would admit in a 1989 interview, the situation was simply "Too big a picture to comprehend. . . . I couldn't believe it. There were two different mothers. It couldn't have happened twice." Happened it had, however, and as soon as they recovered from the initial shock, the Youngs decided to tackle the crisis head-on. It might have been easier (and understandable in the circumstances), especially given Neil's professional commitments, to confine Ben to institutional care; but like many choices Neil made over the years, the easiest was usually not his chosen path.

The front cover and inner pages of an interview with Neil in *Rolling Stone*, 1979.

or Dylan album came out, you knew they were way beyond it. They were always doing something else, always moving down the line.

Moving back to Toronto, Young soon took up a twelve-string acoustic guitar and tried folk singing around the coffeehouses. He made friends easily with other musicians like Stephen Stills, Joni Mitchell and Richie Furay, who were traveling along the same path. Mitchell wrote "The Circle Game" for him after hearing "Sugar Mountain," which was about growing too old to get into the local teen club.

Rock & roll, meanwhile, was booming. One of the biggest bands around Toronto was a group called Ricky James and the Mynah Birds. "We played rock and blues," James, now a disco star, recalls in Los Angeles. "I remember our first solo," continues James, "When Neil took his first solo, he was so excited he leaped off the stage, the plug came out and nobody heard anything."

The Mynah Birds broke up after a flirtation with Motown when James, AWOL from the navy, was pressed back into the service. Their young career at a standstill, James and Young spent a teary afternoon promising each other that they would form another band after James returned. "It was heavy, man," recalls James. "I had really gotten close to the cat. He was never very healthy—he got bad epileptic fits sometimes—but he had balls like you wouldn't believe."

After a few months, money ran out and Young had to sell the Mynah Birds' equipment. Typical of his sense of humor, he used the money to buy a long, black Pontiac hearse and headed for Los Angeles with Mynah Birds' bassist Bruce Palmer. Neither had working permits or the proper papers. "But if you were looking for a break," says Young, "the great Canadian Dream is to get out. So we came down anyway."

They were lumbering down Hollywood Boulevard when the Ontario license plates were spotted by two folkies Young had met up in Canada. Stephen Stills and Richie Furay pulled Young and Palmer over. There, on the street, they talked of their stalled careers. Stills and Furay's folk group had broken up. Stills had even failed an audition to join the Monkees because of his teeth. They decided to form a group, later adding Dewey Martin on drums. They named themselves after a tractor, the Buffalo Springfield.

THE BUFFALO SPRINGFIELD WERE largely a West Coast phenomenon for most of their stormy two-year existence. Around Los Angeles, where their single, "For What It's Worth," became an anthem for the budding hippies battling cops on Sunset Strip, they were a sensation—a tougher, younger brother to the Byrds. Their live shows centered around incredible lead-guitar battles between Stills, the fair-haired, bluesy Southerner, and Young, the dark and fiery "Hollywood Indian" who was always either quitting or rejoining the group. Their fans split into camps and argued for years about why the group broke up.

"Stills and I have always gotten along," explained Young on his bus during his 1976 tour, as we headed for a show in Madison, Wisconsin. "I just had too much energy and so much creative flow coming out that when I wanted to get something down, I just felt like, 'This is my fucking trip' and I don't have to listen to anybody else's. I'd do what they wanted with their band, but I needed more space with my own. And that was a constant problem in my head. So that was why I had to quit. Then I'd come back 'cause it wouldn't sound so good. I just wasn't mature enough to deal with it. Everything was going much too fast."

By late 1968, the intense chemistry of the group had lit a fire under all its members. Everyone had scattered in different directions, leaving bassist and then engineer Jim Messina to assemble the band's third and final album, Last Time Around, at Sunset Sound studios. While Young was recording, though, Joni Mitchell was down the hall, beginning her first solo album produced by her then-boyfriend David Crosby.

"I don't really want to go down there," said Crosby at the time. "That guy Neil Young is strange."

Mitchell turned to her manager. "Elliot," she said, "you have to meet Neil Young. You'll love his sense of humor."

The possessor of a mercurial wit, Brooklyn-born Elliot Roberts immediately hit it off with Young. "Everybody was intimidated by Neil," says Roberts. "I heard all these stories—Neil had left the band twice... Everyone was always on eggshells around Neil. Say the wrong word, he's gone. That is all I ever heard. Well, I found it easier to deal with Neil than Stephen. I used to tell people the funny things Neil had said. They'd say, 'Neil?'"

After the Springfield's demise, Roberts became Young's manager, and launched him on a solo career. Roberts tested Young's appeal by getting him a guest appearance during a Dave Van Ronk show at a Pasadena nightclub. "We stayed up all night because we were so thrilled he didn't get booed off," recalls Roberts. "He hated his voice and thought all his songs were depressing."

AFTER THE SPRINGFIELD, YOUNG said during that ride on his tour bus, "I wanted to get out to the sticks and think everything over." Along with his wife, Susan, Young moved into a spindly house high atop a hill in Topanga Canyon. After finishing his first solo album, Neil Young, in a local studio—which, these days, he fondly characterizes as "Overdub City"—he built his own studio in his garage.

"The problem was, I needed a band again," Young said. "I met these guys that were, to me, the American Rolling Stones. There has never been a bad night with them, to this day, Crazy Horse.

Young met Whitten through a mutual girlfriend while he was still with Buffalo Springfield, and they began playing together. Whitten's guitar playing cut slashing patterns across Young's. After working on the first Buffalo Springfield album during the day, Neil fell into the habit of dropping by Talbot and Whitten's house in Laurel Canyon at night. "We used to have a great time," remembers Talbot, "sitting around, singing 'Mr. Soul' in D-modal tuning—all four of us singing harmony."

Young eventually enticed Whitten, Talbot and Molina to come up to his Topanga home/studio and record some "strange songs" he'd written while being laid up with the flu. "In a single day," Talbot says, "we did 'Cinnamon Girl,' 'Down by the River' and 'Cowgirl in the Sand.' There wasn't much to discuss it..."

Everybody Knows This Is Nowhere—still Neil Young's favorite of all his albums—was finished in two weeks. He and his new band toured small halls as Neil Young and Crazy Horse, and together they built a lasting reputation for hard, metallic rock. Young would spin off on searing guitar solos during which he wildly tipped back and forth on his heels. Because he acted so quickly, Young was never considered as a leftover piece of the Buffalo Springfield for long.

Neither was Stephen Stills, who had meanwhile teamed with David Crosby and Graham Nash as Crosby, Stills & Nash. When the trio finished their album and realized they needed another guitarist to hold up the instrumental end of things on the road, Stills visited Neil.

Danny Whitten was the leader of Crazy Horse. A husky, blond guitarist/surfer, the intensely sensitive Whitten wrote all his songs about the same sixteen-year-old girl who had broken his heart. He had moved to California from back East with Ralph Molina and Billy Talbot, as part of a vocal group called Danny and the Memories.

"You had the impression," Elliot Roberts recalls, "that he had been through a lot and was very soulful. Whatever very soulful is, he had it. Very strong guy, but you could see that you say the wrong word and you'd slap him in the face. We all liked Danny. He was obviously very talented and Neil was drawn to him instantly."

Young. Just beginning his career with Crazy Horse, Young knew he had a decision to make.

"I decided to do both," Young has said. "The obligation with Crosby, Stills and Nash wasn't going to be that heavy, a few songs and lead guitar." It became much, much bigger than that. Or, as Billy Talbot says, "Neil joined up with those guys, man, and everything went crazy."

Young punched the clock twice a day for a year, touring with Crosby, Stills, Nash and Young, then Crazy Horse, then CSNY again. "I never really fit into CSNY as well as Joe Walsh does with the Eagles," he explains. "Everybody had a different viewpoint on what's happening and it takes

PHOTOGRAPH BY JOEL BERNSTEIN

a whole lot to get them all together. It's a great group for that. Four totally different people who all know how it should be done, whatever it is."

Young went straight from Déjà Vu, the first CSNY album, into recording his own third solo album, inspired by actor Dean Stockwell when he unraveled a screenplay idea of his. It was about three lives—one of them a moody musician—on the day that a mythical tidal wave swallowed Topanga Canyon and was called After the Goldrush. The apocalyptic theme influenced the bulk of material for Young's album of the same name.

"The film fell through," says Young, "and there I was with a record. So I put it out. Would I have made a great movie?"

It was a more poetic album than Everybody Knows This Is Nowhere, due in part to the fact that the tenacious, black Les Paul guitar he played throughout the previous album had been lost. "I took it to this store to be repaired," says Young. "I came back to pick it up the next week and the store was gone."

WITH AFTER THE GOLDRUSH just released, Neil Young embarked on a solo acoustic tour of small halls, performing the best of his old work and a slew of new songs, written about his new stopover in Nashville to tape The Johnny Cash Show. During a began recording a followup to After the Goldrush away the show's other two guests, James Taylor, he recorded "Old Man" and "Heart of Gold," with Taylor on banjo, at a local studio. But a lingering back ailment worsened as he continued on the tour, and after it ended, Young suffered a slipped disk on his left side. He underwent operations and a long confinement on

get high," he says, "I'm a basket case." He has never taken acid and never tried heroin. And Whitten's strong aura of junk scared Young considerably—in fact, he wrote "The Needle and the Damage Done" for him.

In the fall of 1972, Young seclusion and undertake his months long and recorded (Time Fades Away) of new m producer of his first solo tra ville rhythm-section core from drums, Tim Drummond on ba guitar; and the rumored-to- Whitten on lead guitar. A hu brought in, and the mammoth Young's Broken Arrow ranch.

NEIL WAS PRETTY S bug tour," recalls forme Makota. "He'd alread changes with Danny, the go and Danny reads th having it anymore...and kills himself. T And are you ready to play God? But tha happened.

"Neil was trying to get a certain soun that he apparently could never find. The sound checks in the afternoons and so they'd come in and do the show at night Neil's mood never seemed happy or con have a situation where everybody is try and nobody really pleased him."

One reason, conjectures Makota (who ter), is that everyone got a little money those full houses every night. The band more dollars and a percentage. Makota him tiating for a bigger crew price. "I admit," he should have just done the job that was at ha

The revolt took Neil by surprise. "It turn everything," Elliot Roberts recalls. "He didn handle his friends constantly hitting on hi money. He rebelled against the success, start it did to people. I was afraid to leave. I knew was gone."

Meanwhile, puzzled audiences were treate versions of his new songs. ("Every time I go road," Young says now, "the album that just behind me. I don't want to lose the tune material.") Young took to drinking tequila to those expectant faces waiting for "Heart of G to look, as he would later write, like an ocean hands that grab at the sky. They were his demo Cleveland, he began to scream at them. "Wake land. Get up..." The rest of the tour was bidin

He returned to the solitude of his ranch, bu saddled with problems from Journey through the deeply upset. "For the first time in my life," he couldn't get anything to turn out the way I wanted the beginning of a time he would later call h Period.

THERE WAS A BRIEF TRY AT A reunion in Hawaii in the summer of 19 Young left the proceedings because "too tired to start another cycle." Gau small resentment within the group, returned to Los Angeles, where he found anoth close to him had ODed—CSNY guitar tuner Bruce For the first time since Danny Whitten's death, Y rounded up the remainder of Crazy Horse, and started recording at a small rehearsal room. The sess began after midnight, after everyone had drunk eno tequila and played enough pool to do songs in memo

chosen an enigmatic cover for the album, a shot of him passing an old lady on his way to a show in New York City. It symbolized his own breakup with Susan and a farewell to the muse that had already started to become overrun. "I came home to find people I didn't know in

The album captured a huge audience for solo artist, and that success brought more ye Young did After the Goldrush, he'd fired us," ot," "Danny was doing... you know." his arm.

He surprised when Danny became a junkie. reason. In those days, people just started p. Didn't snort nothin'. He just shot some my some smack and from then on, he was a lways a strong person and he was also a f more than anyone else, they tell me." eveled looks and maybe-I-know-where- n't stage presence, Neil Young is not a ning time, according to friends, he would ss," before accepting a joint. ("When I

his ranch. Doctor's orders allowed him only four hours a day on his feet.

"I tried to stay away from the success as much as possible," Young says. "And being laid up in bed gave me a lot of time to think about what had happened. I thought the popularity was good, but I also knew that something else was dying. I became really reclusive.

"There was a long time when I felt connected with the outer world 'cause I was still looking. Then you get everything the way you want it. You stop looking out so much and start looking in. And that's why in my head I felt something change; I was thinking about all these things. I was lying on my back for a long time. It affected my music. My whole spirit was prone."

The lethargic downbeat of much of Harvest, Young's next album, was partially a result of the sedation he was under during much of the recording. Released in February of 1972, it was the biggest-selling album of that year and influenced an entire genre of country rockers.

Young's back gradually improved; he began writing and playing electric guitar again, and used some of his wealth from Harvest to finance his movie, Journey through the Past.

PHOTOGRAPHS BY JOEL BER

---

The couple were told about the Institute of Human Potential in Philadelphia, where in the fall of 1980 they attended seminars and then immersed themselves in a program involving their looking after Ben themselves. The rigorous regime required their commitment to teaching Ben to recognize words and numbers, to crawl, and do other physical tasks within his limited capabilities, while stretching those capabilities to their full potential.

Despite the focus on Ben, however, just as the child was officially enrolled in the institute's program in October 1980, Neil was able to release his first recording since the four-pronged album, tour, album, and film Rust attack of the previous year.

## Hawks & Doves

Interpreted by many as a "political" release (it came out just days before a presidential election), Hawks & Doves was split into two sections, one on each side of the disc. Side One, the "Doves" side, featured tracks recorded back in 1974 as part of the Homegrown sessions, plus a mix of other material from sessions at the Triad and Indigo studios. These were regular Neil Young songs, with rich, often dream-like imagery offering a variety of interpretations—only "Captain Kennedy," addressing the issues of war and peace, life and death, is particularly clear-cut in its narrative.

NEIL YOUNG HAWKS & DOVES

# Hawks & Doves

**ALBUM**

On the original vinyl release as listed here, *Hawks & Doves* was spilt into two distinct sections, one on each side of the disc. Side One was gentle and acoustic, the second being the nearest that Neil had gotten to a straight country sound at this point. The acoustic set has all the hallmarks of a regular Neil Young release, with rich lyrics conjuring up a variety of ethereal images—"Captain Kennedy" is the only acoustic track with a straightforward narrative content. The "country" section, however, is a different matter, with Young taking the opportunity to give vent to feelings that had many of his faithful fans worried. There is a patriotic, almost flag-waving mood evident in tracks like "Comin' Apart at Every Nail," a tribute to the hard lot endured by the ordinary working man—while the more prosaic "Union Man" has as its target the American Musicians Union.

## SIDE ONE

Little Wing ★ The Old Homestead* ★ Lost in Space ★ Captain Kennedy

## SIDE TWO

Stayin' Power ★ Coastline ★ Union Man ★ Comin' Apart at Every Nail ★ Hawks & Doves

All songs written by Neil Young.

## RECORDED

December 8, 1974–July 5, 1980, Quadrafonic, Nashville ★ Village Recorders, Los Angeles ★ Indigo Recording, Malibu ★ Triad Recording, Fort Lauderdale, Florida ★ Gold Star Recording, Los Angeles

## RELEASED

October 29, 1980

## PERSONNEL

Neil Young (guitar, piano, vocals) ★ Greg Thomas (drums) ★ Dennis Belfield (bass) ★ Ben Keith (steel guitar) ★ Ddobro (vocals) ★ Rufus Thibodeaux (fiddle) ★ Ann Hillary O'Brien (vocals) ★ *Neil Young (vocals, guitars, harmonica) ★ Levon Helm (drums) ★ Tim Drummond (bass) ★ Tom Seribner (saw)

## LABEL

Reprise/Warner Bros.

## PRODUCERS

David Briggs ★ Tim Mulligan ★ Neil Young ★ Elliot Mazer

Side Two, the "Hawks" side, was what would worry a lot of Neil Young fans. In the nearest he had ever got to a straight down-the-middle country sound, Neil appeared to be revealing an almost redneck side to his character that many found surprising and faintly disturbing. There was a strong satirical element to much of this, of course, a concept many in his American audience failed to appreciate, along with a genuine concern for the urban workingman (exemplified in "Comin' Apart at Every Nail") that came over as sounding overtly patriotic to those steeped in the often myopic hippie ideals of yesteryear. His targets included the inept policies of the American musicians' union ("Union Man"), and the perceived threat from foreign powers in the title track, in which he chants, "Ready to go, willin' to stay and pay/U.S.A., U.S.A."

Below the surface, however, the very fact that Neil decided to present a two-sided format suggests he was standing one step beyond the issues, willing to voice his concerns while tacitly acknowledging there were no definitive answers.

Whatever his true motive, the aim to sell records was certainly frustrated with *Hawks & Doves*; his first album not to earn a gold disc, the record only reached the Top 10 listings in the numerically insignificant overseas markets of Australia and New Zealand.

## Re-ac-tor

Recorded against the background of Neil's grueling therapy program for his son Ben, which would preoccupy him and Pegi for most of 1981, *Re-ac-tor* was one of his least satisfactory releases to date.

Although inflected with the rhythms of the early 1980s new wave bands, Crazy Horse's delivery came over as mannered and often listless—many saw it as the beginning of a steady decline as far as the band was concerned. It seemed as if they were infected by the sheer sense of exhaustion that must have prevailed in the Young household over those months, during a period also marked by stark events in America at large.

The November election in 1980 had seen the Hollywood actor-turned-arch-Republican Ronald Reagan made president; then on December 8, the whole country—and the musical community in particular—was traumatized by the killing of John Lennon on the streets of New York. In March 1981, a would-be assassin's gun was turned on Reagan himself, his survival and return to work within two weeks guaranteeing his hero status among many Americans. And to the amazement of his legions of liberal-minded followers, Neil Young would be among the neoconservative's vocal supporters.

# Re-ac-tor

**SIDE ONE**

Opera Star ★ Surfer Joe and Moe the Sleaze ★ T-Bone ★ Get Back on It

**SIDE TWO**

Southern Pacific ★ Motor City ★ Rapid Transit 8 Shots

All songs written by Neil Young.

**RELEASED**

October 28, 1981

**RECORDED**

October 9, 1980—July 21, 1981, Modern Recorders, Redwood City, California

**LABEL**

Reprise

**PRODUCERS**

David Briggs ★ Tim Mulligan ★ Neil Young ★ Jerry Napier

# Trans

ALBUM

**SIDE ONE**

Little Thing Called Love ★ Computer Age ★ We R in Control ★ Transformer Man ★ Computer Cowboy (aka Syscrusher)

**SIDE TWO**

Hold On to Your Love ★ Sample and Hold ★ Mr. Soul ★ Like an Inca

All songs written by Neil Young.

**RECORDED**

September 24, 1981–May 12, 1982, Modern Recorders, Redwood City, California; Commercial Recorders, Honolulu

**RELEASED**

December 29, 1982

**LABEL**

Geffen

**PRODUCERS**

Neil Young ★ David Briggs ★ Tim Mulligan

## Trans

With the pressure of Ben's home care being his top priority, Neil didn't tour in support of either *Hawks & Doves* or its follow-up, and apart from a set at the Bread and Roses Festival in Berkeley in 1980, he would not play a live show between his Crazy Horse tour of 1978 and concerts set to promote his 1982 album *Trans*.

*Trans* represented yet another surprising change of direction on the part of Neil Young, both business-wise and musically. On the business front, it would be the first album he recorded with the relatively new label Geffen Records, set up by David Geffen in 1980, which had as its first release John Lennon and Yoko Ono's *Double Fantasy*. The label, however, distributed by Warner Bros., would not prove a long-term home for Neil's work.

Influenced heavily by the German electronic sounds of Kraftwerk, and other techno-pop artists including David Bowie who had followed in their wake, Neil had begun experimenting with tape loops, synthesizers, electronic drum machines, and the vocoder (which "electronicized" the sound of the human voice to give a science-fiction robotic effect). He was also impressed by the technology that he had become familiar with in Ben's therapy work, and now that the pressure was off a little on that front (he and Pegi were able to wind down their hands-on commitment to a couple of hours a day) he had time to explore new musical territory once again.

**Touring in early 1983, promoting the *Trans* album.**

**Neil performing on the *Trans* tour and a ticket from one of his gigs in Rome in 1982.**

When the call came to start preparing a first album for his new label, however, Neil initially put to one side his techno-gadgetry and set about recording a straightforward set of smooth-sounding numbers—using the Commercial Recorders studio in Hawaii, the collection was to be appropriately called *Island in the Sun*. The songs, with titles like "Raining in Paradise" and "Big Pearl," were mellow, easy on the ear, and verging on the bland. When he came out to Hawaii to hear what was being laid down, new label boss David Geffen was distinctly unimpressed.

More than a little miffed that his new label was talking about rejecting his first project with them even before it got to the final mixing stage, Neil then

podromo Le Capannelle
ROMA

*Francesco Sanavio presenta:*

# Neil Young

№ 12609

decided to introduce some of the electronic sounds that he'd been playing with at home for months, eventually producing *Trans*, which was released at the end of 1982. For the Hawaii sessions, he had assembled a remarkable lineup consisting of musicians from various points in his career: Crazy Horse's Ralph Molina on drums, Ben Keith from the *Harvest* ensemble on steel guitar, the now-famous Nils Lofgren on guitar, Joe Lala (from the 1974 CSNY tour) on percussion, and—most surprisingly for longtime Neil Young followers—the former Buffalo Springfield bass player Bruce Palmer.

This was the band that would tour as the Trans-Band, on a huge trek of Europe that proved a financial disaster. Inspired by the Rolling Stones' latest stage extravaganzas, Neil brought in legendary stage manager Chip Monck (who had masterminded the setup at Woodstock all those years earlier) to oversee the construction of a huge set involving a forty-foot runway projecting into the crowd, along with a stage that needed three trucks just to transport.

The album itself, which tempered the six electronic songs with three from the melodic Hawaiian recordings, simply bombed, just scraping into the U.S. Top 20. Despite Neil's protestations that the underlying theme of the songs, particularly the track "Transformer Man," was his communication with his son Ben, the staff at Geffen Records were already becoming wary of their recent signing.

## Everybody's Rockin'

No sooner was *Trans* in the stores than Neil, home from the European trek that had preceded the late December release date, was out on the road for a solo acoustic tour of the United States and Canada, on which he showcased a few electronic songs alongside a "greatest hits" selection from previous albums plus some new country-flavored material. And it was the country songs that would be a clue to what the chameleon-like performer was up to next.

Taking time out from the tour at the end of January 1983, Neil booked a studio in Nashville to record what would be his most authentic-sounding country collection so far. He used the tried-and-tested lineup of Ben Keith, Spooner Oldham, Rufus Thibodeaux, Tim Drummond, and Carl Himmel, with some pedigree Nashville backup singers, to come up with a collection that was a plea for an old-time America and its traditions that would have made Ronald Reagan proud.

# Everybody's Rockin'

ALBUM

This is Neil revisiting his 1950s rock 'n' roll roots with a rockabilly-style collection of oldies and originals. Using some of his usual session players, this time renamed the Shocking Pinks, he captures the flavor of the era with a slapped upright bass sound and "echo chamber" effects—though the latter was achieved somewhat inauthentically through a digital delay process, and sounds like it. The covers include "Mystery Train" (featured among Elvis Presley's earliest recordings in Memphis), and Bobby Freeman's evocatively titled "Betty Lou's Got a Brand New Pair of Shoes." Neil's own songs are equally tailored to the genre, including a Hank Williams pastiche on "Rain," and the sharply caustic "Payola Blues," dedicated to the memory of the pioneering rock 'n' roll DJ Alan Freed.

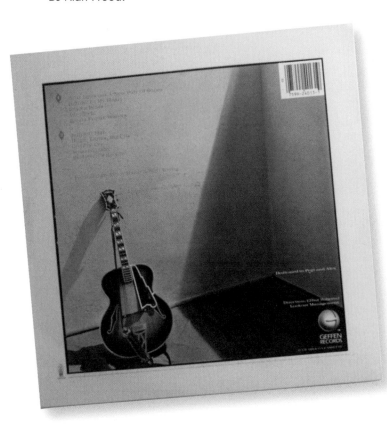

### SIDE ONE

Betty Lou's Got a New Pair of Shoes [Bobby Freeman] ★ Rainin' in My Heart [Slim Harpo, Jerry West] ★ Payola Blues [Ben Keith, Neil Young] ★ Wonderin ★ Kinda Fonda Wanda [Tim Drummond, Neil Young]

### SIDE TWO

Jellyroll Man ★ Bright Lights, Big City [Jimmy Reed] ★ Cry, Cry, Cry ★ Mystery Train [Junior Parker, Sam Phillips] ★ Everybody's Rockin'

All songs written by Neil Young except where indicated.

### RECORDED

April 27–May 25, 1983, Modern Recorders, Redwood City, California

### RELEASED

July 27, 1983

### PERSONNEL

The Shocking Pinks: Neil Young (piano, guitar, harmonica, vocals), Ben "King" Keith (alto sax, guitar), Tim Drummond (double bass), Carl Himmel (snare drum), Larry Byrom (piano, vocals), Anthony Crawford (vocals), Rick Palombi (vocals)

### LABEL

Geffen

### PRODUCERS

Elliot Mazer ★ Neil Young

This was a Neil Young a life away from the hippie hero, in songs like "Silver and Gold," "Depression Blues," and "Are There Any More Real Cowboys," mourning the loss of community in modern suburban America and the threatened disappearance of family values as a consequence. To all intents and purposes, it represented Neil Young as a born-again conservative. What his public, and David Geffen for that matter, would make of it was anybody's guess.

On April 1, Neil resumed recording, now back at his California ranch. This time the country angle had shifted, to the rockabilly sound of embryonic rock 'n' roll, epitomized by Elvis's debut recordings for the Memphis-based Sun Records. In fact he included two covers of those early Presley tracks—"That's All Right, Mama," and "Mystery Train"—in the tapes that he added to the Nashville material and sent off to Geffen Records as his next album release.

Much to Neil's chagrin, the record company dismissed the project almost out of hand, declaring it to be "too country" for a release. They did concede that the rockabilly tracks had some commercial potential—at the time the retro genre was something of a trend—and so Neil Young, "almost vindictively" as he would put it, gave them what they wanted.

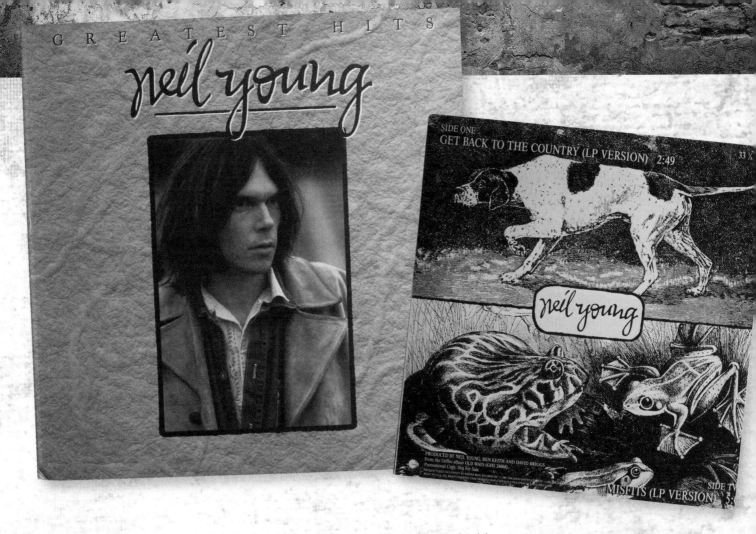

SIDE ONE
GET BACK TO THE COUNTRY (LP VERSION) 2:49          33⅓

neil young

PRODUCED BY NEIL YOUNG, BEN KEITH AND DAVID BRIGGS
From the Geffen album OLD WAYS (GHS 24068)
Promotional Copy. Not For Sale.

MISFITS (LP VERSION)          SIDE TV

Bringing in Carl Himmel, Tim Drummond (this time on stand-up double bass), and Ben Keith from the previous sessions—calling them the Shocking Pinks—Neil created a rockabilly pastiche titled *Everybody's Rockin'* that was certainly weird, with the authentic Sun echo-chamber sound replaced with a digital delay gimmick. Released in July 1983, the album—less than twenty-five minutes in length, and almost universally panned by the critics—only made it to #46 on the U.S. charts, Neil Young's worst rating since he began making solo records.

## Old Ways

Executives at Geffen Records were so frustrated at Neil Young's failure to deliver on their considerable investment in him that in November 1983 they served papers on their artist, suing for damages of over three million dollars on the grounds that both *Trans* and *Everybody Rockin'* were uncommercial and "unrepresentative" of his previous recordings.

Neil meanwhile, while fighting these new battles, went back on tour with a re-formed band, intent on plugging the unreleased Nashville material (collectively known as *Old Ways*) that was "too country" for Geffen, and forging a new identity as a country artist in the process. Called the International Harvesters, the outfit was based around Drummond, Keith, Himmel, Oldham, and Thibodeaux from the 1983 Nashville sessions. Meanwhile, Neil and Pegi added to their family in May 1984, with the birth of their daughter Amber Jean, who would later be diagnosed with epilepsy inherited from her father.

Above left: a special edition of the *Greatest Hits*, released in Australia, and, right, the back of the *Country Ways* single.

Court cases notwithstanding, Young was still signed to Geffen, so for the label it was a public relations minefield as Neil made very public his avowed abandonment of rock music in favor of "real" country. Plus there was the issue of his increasingly strident political opinions—in the main very much to the right of the liberal mainstream—which he took every chance to air during interviews and press conferences on the road. Some views were clearly knee-jerk reactions to current events, others deliberately over-the-top in order to provoke journalists. Hoping that the legal pressure would force their renegade star to return to the fold of "marketable" artists, the company continued with its litigation.

Eventually involving the high-profile country stars Waylon Jennings and Willie Nelson, plus a plethora of top Nashville session players, backing singers, and a string section, a revamped *Old Ways* would be released in August 1985, as a deal-breaker for the lawsuits to be dropped. Unfortunately the record did little on the sales charts to reaffirm any faith Geffen still had in its single-minded and usually stubborn artist.

Opposite: Neil Young playing at the Philadelphia segment of the Live Aid concert, July 13, 1985.

Below: A flyer and ticket for the International Harvesters.

"AS A group of MUSICIANS, they WERE absolutely the PEAK."

Neil Young on INTERNATIONAL HARVESTERS

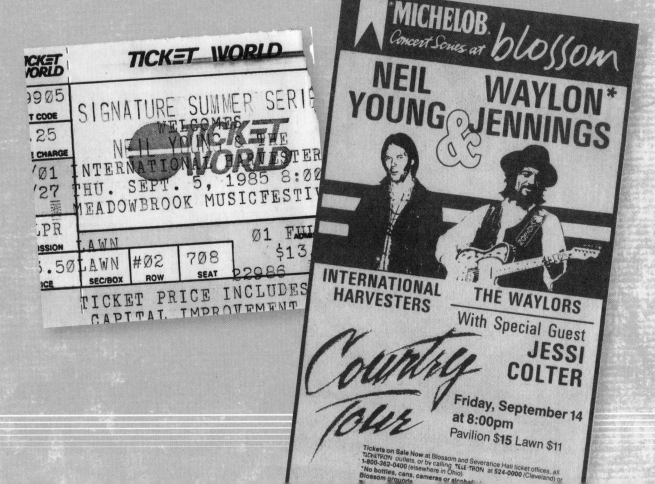

neil young

old ways

# Old Ways

ALBUM

For this album, steeped in the country feel that had been heralded on *Hawks & Doves*, Neil gathered together some of Nashville's finest—including the legendary duo of Waylon Jennings and Willie Nelson—to produce his most thoroughly "down home" album yet. Among several memorable tracks, a cover of the old Gogi Grant hit "The Wayward Wind" sees him working once again with the huge Gone With the Wind Orchestra from *Comes a Time*. Many of the songs—including the title track, the ironic "Are There Any More Real Cowboys," and "Get Back to the Country"—reflect a wish to return to the old-time American values of a simpler age. A track like "Misfits," however, reassures us that underneath the good ol' boy posturing, an inquiring, always skeptical mind is still at work.

### SIDE ONE

The Wayward Wind [Herb Newman, Stanley Lebowsky] ★ Get Back to the Country ★ Are There Any More Real Cowboys?* ★ Once an Angel ★ Misfits

### SIDE TWO

California Sunset* ★ Old Ways ★ My Boy** ★ Bound for Glory ★ Where Is the Highway Tonight?

All songs written by Neil Young except where indicated

### RECORDED

January 28–29, 1983, House of David, Nashville ★ April 20–30, 1985, The Castle, Franklin, Tennessee, Pedernales Recording Studio, Spicewood, Texas ★ June 22, 1984, live at The Opry, Austin, Texas, June 22, 1984 ("California Sunset")

### RELEASED

August 12, 1985

### PERSONNEL

Neil Young (guitar, banjo-guitar, harmonica, vocals) ★ Waylon Jennings (guitar, vocals) ★ Willie Nelson (guitar, vocals), Rufus Thibodeaux (fiddle) ★ Ben Keith (pedal steel guitar, Dobro) ★ Tim Drummond (bass) ★ Carl Himmel (drums) ★ Joe Allen (bass) ★ Ralph Mooney (pedal steel guitar) ★ Hargus "Pig" Robbins (piano) ★ Gordon Terry (fiddle) ★ Joe Osborne (bass) ★ Anthony Crawford (mandolin, vocal) ★ Terry McMillan (harmonica, Jew's harp) ★ Béla Fleck (banjo) ★ Bobby Thompson (banjo) ★ David Kirby (guitar) ★ Grant Boatwright (guitar) ★ Johnny Christopher (guitar) ★ Ray Edenton (guitar) ★ Gove Scrivenor (autoharp) ★ Farrell Morris (percussion) ★ Marty Stuart (mandolin) ★ Carl Gorodetzky (violin) ★ Spooner Oldham (piano, vocals, strings)

### LABEL

Geffen

### PRODUCERS

Neil Young ★ Ben Keith ★ David Briggs ★ *Neil Young, Elliot Mazer, David Briggs, Ben Keith ★ **Neil Young, Elliot Mazer, David Briggs

And just a month before the album's release, Neil Young made what was now a rare appearance with his old comrades Crosby, Stills & Nash on the Philadelphia section of the trans-world TV charity broadcast Live Aid, teaming up with the trio—performing "Only Love Can Break Your Heart," and "Daylight Again/Find the Cost of Freedom"—for their first public performance together in over ten years.

## Landing on Water

After the stylistic acrobatics that Neil Young had appeared to be performing since signing with Geffen in 1981, in 1986 he delivered what would be his first straightforward rock album for the label.

For *Landing on Water*, Neil used just a duo consisting of co-producer Danny Kortchmar on synthesizer-bass and ace session drummer Steve Jordan, plus himself on guitar and synthesizer. To say it was a straightforward rock album is relative, of course; by Neil's erratic standards it was certainly "rock" in that it was aimed at the rock section of the record stores, but the end product itself was far from basic. Notorious for tinkering until he got the sound he wanted, Neil would overdub and overdub—including on material resurrected from failed Crazy Horse sessions two years previous—to the point where Kortchmar walked out. To call the album overproduced is an understatement.

> ## "To call the album overproduced is an understatement."
>
> NEIL YOUNG ON "LANDING ON WATER"

**Neil Young**

LANDING ON WATER

# Landing on Water

ALBUM

**R**ecorded with just two other musicians (apart from two tracks featuring the San Francisco Boys Choir), this synthesizer-dominated offering seemed to be aimed fairly and squarely at the lucrative, middle-of-the-road, adult rock market. The result satisfied neither Neil's committed fan following nor the contemporary pop audience at large. Overdubbed to the point of it being overproduced—even songs "rescued" from aborted Crazy Horse sessions get the revisionary treatment—the only saving grace of interest is in some of the lyrics. "Hippie Dream" is a good case in point, which although ostensibly a message to David Crosby struggling with his drug problems, can be read as another contemplation on the optimistic ideals of the 1960s having turned sour.

## SIDE ONE

Weight of the World ★ Violent Side* ★ Hippie Dream ★ Bad News Beat ★ Touch the Night*

## SIDE TWO

People on the Street ★ Hard Luck Stories ★ I Got a Problem ★ Pressure ★ Drifter

All songs written by Neil Young.

## RECORDED

August 1983–March 1986, Broken Arrow Ranch, Woodside, California, and Record One, Los Angeles

## RELEASED

July 21, 1986

## PERSONNEL

Neil Young (guitar, synthesizer, vocals) ★ Danny Kortchmar (guitar, synthesizer, vocals) ★ Steve Jordan (drums, synthesizer, vocals) ★ * also featuring tThe San Francisco Boys Chorus

## ADDITIONAL PERSONNEL

Norris Badeaux (baritone saxophone on Good Time Boy) ★ Hal Blaine (drums) ★ Merry Clayton (vocals) ★ James Burton (Dobro, guitar) ★ Charlie Chin (banjo) ★ David Crosby (backing vocal on Rock & Roll Woman) ★ Jim Fielder (bass) ★ Jim Gordon (drums) ★ Doug Hastings (guitar) ★ Brenda Holloway (vocal) ★ Patrice Holloway (vocal) ★ Jim Horn (clarinet) ★ Gloria Jones (vocal) ★ Carol Kaye (bass) ★ Shirley Matthews (vocal) ★ Harvey Newmark (bass) ★ Gracia Nitzsche (vocal) ★ Jack Nitzsche (electric piano) ★ Don Randi (piano, harpsichord) ★ Chris Sarns (guitar) ★ Ryss Titelman (guitar) ★ Bobby West (bass)

## LABEL

Geffen

## PRODUCERS

Neil Young ★ Danny Kortchmar

Pages 206–207: Neil Young with Keith Richards and Chuck Berry at Berry's induction into the Rock and Roll Hall of Fame, 1986.

Neil took Crazy Horse out on the road to promote the album, the seasoned rockers making the best job they could of trying to substitute for the synthetic sounds achieved in the studio. And again, a costly presentation almost guaranteed that the whole U.S. and Europe exercise would be losing money from the start.

As if to salvage something from the tour, David Briggs was recruited to make a live album out of the concerts. Fraught with tension within the ranks, as the circus moved to Europe, things got more chaotic—some dates were even canceled because of poor box-office sales—and Briggs left just before the trek ended. With the majority of tracks recorded during the early American phase of the tour, at the Universal Amphitheatre in Universal City, California, *Life*, released in July 1987, would be one of Neil Young's worst-selling albums. Despite—or perhaps because of—the strong political content of some of the songs, it was a sad if predictable swan song for his time with Geffen. By October 1987, Elliot Roberts had negotiated Neil's departure from the label, back to his previous record company Reprise.

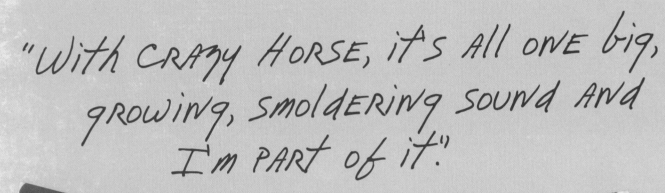

"WITH CRAZY HORSE, IT'S ALL ONE big, growing, smoldering Sound And I'm PART of it."

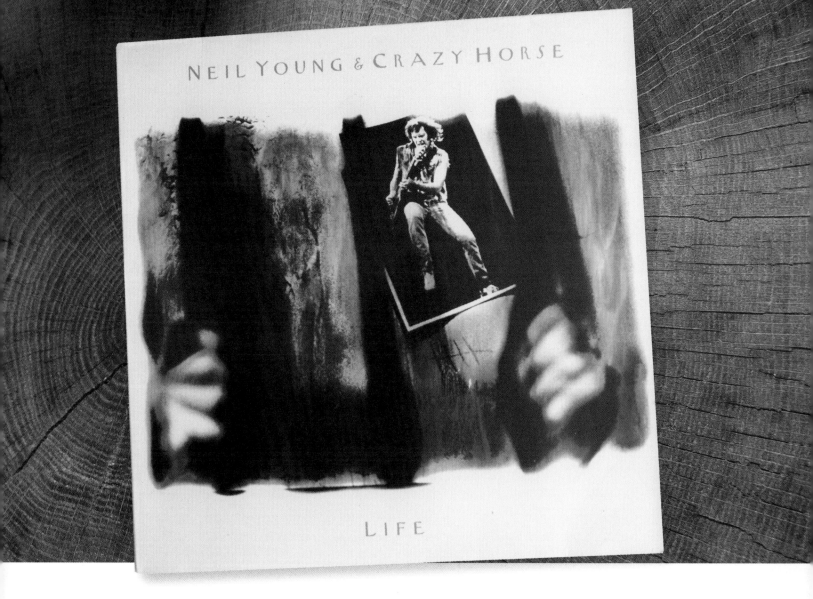

# Life

ALBUM

SIDE ONE

Mideast Vacation ★ Long Walk Home ★ Around the World ★ Inca Queen

SIDE TWO

Too Lonely ★ Prisoners of Rock 'n' Roll ★ Cryin' Eyes ★ When Your Lonely Heart Breaks ★ We Never Danced*

RELEASED

June 30, 1987

RECORDED

November 18-19, 1986, Universal Amphitheatre, Universal City ★ later at Record One, Los Angeles

LABEL

Geffen

PRODUCERS

David Briggs ★ Neil Young ★ *Jack Nitzsche, Neil Young

# BEHIND THE CAMERA

**B**orn in 1945, Neil Young, like most of his generation, grew up in a world where the major mass-cultural influence was undoubtedly the cinema. Although music touched the baby-boom teenagers of the late 1950s profoundly—for the first time young people had their own music in the form of rock 'n' roll—the movies were a common experience shared by all, regardless of age, class, or nationality.

Despite television having invaded virtually every home in the Western world by the end of the decade, it was the movies (alongside music, of course) that captured the imagination of kids like Neil. It hardly came as a surprise, therefore, that when the ever-experimenting musician had the financial wherewithal to indulge other artistic fancies outside the parameters of songwriting and performing, he turned to the medium of film.

Neil's first forays onto the big screen were purely as a contributing songwriter to the soundtracks of *Changes* and *The Strawberry Student* (both released in 1969)—though in the latter picture performing three songs himself. But it was in 1972, with the overtly experimental *Journey through the Past* that he made his cinematic debut behind the camera, as a director. In true art-house tradition, the film was shot in a 16mm format, before being transferred to the conventional 35mm for theatrical release in 1974. Although originally planned as a straightforward compilation of unseen footage from various stages of Young's career (or at least that's what Warner Bros. were led to believe when they first agreed to fund the

Neil strumming a guitar on the set of the 1982 film *Human Highway*, with actor Dennis Hopper (center).

'project), the promised musical clips were interspersed with surreal scenes shot by Neil with the aid of various friends and neighbors from Topanga Canyon, where he was living at the time. Bizarre sequences included an American Legion audience singing "God Bless America," an overlong shot of Neil eating strawberries, President Richard Nixon speaking at a religious meeting, and a group of horsemen dressed as Ku Klux Klan members riding across a beach to the soundtrack of *King of Kings*. Neil would later admit—after it failed to impress critics and audiences alike—that the film was a total indulgence on his part.

Next came *Rust Never Sleeps*, a concert film that was released at the same time as his album *Live Rust* in November 1979; the album, and its predecessor *Rust Never Sleeps*, comprised various live recordings from the 1978 "Rust Never Sleeps" tour, the film being shot at just one show at San Francisco's Cow Palace in October. Neil (who made the movie under his pseudonym of Bernard Shakey) had to do things a little differently, of course. At the Hollywood premiere of the film, he presented the picture as having been shot in "Rust-O-Vision," providing the audience with cardboard glasses reminiscent of 3-D movies from the 1950s—by all accounts, the specs made no difference whatsoever to what was seen onscreen.

Neil's second motion picture under the name of Bernard Shakey appeared in 1982, a whacky comedy that included Hollywood stars Dean Stockwell (who co-directed with

A FILM BY JIM JARMUSCH

YEAR OF THE HORSE
NEIL YOUNG AND CRAZY HORSE LIVE

CRANK IT UP

Above: A poster for the film by Jim Jarmusch, *Year of the Horse*, which came out the year after the tour of the same name.

Below: A *Rolling Stone* article about Neil's film work in May 1973.

# MUSIC

## Neil Young's First Film Shown: A docu-autobio-musico-'Journey'

'*Journey Through the Past*' comes off as sort of a cinematic contemplation of the navel. The film will probably disappoint those fans seeking the music of Young and be of value primarily to those searching souls looking for a view of the outside world from inside the hectic, confused, and confusing world of rock music.
—Bob Porter, Dallas Times-Herald

### BY JANELLE ELLIS

DALLAS, Tex.—Neil Young's first film, *Journey Through the Past*, premiered at the US Film Festival here on April 8th. Only a third of the 3500-seat Memorial Auditorium in the Dallas Convention Center was filled for the Sunday afternoon screening; at Young's request, none of the papers had mentioned anything about Neil Young himself showing up. Still, *Journey*'s two showings that day drew the largest crowds of the week, including the festival's handful of celebrities: Vincent Minnelli, Jack Nicholson, Lou Adler and Carrie Snodgress. Minnelli was being honored during the week with a retrospective of his films; Nicholson, who directed *Drive He Said*, was on a panel discussion; Adler, whose record label is heading toward video (he'll be filming parts of the Carole King tour for a movie or TV special), had a weekend to spare, and Snodgress was there

Neil Young began talking about making movies about four years ago, when

is a morbidly drawn-out scene of a junkie fixing up (Neil later indicated that he had witnessed such scenes backstage); shots of Jesus Freaks on Hollywood Boulevard putting the word on Young, and a re-creation of a recurring dream of his: twelve black-hooded men on black horses sweeping down a beach toward a man and his pickup truck. Although Young said he couldn't explain its significance, the scene serves as the illustration for the soundtrack album.

Another scene has Young in a junkyard under a busy freeway. He sits in a '57 Buick, opens his lunchbox and talks ecology: "Like, man, you know, rebuilding old cars instead of manufacturing new ones."

Bob Porter of the Times-Herald, the only critic who covered the film, called its philosophy "simplistic—unless there is a gigantic put-on taking place. . . . It seems at odds that someone so organized and craftsmanlike in his music would approach another media so unstructured. Young expressed the determination to do other films. He is artist enough that he may grow with that. With *Journey* he stands as a filmmaker somewhat like he would as a beginning musician."

Beaulieux 8mm camera was a new toy, and his dream was to blow up some of the best of his home movies to 16mm for "the big time"—to show to neighbors at the Topanga Community House. Young had recently joined Crosby, Stills and Nash, and they soon began plotting out a movie of themselves—a documentary of their live concerts and of their lives. David Myers began shooting them on the road, with L.A. Johnson doing sound and Underhill as a production assistant.

"After we'd shot a lot of stuff, they looked at it and did nothing." But whoever might want the footage, it was agreed, could have it. Neil then began plans for *Journey Through the Past*, through his own production company, Shaky Pictures, in conjunction with Myers, Johnson and Underhill, whose own company is called Taut and Gripping, Inc., from a Judith Crist film review.

In the credits, *Journey* is identified as "A film by Neil Young." Neil is also credited as editor—"that's what he's most proud of," said Underhill—although he also directed scenes and conceived of most of the fantasy bits. He also went to TV networks in New York to look through stock footage, coming up with, among others, ABC-TV's coverage of Billy Graham and Richard Nixon

By last January, the movie, 80-minutes long, was finished, and Warne Bros., the distributor, released its sound track album. But legal problems developed: Clearances had to be obtained for everything from Jesus Freaks to the man who composed "God Bless America," Irving Berlin. Now, the film scheduled to be released in June, pending a few more clearances, with openings in New York and Los Angeles.

In Dallas, when the film began and Young's name appeared on the screen the audience burst into spontaneous spirited applause. At the end, the applause was more . . . polite, and scattered. Neil had watched the film from inside the projectionist's booth and listened to the response. He judged himself safe and bounded down the aisle completely surprising the audience. Joined by Underhill, Myers and festival director L.M. "Kit" Carson (who'd worked with Myers on *Marjoe* and invited Young's participation in this year's festival), he sat on the edge of the stage, legs dangling over the front row.

"Not used to this," Neil began. "We don't have question and answer periods after our concerts." The audience immediately warmed up and shot questions at him for half an hour—the usual inane ones ("Were you drinking gasoline from that . . .

Posters for two of Neil Young's films: *Journey through the Past* (1972) and the 2008 documentary *CSNY/Déjà Vu*.

Young), Russ Tamblyn, Sally Kirkland, and Dennis Hopper. Like *Journey through the Past*, *Human Highway* developed into something far more eccentric (and financially unviable) than originally intended; what was to have been a semi-documentary of life on the road with a rock band turned into a madcap farce involving a collection of characters in a small town (situated next to a nuclear reactor plant) as an atomic war ensues.

In 1995 Neil returned to the cinema screen, this time composing the entire soundtrack to *Dead Man*, a Western movie directed by the acclaimed Jim Jarmusch. After studying the film over and over at home, Neil improvised the soundtrack "live" while watching the film one more time in the studio. Young and Jarmusch would collaborate once again in 1997, when the director released *Year of the Horse*, a concert film featuring Neil and Crazy Horse.

Neil took a directorial role with the 2004 release of *Greendale*, a spin-off from the "audio novel" album concerning the lives and struggles of the residents of a small rural town in California. Despite its deliberately "amateur" look (some segments were filmed in the "home-movie" Super 8 format), the film—in which actors lip-synched to songs from the album—was taken seriously by a number of critics. In the words of Armond White in the *New York Press*: "Not many contemporary artists have responded to the post-9/11 question of how to make relevant art. Young proposes an answer by emulating the simplicity of folk art: the forcefulness of style, technique, purpose that can be felt in every version of *Greendale*."

At the time of writing, Neil Young's latest excursion into the world of film directing (again as Bernard Shakey) was in collaboration with Crosby, Stills and Nash for *CSNY/Déjà Vu*, a documentary based on the CSNY "Freedom of Speech Tour" in support of his *Living with War* album in 2006. The backdrop to the tour was the war in Iraq, and the 2008 film examines the band's connection with its audience in political and musical terms. It draws a parallel with today's post-9/11 protesters, and the sentiment of the anti-war lobby against the Vietnam conflict. In the film, a Vietnam veteran makes the pertinent comment, "It's déjà vu all over again."

In 2011, Jonathan Demme, who has directed several Neil Young concert documentary films—including 2006's acclaimed *Hearts of Gold*—released his latest Young project, *Neil Young Journeys*, which premiered at the Toronto Film Festival. Described by one reviewer as "So up close and personal it leaves the audience viewing the rocker through his own spit," it is the latest in what will almost certainly not be the last of Neil Young's ongoing love affair with the movie camera, both as subject and director.

Neil Young with director Jim Jarmusch during the filming of *Year of the Horse* in 1996.

SEVEN Freedom

As the 1980s came to a close, and Neil Young was making one of his biggest stylistic shifts yet into a jazz-infected blues sound, there were two schools of thought about his constant changes of musical direction. Many saw it as cynical bandwagoning, jumping on any trend that took his fancy in order to cash in—whether the cash came in, of course, was another matter. Other, more supportive voices recognized an open-minded approach to any musical genre that grabbed his interest, combined with a praiseworthy refusal to be pigeonholed. The closing decade of the twentieth century would see him as eclectic as ever, taking on board the new indie sounds of bands like Nirvana and Sonic Youth (and being dubbed the "Godfather of Grunge" in the process), returning to his folk-rock roots, and as the new millennium dawned, embarking on a record-breaking reunion with Crosby, Stills and Nash. And despite the constant controversy his various projects stimulated, his long-term place in the rock music pantheon was acknowledged with his induction into the Rock and Roll Hall of Fame.

## Bluenotes

Now freed from the trials and tribulations of his Geffen contract, after a short tour with Crazy Horse promoting *Life*, Neil decided to put together a new lineup dominated by a jazz-influenced horn section. Consisting of one trombone, three saxophones, and two trumpets plus the usual rhythm section, the band was named the Bluenotes and began rehearsing a clutch of rhythm-and-blues-based numbers, some harking back to Neil's teen years as a music fan.

During June 1987, he'd enjoyed a one-night reunion with his old group the Squires in Winnipeg, and immediately afterward their former bass player Ken Koblun handed him a sheet of lyrics of songs that Neil had written back in the mid-1960s. Now he was taking these songs, and new material in a similar R&B vein, onto the road. Yet again reinventing his own persona—this time as "Shakey Deal," a hip bluesman sporting a fedora and shades—Neil and his outfit started with some dates around the San Francisco Bay Area.

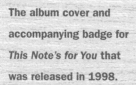

The album cover and accompanying badge for *This Note's for You* that was released in 1998.

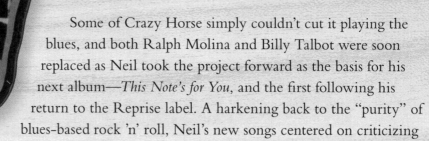

Some of Crazy Horse simply couldn't cut it playing the blues, and both Ralph Molina and Billy Talbot were soon replaced as Neil took the project forward as the basis for his next album—*This Note's for You,* and the first following his return to the Reprise label. A harkening back to the "purity" of blues-based rock 'n' roll, Neil's new songs centered on criticizing the commercialism of the rock business, and concert tours in particular. The title track, which reached #19 on the American singles chart soon after the album's release in April 1988, is a cutting commentary on gig sponsorship, accompanied at the time by a video featuring a Michael Jackson look-alike whose hair catches fire. Bizarrely, despite controversy centered on the MTV network's banning of the video, it went on to win Music Video of the Year at the MTV Music Awards. After the album's release, soul star Harold Melvin threatened to sue Young for use of the name Bluenotes (the title of his own backing outfit); Young rechristened his group Ten Men Workin'.

## American Dream

At the end of 1988, Crosby, Still, Nash & Young were on the market again, with the release of their first album together since 1971's *4 Way Street* and their first studio album since the mega-successful *Déjà Vu* the year before that. Throughout the 1980s, the trio of CSN had gotten together in various permutations, but every collaboration seemed to be overshadowed by David Crosby's descent from creative recreational drug use to hard-core addiction. In 1986 they had reunited with Young for a one-time reunion, a benefit for the Bridge School charity that Neil and Pegi Young were very much involved in, but after that they failed to reconvene until Young's release from Geffen.

The album, called *American Dream*, was an all-around disappointment for fans seeking even a hint at the greatness of *Déjà Vu*. While Neil could have brought a tough edge to the inherent smoothness of the others' contribution (on a collection of largely lackluster songs, it has to be said), he seemed content to be going through the motions on a project he sounded disenchanted with before the tapes had even begun to roll. Being met with a some tough reviews by the critics (*Rolling Stone*'s Anthony DeCurtis commented, "Despite pleasant melodies, the occasional interesting song, and the signature harmonies, *American Dream* is, for the most part, a snoozefest"), the album managed to peak at #16 on the *Billboard* chart, selling over a million copies.

Neil (far right) jamming at the Nordoff-Robbins Music Therapy Foundation's Silver Clef Award and Auction dinner, New York, 1988, with (left to right) Buckwheat Zydeco, Robert Plant, and Curt Smith of the UK band Tears for Fears.

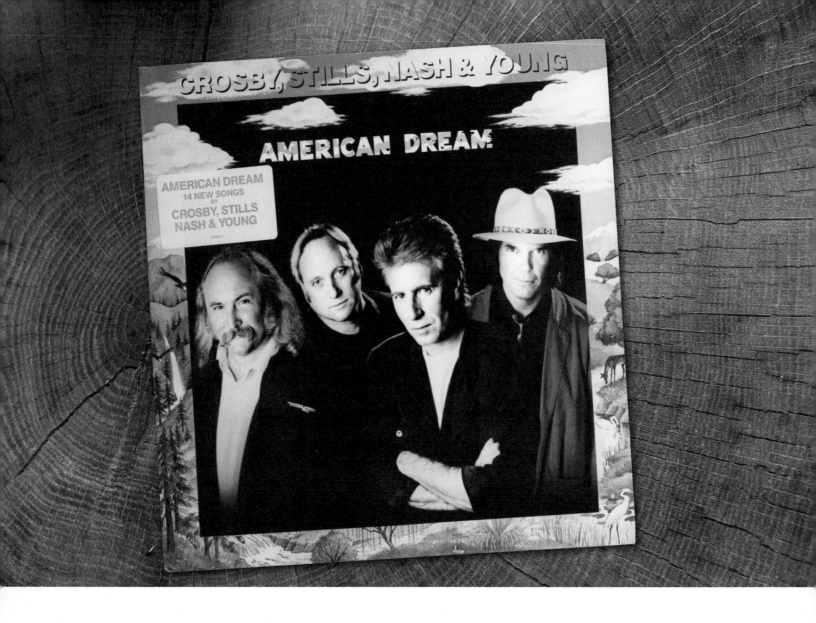

# American Dream

ALBUM

American Dream [Young] ★ Got It Made [Stills/Young] ★ Name of Love [Young] ★ Don't Say Goodbye [Nash/Vitale] ★ This Old House [Young] ★ Nighttime for the Generals [Crosby/Doerge] ★ Shadowland [Ryan/Nash/Vitale]* ★ Drivin' Thunder [Stills/Young] ★ Clear Blue Skies [Nash] ★ That Girl [Stills/Vitale/Glaub] ★ Compass [Crosby] ★ Soldiers of Peace [Nash/Doerge/Vitale] ★ Feel Your Love [Young] ★ Night Song [Stills/Young]

★ RECORDED ★

February 25–July 28, 1988   *April 24, 1987

★ RELEASED ★

November 22, 1988

★ LABEL ★

Atlantic

★ PRODUCERS ★

Niko Bolas ★ David Crosby ★ Stephen Stills ★ Graham Nash ★ Neil Young

## Eldorado

Almost as a reaction to the comfortable, inoffensive sound of the CSNY recordings, Neil's next foray was into the strident, guitar-thrashing world of heavy metal. While not assembling a metal outfit as such, he voiced the opinion that were he a teenager at that time—the late 1980s—he would have formed an HM group himself. Using ex-Bluenotes Chad Cromwell and Rick Rosas on drums and bass, he went into New York's Hit Factory studio and blasted out a battery of earsplitting numbers including "Heavy Love," "Cocaine Eyes," and a mind-bending version of the old pop classic "On Broadway," all initially intended for an album called *Times Square*.

As Neil Young and the Restless, the band—now also including Ben Keith and Frank Sampedro—took to the road across mid-America in January 1989, followed in April and May by a tour of Japan, Australia, and New Zealand (this time renamed the Lost Dogs). Those territories were the only ones to officially see the release of a limited-edition mini album of just five of the Hit Factory recordings, now under the name *Eldorado*. Neil advised fans in America who

**Below: Neil and Frank Sampedro playing together onstage in 1989.**

the bridge

a tribute to neil young

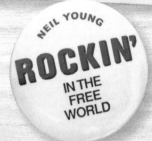

NEIL YOUNG

ROCKIN'
IN THE
FREE
WORLD

Above: The CD cover for
*The Bridge: A Tribute to Neil
Young* and a badge promoting
"Rockin' in the Free World."

asked where they could get a copy, to get hold of a bootleg tape.

## Freedom Rockin'

Having shelved most of the Hit Factory recordings, for the moment at least, Neil busied himself once more in the studio through the summer months of 1989, refreshing recent recordings, re-recording some older material, and bringing in Linda Ronstadt to help out on vocals. Including a couple of edited versions of *Eldorado* tracks, his next album *Freedom*—released in October 1989—featured a distinct use of distortion and feedback on some tracks.

That emphasis would coincide with the rise of "grunge" rock, associated with the Seattle bands Pearl Jam, Nirvana, and Mudhoney. Many of these grunge rockers—including Nirvana's Kurt Cobain and Pearl Jam's Eddie Vedder—named Neil Young as a major influence. Suddenly the forty-four-year-old rocker was at the cutting edge again. There was even a grunge-heavy tribute album released in July 1989, titled *The Bridge: A Tribute to Neil Young*, and featuring covers of his songs by various groups, including Sonic Youth, Soul Asylum, Nick Cave, and the Pixies.

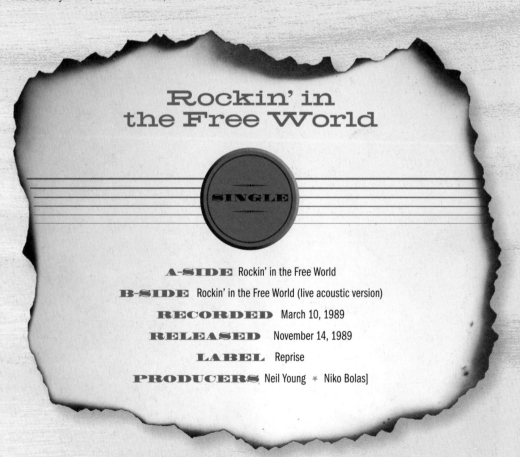

## Rockin' in the Free World

SINGLE

**A-SIDE** Rockin' in the Free World

**B-SIDE** Rockin' in the Free World (live acoustic version)

**RECORDED** March 10, 1989

**RELEASED** November 14, 1989

**LABEL** Reprise

**PRODUCERS** Neil Young ✶ Niko Bolas]

# Freedom

**ALBUM**

★ **SIDE ONE** ★

Rockin' in the Free World* [live acoustic version]  ★  Crime in the City (Sixty to Zero Part I)  ★  Don't Cry  ★  Hangin' on a Limb  ★  Eldorado  ★  The Ways of Love

★ **SIDE TWO** ★

Someday  ★  On Broadway  ★  Wrecking Ball  ★  No More  ★  Too Far Gone  ★  Rockin' in the Free World [electric version]

All songs written by Neil Young except where indicated.

★ **RELEASED** ★

October 2, 1989

★ **RECORDED** ★

July 25, 1988–July 10, 1989  ★  *June 14, 1989, live at Jones Beach

★ **LABEL** ★

Reprise

★ **PRODUCERS** ★

Neil Young  ★  Niko Bolas

Stylistically diverse, however, *Freedom* also included acoustic love songs, plus two featuring the Bluenotes horn section. And it contained what would be one of Neil's best-known political outings: both an acoustic and an electric version of the anthemic "Rockin' in the Free World." Highlighted in the media via a live performance on *Saturday Night Live* on September 30, 1989, the song became one of Neil Young's biggest hits ever.

Touching on urban homelessness and the environment, deeply critical of the policies of President George H. W. Bush, the song was used on the end credits of Michael Moore's celebrated protest documentary *Fahrenheit 9/11*, and was also something of a theme tune for the fall of the Berlin Wall (which occurred a month after the album's release), with its repeated chorus of "Keep on Rockin' in the Free World."

Earning a gold disc in the United States, *Freedom* was Neil Young's most successful long-player of the decade, reaching #35 on the U.S. charts and #17 in the UK, while the single smashed its way up the charts, eventually making the #2 position in the *Billboard* rock listing.

## Ragged Glory

With his career on a high once again, Neil reconvened Crazy Horse in the barn of his Northern California ranch to work on his next collection, which would perpetuate the distortion-heavy style that had featured strongly on *Freedom* and the *Eldorado* tracks. This was straightforward rock with a vengeance, Crazy Horse letting rip on tracks like "Over and Over" in what was Young's strongest and most significant album in years. And songs such as "Love and Only Love" and "Love to Burn" would reveal some of the his best guitar solos in a long time.

Released in September 1990, *Ragged Glory* met with almost universal acclaim from the critics, with Kurt Loder in *Rolling Stone* famously declaring Neil Young "the king of rock and roll" and calling the album "a monument to the spirit of the garage—to the pursuit of passion over precision." It marked a return the mainstream for Young, hitting the U.S. album chart at #31, with the single "Mansion on the Hill" making #3 on *Billboard*'s Mainstream Rock listing.

# Ragged Glory

**ALBUM**

A part from the closing track "Mother Earth (Natural Anthem)," recorded live at a Farm Aid benefit, the entire album was recorded in one frantic week of solid playing with a rejuvenated Crazy Horse. The collaboration sees Neil on a creative roll, the high-energy music earning him accolades both from rock traditionalists—songs like "Love to Burn" featuring his best guitar soloing in a long time—and the new breed of alt-rockers, who would soon acclaim Young as the "Godfather of Grunge." The sheer energy of tracks like "Over and Over," in which Neil and the Horse trade guitar licks gloriously, is a testament to the raw power of no-frills, back-to-basics garage rock.

### SIDE ONE

Country Home ★ White Line ★ F*!#in' Up ★ Over and Over ★ Love to Burn

### SIDE TWO

Farmer John [Don Harris, Dewey Terry] ★ Mansion on the Hill ★ Days That Used to Be ★ Love and Only Love ★ Mother Earth (Natural Anthem)*

All songs written by Neil Young except where indicated.

### RECORDED

April 24–30, 1990, Plywood Digital, Woodside, California ★
*originally recorded live April 7, 1990, Hoosier Dome, with additional vocals recorded later at Redwood Digital

### RELEASED

September 9, 1990

### PERSONNEL

Neil Young (guitar, vocals) ★ Frank Sampedro (guitar, vocals) ★
Billy Talbot (bass, vocals) ★ Ralph Molina (drums, vocals)

### LABEL

Reprise

### PRODUCERS

David Briggs ★ Neil Young

NEIL YOUNG + CRAZY HORSE
MANSION ON THE HILL

Below: Neil making a solo concert appearance in June 1992.

As Neil and Crazy Horse went on tour to promote the album—significantly with the country-punk band Social Distortion and alternative-rock heroes Sonic Youth for support—more and more of the new rock generation (including the Red Hot Chili Peppers, Counting Crows, and Spiritualized) declared Young, and *Ragged Glory*, as profoundly influential. The attention from the alt-rock scene, originally acknowledged back in 1989 with the release of the *Bridge* tribute album, soon earned Neil Young the unlikely title "the Godfather of Grunge" in the music press worldwide.

Just a month after the release of *Ragged Glory*, a personal tragedy occurred when Neil's mother Rassy—who from the start, and throughout her life, had encouraged her son's musical ambitions—died from cancer. Neil, who had attended her bedside frequently over the last months of her life, made all the funeral arrangements. She died on October 15, the day before her seventy-third birthday.

# Weld

**RECORDED**

February–April 1991, North American tour

**RELEASED**

October 23, 1991 (limited-edition three-CD set) ★ November 23, 1991 (two-CD *Weld*)

**LABEL**

Reprise

**PRODUCERS**

David Briggs ★ Neil Young, with Billy Talbot

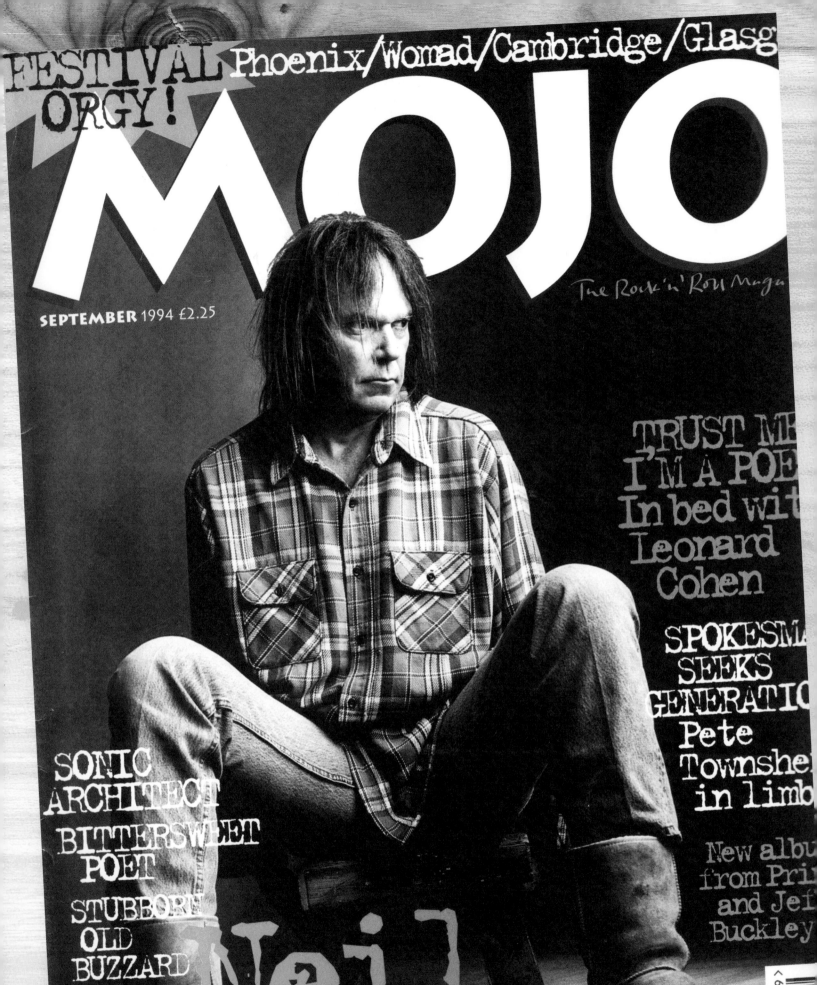

**FESTIVAL ORGY!** Phoenix/Womad/Cambridge/Glasg

# MOJO

*The Rock 'n' Roll Maga*

SEPTEMBER 1994 £2.25

'TRUST ME
I'M A POE
In bed wit
Leonard
Cohen

SPOKESMA
SEEKS
GENERATIO
Pete
Townshe
in limb

New albu
from Pri
and Jef
Buckley

SONIC
ARCHITECT
BITTERSWEET
POET
STUBBORN
OLD
BUZZARD

Neil Young

Released a year later, in October 1991, the two-disc live album *Weld* documented the *Ragged Glory* tour. It also came in a special edition with a third album, *Arc*, consisting of a thirty-five-minute collage of feedback, distortion, and fragmentary lyrics, apparently inspired at the suggestion of Sonic Youth front man Thurston Moore. But although he seemed to be pinning his colors firmly to the alt-rock mast, by the end of 1991 Neil Young was already preparing an abrupt return to the country and folk-rock world of *Harvest* when he embarked on what sounded like a sequel to the classic album of twenty years earlier.

## Harvest Moon

As the recording sessions for the new album *Harvest Moon* progressed through September 1991 into February 1992, it seemed a follow-up to *Harvest* was indeed in the pipeline. Neil had recruited Stray Gators Ben Keith, Kenny Buttrey, and Tim Drummond, along with guest stars Linda Ronstadt and James Taylor, all of whom had appeared on the 1972 album. But as the record company publicity machine began to get into gear prior to the October release date, Young was anxious to identify the new release as a unique collection in its own right, playing down the hype as the record hit the shops; "This is not *Harvest II*," he declared in interviews, insisting that all the two albums had in common was their title and almost identical personnel.

Above: The back cover of *Weld*.

Opposite: Neil appearing on the front cover of British magazine *Mojo* in 1997.

# "This is not HARVEST II."

### NEIL ON HARVEST MOON

After the wild electronic excesses of his recent endeavors, the careful crafting of these tracks veered heavily into the soft rock territory that Neil had so resolutely rejected. Musically most of the tracks couldn't be faulted, but the result, as in the title track, was often bland. Even the song into which Young poured most passion, "Such a Woman," his performance of which could have stood alone as a solo epic, suffered from the overwrought backing of Jack Nitzsche's eighteen-piece string section.

NEIL YOUNG ~ HARVEST MOON

# Harvest Moon

I n what many saw as a sequel after twenty years—though Neil denied it at the time—*Harvest Moon* boasts a very similar personnel to its predecessor *Harvest*. This is Neil Young back in a soft rock mode, with a set of near-faultless recordings, which sometimes, unfortunately, verge on the bland. Stylistically it falls between the 1972 album and 1978's folksy *Comes a Time*, a comfortable excursion into nostalgia territory in which Neil strums his acoustic with considered restraint. Conversely, the stand-out track in many ways is "Such a Woman," in which Jack Nitzsche's eighteen-piece string section is in danger of overwhelming Neil's heartfelt delivery. But whatever its shortcomings, the album was what thousands of fans had been waiting for, and resulted in one of Neil Young's all-time best sellers.

## TRACKS

Unknown Legend  ★  From Hank to Hendrix  ★  You and Me  ★  Harvest Moon  ★  War of Man  ★  One of These Days  ★  Such a Woman**  ★  Old King  ★  Dreamin' Man  ★  Natural Beauty*

All songs written by Neil Young.

## RECORDED

September 20, 1991–February 1, 1992, Redwood Digital, Woodside, California  ★  * January 23, 1992, live at Portland Auditorium, Portland OR, later at Redwood Digital  ★  **strings recorded at Sunset Sound, Hollywood

## RELEASED

November 2, 1992

## PERSONNEL

Neil Young & the Stray Gators: Neil Young (guitar, banjo-guitar, piano, pump organ, vibes, vocals), Ben Keith (pedal steel guitar, Dobro, bass marimba, vocals), Kenny Buttrey (drums), Tim Drummond (bass, marimba, broom), Spooner Oldham (piano, pump organ, keyboards)

## ADDITIONAL PERSONNEL

Linda Ronstadt (vocals)  ★  James Taylor (vocals)  ★  Nicolette Larson (vocals)  ★  Astrid Young (vocals)  ★  Larry Cragg (vocals) and **strings

## LABEL

Reprise

## PRODUCERS

Neil Young  ★  Ben Keith

What the album did reveal was the basic sincerity in Neil Young's approach—this was no trend-chasing exercise, but indeed an attempt to step back and deliver something considered, and deliberately restrained. Unfortunately, the end result would sound, to many recent Young devotees at least, simply uncommitted. But as always, the record-buying public had the last say: *Harvest Moon* made #16 on the U.S. charts, going platinum with million-plus sales by February 1993, and winning the critics' Juno Award for Album of the Year in 1994.

## Unplugged

As sales of *Harvest Moon* passed the million mark in February 1993, Neil was booked to appear on the prestigious *Unplugged* series on MTV, in which artists would appear in a semi-acoustic setting playing live in front of the TV cameras. Neil's performance, which included the previously unreleased song "Stringman," did not go smoothly; there was constant tension with the band, whose playing he didn't think was up to the mark, and the released version would be the second attempt at recording a set suitable for airing. All but four of the songs performed in the TV recording—"Dreamin' Man," "Sample and Hold," "War of Man," and "Winterlong"—would appear on the CD of the show released the following June, the album hitting #23 on the *Billboard* 200.

Following the *Unplugged* release, Neil took another turn in a totally unexpected direction when he teamed up for a tour of Europe and the United States with the bedrock band of Memphis soul music, Booker T. and the MGs. The legendary group—consisting of Booker T. Jones on keyboards, guitarist Steve Cropper, and Donald "Duck" Dunn on bass—had backed most of the soul greats who had recorded at the Stax studios in Memphis through the 1960s and '70s, and first played with Young at the "Bobfest" in October 1992, the marathon concert at Madison Square Garden celebrating Bob Dylan's thirtieth anniversary. A sign of what was to come with later collaborations, some of the European shows closed with guests Pearl Jam playing their version of "Rockin' in the Free World."

# Unplugged

**ALBUM**

**D**espite having his differences with MTV, Neil agreed to take part in an edition of the music channel's *Unplugged* series, in which artists would appear in a semi-acoustic format to play a live set for a TV recording. Significantly, Neil avoided making this a "greatest hits" collection, with notable omissions, including "After the Goldrush," "Sugar Mountain," and even "Heart of Gold." He did, however, include a number from each of his back catalogues with Buffalo Springfield and Crosby, Stills, Nash & Young. Most of the performances sound little different to their more familiar "electric" versions, except for "Like a Hurricane," on which Neil accompanies himself on a pump organ.

### TRACKS

The Old Laughing Lady ★ Mr. Soul ★ World on a String ★ Pocahontas ★ Stringman ★ Like a Hurricane ★ The Needle and the Damage Done ★ Helpless ★ Harvest Moon* ★ Transformer Man ★ Unknown Legend ★ Look Out for My Love ★ Long May You Run ★ From Hank to Hendrix All songs written by Neil Young.

### RECORDED

February 7, 1993, Stage 12, Universal Studios, Universal City, California

### RELEASED

June 8, 1993

### PERSONNEL

Neil Young (guitar, harmonica, piano, pump organ, vocals) ★ Nils Lofgren (guitar, autoharp, accordion, vocals) ★ Astrid Young (vocals) ★ Nicolette Larson (vocals) ★ Ben Keith (Dobro) ★ Spooner Oldham (piano, pump organ) ★ Tim Drummond (bass) ★ Oscar Butterworth (drums) ★ *Larry Cragg (broom)

### LABEL

Reprise

### PRODUCER

David Briggs

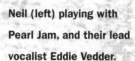

Neil (left) playing with Pearl Jam, and their lead vocalist Eddie Vedder.

"It's better to burn out than fade away."

Also in 1993, Neil Young would be nominated for an Oscar for his song "Philadelphia," used on the soundtrack of the movie of the same name, directed by Jonathan Demme. Neil played the song live at the Sixty-sixth Academy Awards ceremony in Hollywood. It had been a varied year, even by Neil Young's standards.

## Kurt Cobain

On April 5, 1994, the lead singer and songwriter of Seattle indie-rock band Nirvana was found dead at his home in the city, an apparent suicide after a long struggle with heroin addiction. Like many in the rock fraternity, Neil took the news badly, and the circumstances of the singer's death would be central to his next album with Crazy Horse, the dark and brooding *Sleeps with Angels*. Much of the album was recorded before the event, but the title track addressed the tragedy of Cobain's death, though not mentioning the grunge hero by name. In a suicide note, Cobain had quoted Neil Young's line, "It's better to burn out than fade away"—from "My My, Hey Hey (Out of the Blue)"—and it was widely reported that Neil had tried to contact Cobain prior to his untimely death.

Still feeling a strong connection with the grunge scene, Neil would reconvene with Pearl Jam in 1995 for the "live" studio album *Mirror Ball*, but not without some troubling negotiation with the band's label Epic; eventually the album had to be released without Pearl Jam's name on the CD cover, and the band members were forbidden from promoting it in any way. Neil's alliance with their lead singer Eddie Vedder continued the same year, however, when he was inducted into the Rock and Roll Hall of Fame, his induction ceremony, fittingly many thought, being conducted by Vedder.

## Dead Men

That same year Young worked on his first film soundtrack when the high-profile art-house director Jim Jarmusch asked him to compose the soundtrack to his black-and-white western movie *Dead Man*. Ever the innovator, Neil viewed the film several times at home, then laid down a haunting improvised soundtrack (using a pump organ and detuned piano alongside the more conventional guitars) while watching the film one more time in the studio.

Late in 1995, tragedy struck once again when Neil's longtime collaborator and producer David Briggs died after a yearlong battle with lung cancer. Although the two had not worked together after *Sleeps with Angels* was completed in April 1994, their career-spanning association meant that for Neil Young it was a traumatic loss.

To some degree a reaction to Briggs's death, in the spring of 1996 Neil Young once again went on the road with Crazy Horse. The tour, if it could be so called, was a hit-and-miss affair of mainly unannounced gigs at which the traveling entourage would arrive in a caravan of pickup trucks and trailers like medieval players, setting up camp and performing as the spirit took them. With audiences literally within touching distance of the musicians, they were certainly the most intimate dates Neil had played for many years. As was his habit, he renamed the band for the occasion, dubbing them the Echoes.

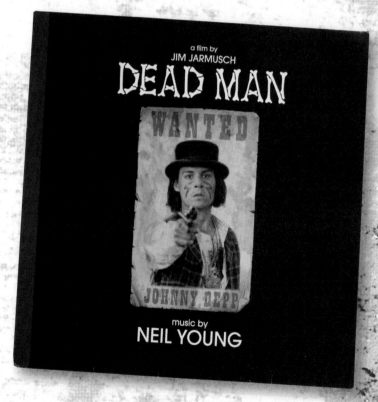

Below: The CD cover design for the sountrack to *Dead Man*, released in 1996 and featuring Johnny Depp reading poetry and Neil's music.

sleeps
with angels
happen
too late too soon
too late too soon
neil young and crazy horse

# Sleeps with Angels

ALBUM

**T**he album was planned by Neil as a deliberate attempt to revisit some of the experiments that he and Crazy Horse had indulged in during the *After the Gold Rush* period in early 1970s. After Kurt Cobain's death, although much of the collection was already recorded, it took on a darker, brooding mood more reminiscent of 1975's *Tonight's the Night*, with the title track a direct response to the Nirvana leader's suicide. One exception to the overriding gloom generated throughout is the punk-influenced "Piece of Crap," while (oddly) two of the songs—"Western Hero" and "Train of Love"—utilize the same music but with different lyrics.

### ★ TRACKS ★

My Heart ★ Prime of Life ★ Driveby ★ Sleeps with Angels ★ Western Hero ★ Change Your Mind ★ Blue Eden [Ralph Molina, Frank Sampedro, Billy Talbot, Neil Young] ★ Safeway Cart ★ Train of Love ★ Trans Am ★ Piece of Crap ★ A Dream That Can Last

All songs written by Neil Young except where indicated.

### ★ RECORDED ★

November 8, 1993–April 25, 1994, The Complex Studios, Los Angeles

### ★ RELEASED ★

August 6, 1994

### ★ PERSONNEL ★

Neil Young (guitar, tack piano, accordion, flute, harmonica, vocals) ★ Frank Sampedro (guitar, grand piano, electric piano, keyboards, bass marimba, vocals) ★ Billy Talbot (bass, vibes, bass marimba, vocals) ★ Ralph Molina (drums, vocals)

### ★ LABEL ★

Reprise

### ★ PRODUCERS ★

David Briggs ★ Neil Young

Previous pages: *Year of the Horse* director Jim Jarmusch poses with Neil in Los Angeles, February 1996.

Right: A promotional poster for *Year of the Horse*.

Below: Neil Young on the cover of *Mojo* magazine, July 1997.

**ANGELIKA FILMBILL**

OCTOBER / NOVEMBER 1997

A FILM BY JIM JARMUSCH

YEAR OF THE HORSE
NEIL YOUNG AND CRAZY HORSE LIVE

OCTOBER FILMS

Nick Kent reviews Radio
plus 50 pages of this month's bes

JULY
1997 · £2.95
USA $6.95

THE OJO LTER

MOJO
*The Music Magazine*

"When a crowd goes nuts, then *that's* playing live..."

Onstage with **Neil Young**

Teenage
Echo & The Bunnymen
Aerosmith vs Kula Shaker
Mark Lamarr meets Sir Cliff!
Supertramp

Free inside!
Classic prints of Marianne Faithfu and James Brown

During the tour, most of which took place within easy driving distance of Young's home, Neil and Crazy Horse took time off at the ranch to lay down tracks for an album, *Broken Arrow*. Released in July 1996, it perfectly captured the loose nature of the tour performances—too perfectly, in many ways. In parts sounding no better than a badly recorded bootleg, the album met with almost universally bad reviews, and sales-wise it failed to get higher than #31 on the U.S. album charts. A year later a concert film of Neil Young and Crazy Horse was released, directed by *Dead Man* director Jim Jarmusch. Titled *Year of the Horse*, it used footage from both the "Echoes" tour and more conventionally organized dates staged later in 1996 in Europe and North America. With a different track list from the film, a live album also called *Year of the Horse* was released in 1997. Regarded as an epitaph to David Briggs, it featured songs that were among the late producer's favorites.

## Looking Forward

In 1998, Neil embarked on another of his frequent collaborations, this time with the rock band Phish. Formed in 1983 at the University of Vermont, Phish is a multigenre outfit that over nearly three decades has explored a variety of styles from jazz to folk to punk, utilizing long improvised jams reminiscent of the Grateful Dead. Young even invited them to back him on a 1999 U.S. tour, but they declined the offer.

The band shared the bill with Neil—he joined them onstage—at benefit concerts for Farm Aid and the Bridge School Benefit, two causes close to Young's heart and which he had been intimately involved with; he would become more so as the years progressed. But although the new millennium would be characterized by Neil Young spending more of his time exploring extramusical activities, it was with his ex-compatriots Crosby, Stills and Nash that he closed the old decade and opened the new, with an album aptly titled *Looking Forward* and the quartet's highest-grossing tour ever.

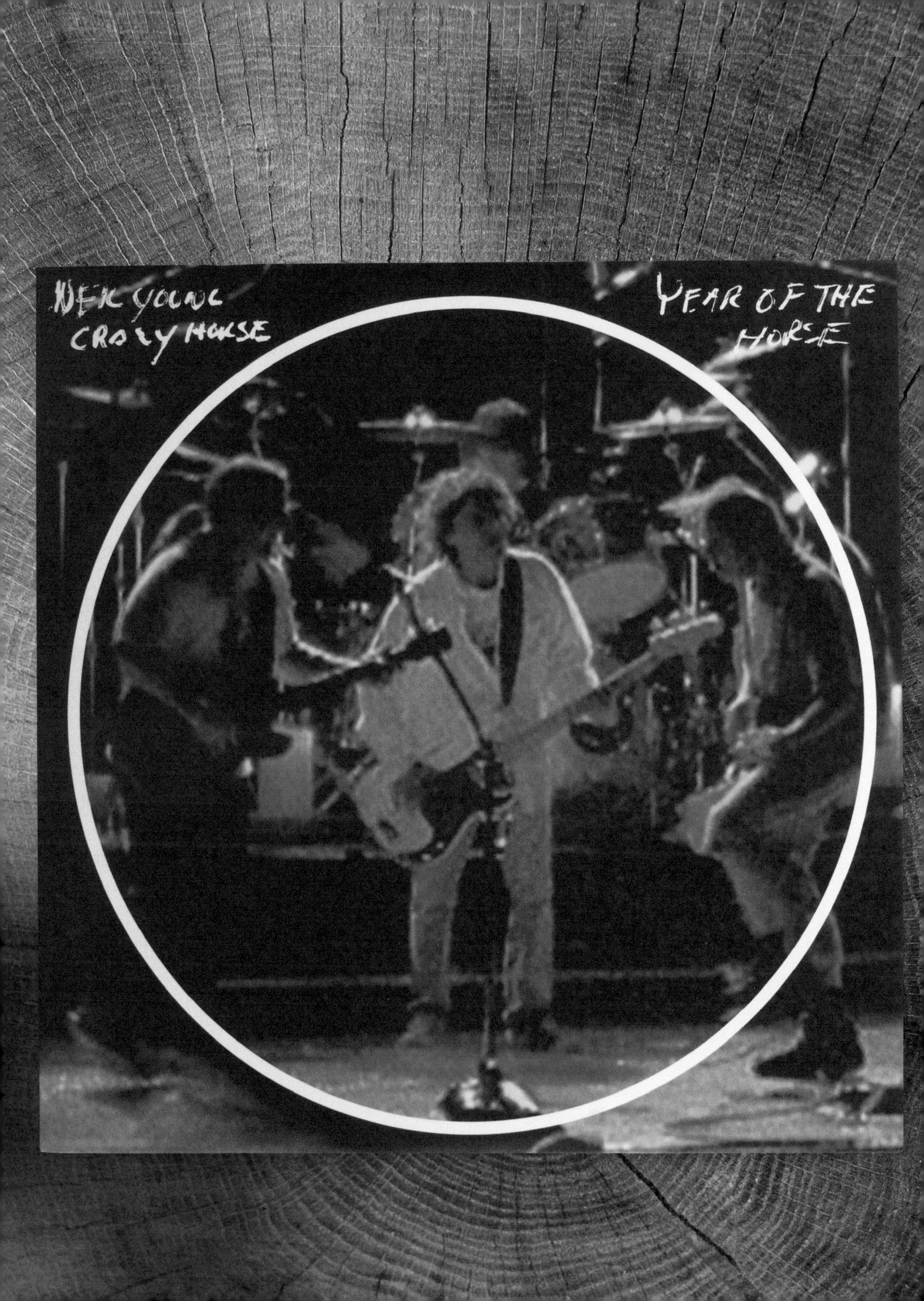
NEIL YOUNG
CRAZY HORSE
YEAR OF THE
HORSE

# Year of the Horse

**R**eleased in 1977 on the back of the Jim Jarmusch–directed concert film of the same name, the live album—with a different track listing from the movie—features recordings from the North American leg of Neil Young and Crazy Horse's 1996 tour. Many might ask how many live recordings of Neil's standbys like "When You Dance, I Can Really Love," "Mr. Soul," or "Pocahontas," do we need? The choice here, however, was largely governed by the notion of the album as an epitaph to David Briggs, including some of the late producer's favorites, alongside songs from more recent albums. The listing here, from the double-disc CD release, includes "Sedan Delivery," which was not included on the vinyl pressings.

### DISC ONE

When You Dance, I Can Really Love ★ Barstool Blues ★
When Your Lonely Heart Breaks ★
Mr. Soul ★ Big Time ★ Pocahontas ★ Human Highway

### DISC TWO

Slip Away ★ Scattered ★ Dangerbird ★ Prisoners ★
Sedan Delivery
All songs written by Neil Young.

### RELEASED

June 17, 1997

### RECORDED

May 9–November 8, 1996, on tour

### PERSONNEL

Neil Young (guitar, piano, harmonica, vocals) ★
Poncho Sampedro (guitar, keyboards, vocals) ★ Billy Talbot
(bass, vocals) ★ Ralph Molina (drums, percussion, vocals)

### LABEL

Reprise

### PRODUCERS

"A Punk David Production—Produced by Horse"

# FARM AID

**N**eil Young has been a driving force in Farm Aid, a uniquely American charity and advocacy group, from its inception in 1985 for nearly three decades. The initial inspiration for Farm Aid came out of the Live Aid concert on July 13, 1985, set up specifically to raise money for drought-stricken regions of Africa. During his set at that event, which was broadcast live worldwide, Bob Dylan declared from the stage, "Wouldn't it be great if we did something for our own farmers right here in America?"—referring to the great many American farmers losing their farms and livelihoods through mortgage debt.

Taking their cue from Dylan's plea, Willie Nelson, Neil Young, and John Mellencamp—recognizing that U.S. farmers were in urgent need of help—organized the first Farm Aid concert. It took them just six weeks to put the show together, which was staged at the University of Illinois' Memorial Stadium in Champaign on September 22, 1985, in front of an audience of eighty thousand. Stars performing included Dylan, Billy Joel, Roy Orbison, Tom Petty, B. B. King, Loretta Lynn, and of course Neil Young. The event raised more than nine million dollars for America's family farmers.

Immediately after that first concert, the newly formed Farm Aid established emergency hotlines for farmers and farming associations. Nelson and Mellencamp then brought family farmers before Congress to testify on the plight of

Neil with Emmylou Harris at the Farm Aid concert at the First Midwest Bank Amphitheatre, Tinley Park, Illinois, on September 18, 2005.

family farmers in the country. A direct consequence of this was the passage of the Agricultural Credit Act of 1987, an attempt to save family farms from foreclosure.

The organization, with a board of directors that includes Nelson, Mellencamp, Young, and Dave Matthews, decided to stage an annual concert of country music, blues, and rock, to raise funds and keep the issue in the public eye.

In 1989 Farm Aid president Willie Nelson took Farm Aid on the road for sixteen of his own show dates, holding press conferences at each site to bring attention to the ongoing farm crisis, local farm issues, and future farm policy. Spotlighting area farmers and their struggles, he invited the media to meet with local farmers and discuss the issues facing them, drawing support for local Farm Aid–funded organizations. Farmers from New York to Oregon met with Willie and the media to assert that the farm crisis was not over, and that the effects were still being felt across rural America.

Farm Aid also established emergency hotlines for farmers who lost their crops and even homes through natural disasters, such as the victims of Hurricane Katrina and the tornadoes that swept rural areas in 2011.

Willie Nelson, John Mellencamp, Neil Young, Dave Matthews, and other performers and farmers before the start of the Farm Aid concert on September 21, 2002 in Burgettstown, Pennsylvania.

The funds raised in this way are used to pay farmers' expenses and provide food as well as legal, financial, and psychological support.

In 2010, Farm Aid celebrated its twenty-fifth anniversary with a concert called Growing Hope for America, held at Miller Park in Milwaukee, Wisconsin, on October 2. A huge crowd of thirty-five thousand enjoyed performances by Willie Nelson, John Mellencamp, Neil Young, and Dave Matthews with Tim Reynolds. Other artists included Jason Mraz, Jamey Johnson, Norah Jones, Jeff Tweedy, Kenny Chesney, Band of Horses, Robert Francis, Amos Lee, Lukas Nelson and Promise of the Real, Randy Rogers Band, the Blackwood Quartet, and the BoDeans. All of the artists donated their time and travel expenses.

With the support of key activists like Neil Young, Farm Aid has become the longest-running benefit concert series in America, raising more than thirty-nine million dollars to help family farmers thrive all over the country.

# Old Master, New Tricks

Below: Neil on tour in 2008.

Opposite: The tour program
from the 2000 CSNY shows.

THE most significant changes that came about in popular music during the first decade of the twenty-first century were not in the music itself but in its dissemination and consumption. During Neil Young's own lifetime the record industry had undergone some major changes: the move from a singles-only market to the long-player album, the perceived threat of people copying music on cassette tapes, the introduction of digital recording and the CD disc. Still, the biggest technical revolution was to come with the advent of the Internet and the subsequent downloading of music. Typically, Neil took this in stride, as he had various artistic challenges throughout his career. When he rush-released *Living with War* in 2006—an album in the antiwar protest song tradition of the early 1960s—he first made it available as an online download, a week before any hard copies hit the record stores. And in 2009, his first releases in the career-spanning Archives project would be his earliest singles and albums, reissued as remastered high-definition discs and digital downloads—a classic case of the old master embracing the new technology.

## Millennial Reunion

During the early months of 1999, Neil Young's involvement in a new project with Crosby, Stills and Nash was a gradual process. Initially Stephen Stills had approached his old sparring partner with a view to playing on one new song he had written, but over the following months Neil would drop in on a number of sessions; neither he nor any of the other three acknowledged publicly that there would indeed be a new CSNY album in the offing.

Various potential compilations of old and new tracks were juggled for a possible release, with industry onlookers naturally skeptical given the history of abandoned CSNY projects in the past; rumors of a tour were greeted with even more suspicion. It had been almost a quarter century since they had been on the road together on a full-fledged tour, but nevertheless word got around that there might be a summer trek with a half-million-dollar guarantee for each show. Nothing came of it, however, and Neil embarked on a spring tour of the United States that included performances of songs that

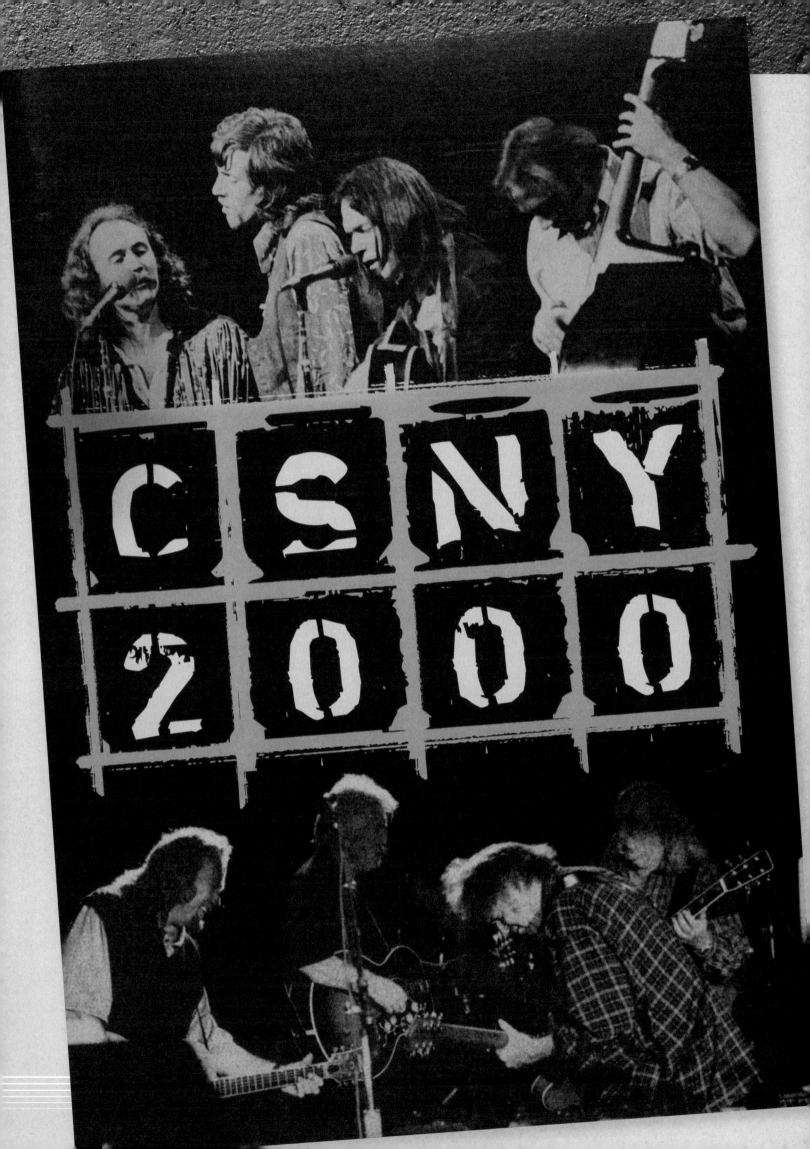

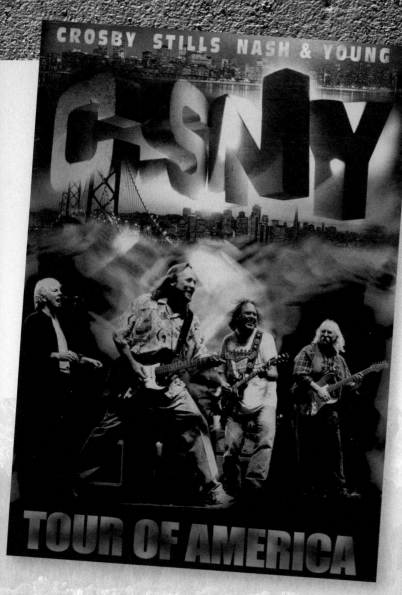

A poster for the 2000 CSNY
Tour of America.

would appear on the next, still-unannounced CSNY album.

The tour prompted alternative speculation about a new Neil Young solo album, but everyone was taken by surprise when a CSNY release—*Looking Forward*—was set for October 1999. With studio material from November 1996 to July 1999, the album wasn't a spectacular success—despite being the quartet's first studio release since *American Dream* in 1988—but the live tour that followed was another matter altogether. Kicking off as the world celebrated the new millennium, the tour of the United States and Canada earned the foursome over $41 million. It was the eighth-largest-grossing tour of 2000.

## Silver, Gold, and Road Rock

It was something of an irony that a reunion with CSN should be Neil Young's first activity of the new century. Despite its huge success, however, the short-lived reunion was put into its rightful perspective when two more Neil Young albums were released under his own name during 2000. In fact the get-together with Crosby, Stills and Nash confirmed once again what had been the essential precept of their alliance in the first place—a collaboration of four independent artists, still free to pursue their own careers, rather than a formal band.

Featuring material from the late 1990s up to its April 2000 release, *Silver & Gold* marked a return to the country and folk textures of albums like *Harvest*, but now the lyrics reflected a more settled, complete attitude toward life. There's a touch of nostalgia in the songs, not least in "Buffalo Springfield Again," in which Young even hints at a reunion with his original 1960s hitmakers. A live video, *Neil Young: Silver & Gold*, featured performances from his 1999 tour.

Selling moderately well, and hitting #5 in Neil's native Canada, the studio album was followed by the live album *Road Rock Vol. 1: Friends & Relatives*. Released in December 2000, all the tracks were culled from a North American tour the previous fall, with a lineup that included Ben Keith, bass player "Duck" Dunn, Spooner Oldham on keyboards, and ace session drummer Jim Keltner, plus Young's wife Pegi and sister Astrid on backing vocals, and guest vocalist Chrissie Hynde on a cover version of Bob Dylan's "All Along the Watchtower." There was also a companion DVD and videotape release to this album, titled *Red Rocks Live: Neil Young Friends & Relatives*.

# Silver & Gold

ALBUM

## ★ TRACKS ★

Good to See You ★ Silver & Gold ★ Daddy Went Walkin' ★ Buffalo Springfield Again*

The Great Divide* ★ Horseshoe Man ★ Red Sun** ★ Distant Camera ★ Razor Love ★ Without Rings

All songs written by Neil Young

## ★ RECORDED ★

August 26, 1997–November 2, 1998 ★ *May 28, 1999

## ★ RELEASED ★

April 25, 2000

## ★ LABEL ★

Reprise

## ★ PRODUCERS ★

Neil Young ★ Ben Keith

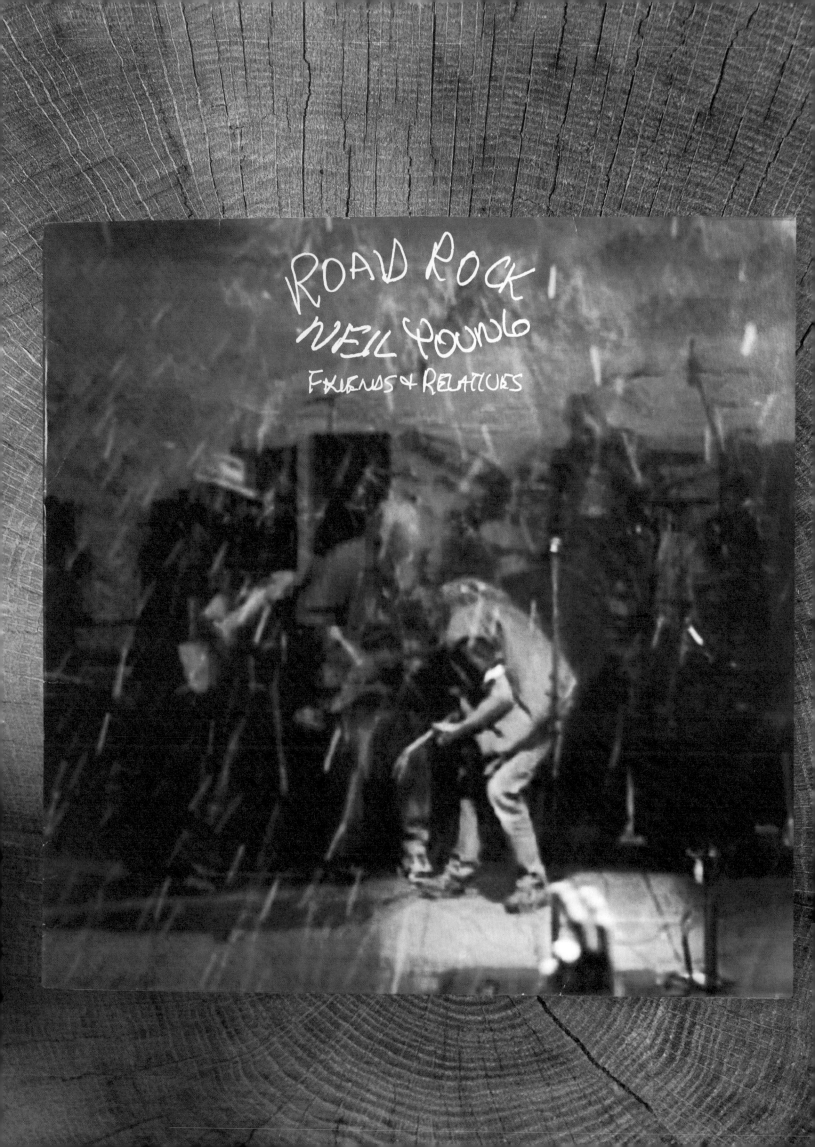

# Road Rock Vol I: Friends and Relatives

ALBUM

This album includes live tracks from Neil (and "Friends & Relatives") on his fall 2000 North American "Music in Head" tour. With instrumental maestros at the helm, including the formidable rhythm section of "Duck" Dunn on bass and Jim Keltner on drums, this is country-oriented rock of the highest caliber. The sound quality on much of the recording is, unfortunately, below par, but what comes through unmistakably on tracks like the eighteen-minute marathon "Cowgirl in the Sand," and the down-home waltz time of "Words" is the sheer glow of satisfaction of seasoned rockers simply having a good time.

## TRACKS

Cowgirl in the Sand ** ★ Walk On ****
Fool for Your Love *** ★ Peace of Mind **** ★ Words ****
Motorcycle Mama ** ★ Tonight's the Night **
All Along the Watchtower [Bob Dylan]
All songs written by Neil Young except where indicated.

## RELEASED

December 5, 2000

## RECORDED

August 29–October 1, 2000: live at Blossom Music Center Cuyhoga
Falls, OH* ★ Coors Amphitheatre San Diego** ★
Santa Barbara Bowl *** ★ GM Place, Vancouver****

## PERSONNEL

Neil Young (guitars, piano, vocal) ★ Ben Keith (guitar, pedal steel guitar,
lap slide guitar, vocal) ★ Spooner Oldham (piano, electric
piano, organ) ★ Donald "Duck" Dunn (bass)
★ Jim Keltner (drums, percussion) ★ Pegi Young (vocal)
★ Astrid Young (vocal) ★ *Chrissie Hynde (guitar, vocals)

## LABEL

Reprise

## PRODUCERS

Neil Young ★ Ben Keith

## "Let's Roll"

Like the rest of America, and indeed the world, Neil Young was traumatized by the September 11, 2001, terrorist attacks. His musical response was the song "Let's Roll," released in November 2001. The lyrics were inspired by the final recorded words of Todd Beamer, a passenger on Flight 93, one of the four highjacked aircraft. On this flight, the passengers attempted to regain control of the plane, forcing it to crash in a field in Pennsylvania rather than its intended target of Washington, D.C. Beamer ended his final cell phone call with "Let's roll" as passengers readied themselves to rush the cockpit. Everyone on the airliner was killed in the crash.

Immediately after the 9/11 attacks, Neil took part in the *America: A Tribute to Heroes* television benefit concert for the families of the victims, held on September 21 and later released on DVD in December 2001. He performed John Lennon's "Imagine," and also accompanied Pearl Jam's Eddie Vedder on "Long

Road," a song written with Young during the *Mirror Ball* sessions.

Backed by Booker T. and the MGs and others, the track was also included on Neil's next album, *Are You Passionate?*, released in April 2002. Except for "Let's Roll" and the rocker "Goin' Home" (recorded with Crazy Horse), the entire album was an unprecedented foray into soul music for Neil Young, comprising mostly laid-back love songs dedicated to his wife, Pegi.

## Greendale

Current events in the news grabbed Neil Young's attention once again in 2002, with the murder of a police officer in a small California town. The event, and the effect it had on the town's inhabitants, served as inspiration for an ambitious concept album, movie, and graphic novel project. Loosely based on the real place, Greendale was a fictional seaside town in which Neil set his ten-song "rock opera" recorded with Crazy Horse.

Based on the saga of the Green family, the exploration of life in small-town America addressed issues including corruption, post-9/11 America, and the environment. Alongside the CD release, Neil directed an accompanying film under his pseudonym of Bernard Shakey, in which actors lip-synched to the songs from the album. The album and film attracted a divergence of critical responses, from comparisons to literary classics like Thornton Wilder's *Our Town*, to accusations of amateurism, to being voted one of the best albums of 2003 by the music writers in *Rolling Stone*. Young took *Greendale* on the road through 2003 and 2004, first with a solo acoustic show across European cities, then with a full-cast stage show in the United States, Canada, Japan, and Australia. It was during the 2004 stage of the trek that he began using biodiesel fuel for his tour trucks and buses, a solid signal of his increasing commitment to environmental issues. "Our Greendale Tour is now ozone friendly," Neil said. "I plan to continue to use this

government-approved-and-regulated fuel exclusively from now on to prove that it is possible to deliver the goods anywhere in North America without using foreign oil, while being environmentally responsible." In June 2010, the graphic novel of *Greendale* appeared, with words by Joshua Dysart and artwork by Cliff Chiang.

## Prairie Wind

In March 2005, Neil Young went into Master-Link in Nashville to record what would be his twenty-eighth studio album. Like *Silver & Gold* at the beginning of the decade, *Prairie Wind* was once again a return to the acoustic-based sound of his big commercial successes, *Harvest* and *Harvest Moon*. Initially the album was a response to the recent death of his father, Scott Young, but during the recording Neil was forced to confront the issue of his own mortality.

While working on the album he was diagnosed with a potentially fatal brain aneurism that required minimally invasive neuroradiological surgery. The operation was conducted in New York on March 29. Two days later Young passed out in the street due to bleeding in the artery that surgeons had used to access his brain. Neil had to cancel various dates, but he was back onstage on July 2, 2005, appearing at the Live 8 concert in Barrie, Ontario, where he debuted the album's closing track, "When God Made Me," a direct reflection on his brush with death.

A live performance premiering the entire album took place at the Ryman Auditorium in Nashville on August 18 and 19. The two concerts were the subject of the 2006 film *Neil Young: Heart of Gold*, made by *Silence of the Lambs* director Jonathan Demme, for whom Neil had provided the soundtrack to *Philadelphia* in 1993.

**Opposite:** Neil at a press conference discussing his film *Greendale* at the Twenty-eighth Toronto International Film Festival in 2003.

**Below:** Fans printed as promotional items for the *Prairie Wind* album.

**Following pages:** Neil (left) with Willie Nelson at the 2003 Farm Aid concert in Columbus, Ohio.

# Prairie Wind

ALBUM

Considered by many on its release to be a completion of his acoustic *Harvest/Harvest Moon* trilogy, *Prairie Wind* features Neil backed once again by longtime Nashville collaborators such as keyboards man Spooner Oldham, guitarist Ben Keith, and the always wonderful vocals of Emmylou Harris. The lush pedal steel sound supports a basically acoustic set, in which Neil is coming to terms with mortality—in "Falling off the Face of the Earth," and "When God Made Me"—while reflecting on his own childhood roots in the title track. Some of the arrangements may seem a little too sentimental-sounding for many tastes, but the essence of the simple acoustic approach remains pure Neil Young.

## TRACKS

The Painter ★ No Wonder ★ Falling off the Face of the Earth
Far from Home ★ It's a Dream ★ Prairie Wind ★
Here for You ★ This Old Guitar ★ He Was
the King ★ When God Made Me
All songs written by Neil Young.

## RECORDED

March 2005, Master-Link, Nashville

## RELEASED

September 27, 2005

## PERSONNEL

Neil Young (acoustic and electric guitar, harmonica, piano, vocals)
Ben Keith (Dobro, pedal steel, slide guitar) ★ Spooner Oldham
(piano, Hammond B-3 organ, Wurlitzer electric piano) ★ Rick Rosa
(bass guitar) ★ Karl Himmel (drums, percussion) ★ Chad Cromwell
(drums, percussion) ★ Grant Boatwright (acoustic guitar, vocals),
Clinton Gregory (fiddle) ★ Wayne Jackson (horns) ★ Thomas
McGinley (horns) ★ Emmylou Harris (vocals) ★ Pegi Young
(vocals) Diana Dewitt (vocals) ★ Anthony Crawford (vocals) ★ Gary
Pigg (vocals) ★ Curtis Wright (vocals) ★ Strings ("Here for You,"
"It's a Dream") arranged by Chuck Cochran ★ Fisk University Jubilee
Choir ("No Wonder," "When God Made Me") directed by Paul Kwami

## LABEL

Reprise

## PRODUCERS

Ben Keith ★ Neil Young

## Living with War

Neil Young featured on the front cover and inside *Rolling Stone* magazine, 2006.

Before *Living with War* was released in May 2006, Neil had not come out with an overtly political album since 1989's *Freedom*, in which he launched an attack on President Reagan's policies. A direct criticism of George W. Bush and his conduct of the war in Iraq, the lyrics of *Living with War* are in the tradition of early 1960s folk-protest singers like Tom Paxton, Phil Ochs, and Bob Dylan.

Accompanied by bass player Rick Rosas, drummer Chad Cromwell, and trumpeter Tommy Bray (who also featured heavily on *Freedom*)—plus a hundred-voice choir—Young recorded the entire album over the course of nine days in March and April. It was premiered on Los Angeles radio on April 28, released onto the Internet on May 2, and rush-released into retail outlets just a week later. Neil made it plain from the start that he wanted the album to be listened to as a whole, in the order of release; consequently, the Internet streaming was of was the entire album, not individually selectable tracks. He also worked once again with Crosby, Stills, and Nash on a "Freedom of Speech" tour in support of the album.

Striking a chord with the huge body of opinion worldwide that was disenchanted by the war and Bush's policies generally, the album made #15 on the U.S. charts, #7 in Canada, and #14 in the United Kingdom, and was nominated for three Grammy Awards in the categories of Best Rock Album, Best Rock Song, and Best Rock Solo Performance—both latter awards for the song "Lookin' for a Leader."

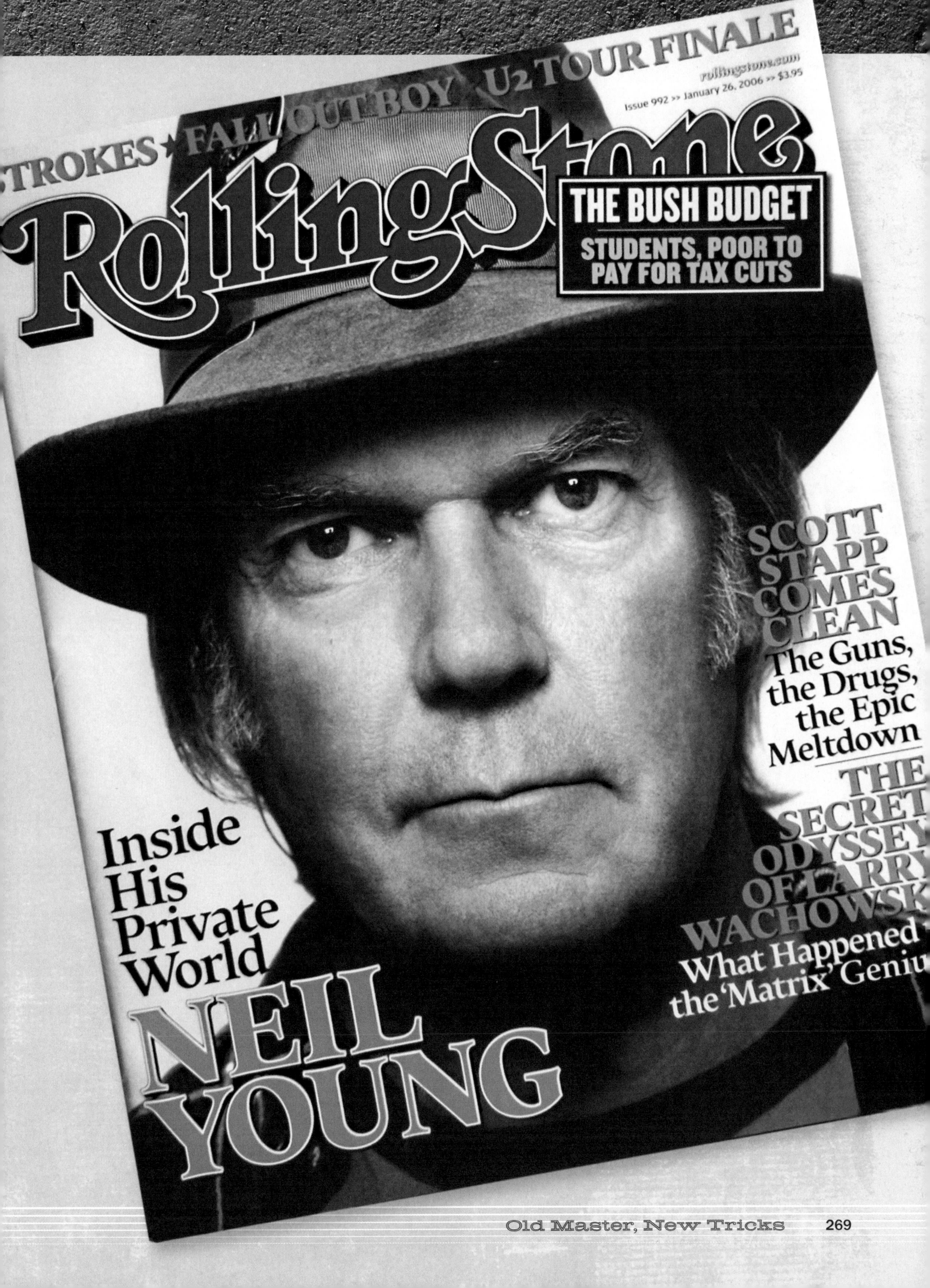

STROKES ★ FALL OUT BOY   U2 TOUR FINALE

rollingstone.com
Issue 992 >> January 26, 2006 >> $3.95

# Rolling Stone

**THE BUSH BUDGET**
STUDENTS, POOR TO
PAY FOR TAX CUTS

SCOTT
STAPP
COMES
CLEAN

The Guns,
the Drugs,
the Epic
Meltdown

THE
SECRET
ODYSSEY
OF LARRY
WACHOWSK

What Happened
the 'Matrix' Geniu

Inside
His
Private
World

## NEIL YOUNG

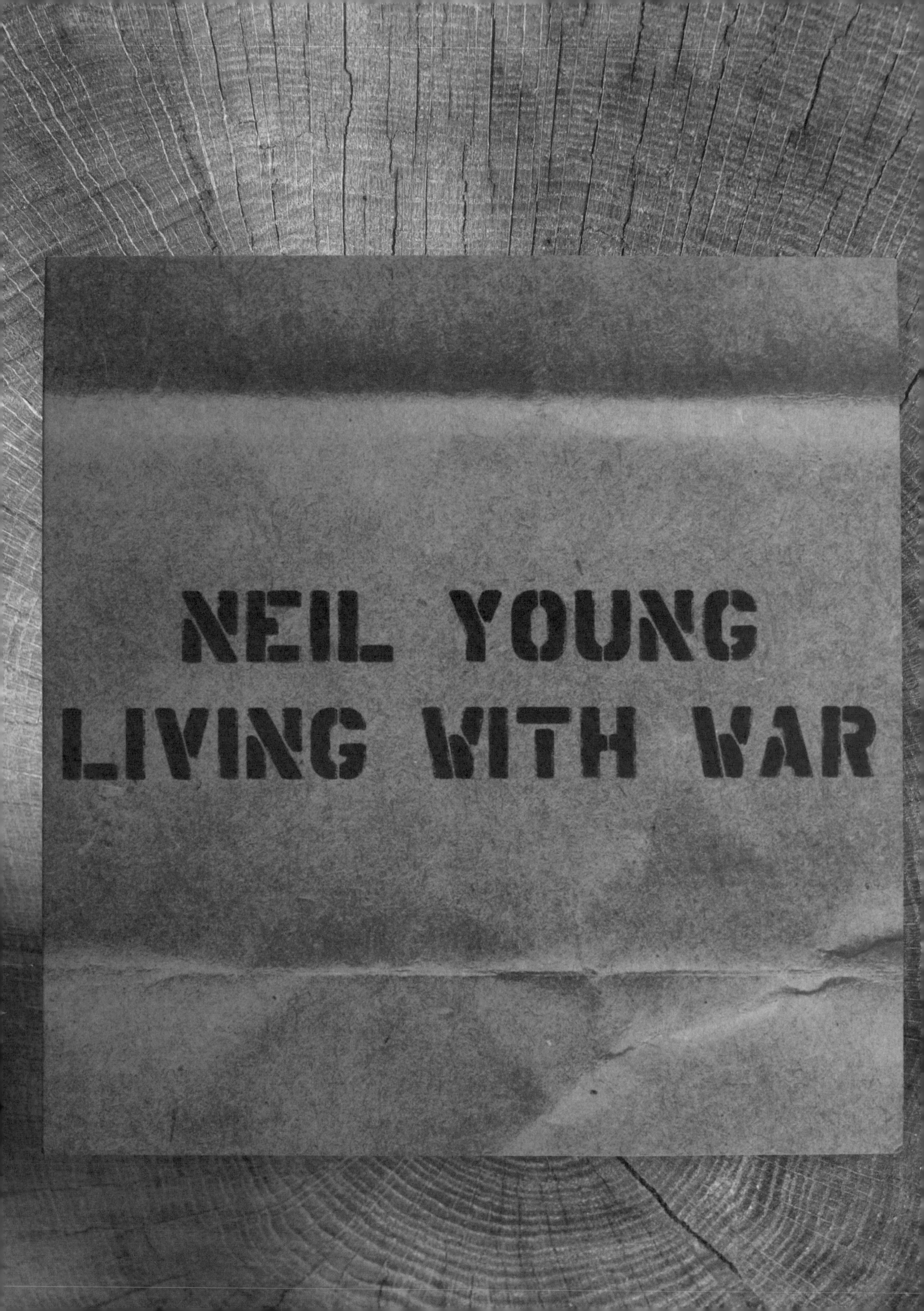
NEIL YOUNG
LIVING WITH WAR

## Eco Dreams

Neil Young's continuing concern about environmental issues and his activism in that direction was increasingly evident into the second half of the 2000s, although his next album release—2007's *Chrome Dreams II*—was of a more personally spiritual nature. The record was a sequel to *Chrome Dreams*, the unreleased 1977 album that was eventually shelved in favor of *American Stars 'n Bars*. Produced by Neil and Niko Bolas, the new album featured Crazy Horse drummer Ralph Molina, bassist Rick Rosas, and Ben Keith on pedal steel and Dobro. Debuting in the *Billboard* Top 200 chart at #11, it sold over fifty thousand copies in its first week. Critical opinion was highly favorable, citing it as a "spiritual" statement on Young's part, but, as ever, Neil had his own view: "Some early listeners have said that this album is positive and spiritual. I like to think it focuses on the human condition."

Indulging a lifelong passion for vintage cars with an eco-concious eye on technical developments, in 2008 Neil revealed the latest project he had been working on—the production of a hybrid engine, combining a conventional combustion engine with an electric system. Because it used a 1959 model Lincoln automobile, he dubbed the experimental vehicle Lincvolt; there was even an album loosely based on the project, *Fork in the Road*, released in April 2009. A major setback occurred in November 2010, however, when a fire swept

Neil proudly unveils his eco-friendly Lincvolt automobile, 2008.

Opposite: Performing at the
ACV hall in Vienna, Austria,
February 22, 2008.

the California warehouse where the car was garaged. The fire destroyed the Lincvolt as well as nearly a million dollars' worth of Neil's extensive collection of rock 'n' roll memorabilia.

Afterward he explained that the vehicle's plug-in charging setup was probably at fault, pledging that he and his team would continue developing the car. "The wall-charging system was not completely tested and had never been left unattended," he said after the incident. "A mistake was made. It was not the fault of the car."

Alongside the hybrid engine project, 2009 saw Neil Young still active on the musical front. An instrumental album called *Potato Hole* by organist Booker T. Jones (of Booker T. and the MGs) featured Young on guitar on nine of the ten tracks, with the Drive-By Truckers as Booker T.'s backup group for the occasion. Neil also toured internationally, with prestige gigs including the UK's major rock gathering the Glastonbury Festival, the Hard Rock Calling event in London (where he was joined onstage by Paul McCartney to sing the Beatles classic "A Day in the Life"), the Isle of Wight Festival in the south of England, the Primavera Sound Festival in Barcelona, Spain, and appearances at the Big Day Out festivals in Australia and New Zealand.

Along with his continuous work on behalf of both Farm Aid and the Bridge School, Neil Young has continued to give his time freely to causes and charities in need of urgent support—in 2010, for instance, when he appeared on the *Hope for Haiti Now: A Global Benefit for Earthquake Relief* fund-raising telethon in aid of the victims of the earthquake in Haiti.

PIANO - VOCAL - GUITAR

NEIL YOUNG

FORK IN THE ROAD

## Treasures Old and New

As has been the case since his teenage years, a seemingly never-ceasing musical output lies at the core of Neil Young's life as he moves through his mid-to-late sixties. In May 2010, it was announced that he was working on a new album with the eminent Canadian producer Daniel Lanois; the result, *Le Noise*, was a stark, pared-down affair featuring Neil with a basically self-accompanying electronic backing. It went on to hit #2 on the Canadian charts and #14 in the *Billboard* U.S. Top 200, with the track "Angry World" winning the 2011 Grammy Award for Best Rock Song. At the same time, Neil had been delving back into his own past with the development of his monumental Archives project, which had first seen the light of day with the release in 2006 of *Live at the Fillmore East 1970*.

The sheer multitude of recordings potentially set for release, many for the first time, was evidenced by the fact that the Archives releases would be subdivided into the "Performance Series," "Special Edition Series," and so on.

# Le Noise

**C**ertainly one of Neil Young's strangest offerings, the album was recorded with just the singer and his guitar, but embellished with all the electronic trickery that producer Daniel Lanois could pull out for the occasion. In many ways, the paired-down quality gives it a natural, intimate, feel—the lyrics somehow isolated against the stark, uncompromising background of fuzz and distortion—as Neil relentlessly explores a landscape of ideas; in just one song, "Peaceful Valley Boulevard," he manages to reference the sweep of American history, from the nineteenth-century "Indian wars" to his vision of electric automobiles. Numbers like "Angry World" and "Rumblin'" hint at nameless uncertainties and fears—overall, this decidedly noir collection may be difficult to listen to, but in most cases worth the effort.

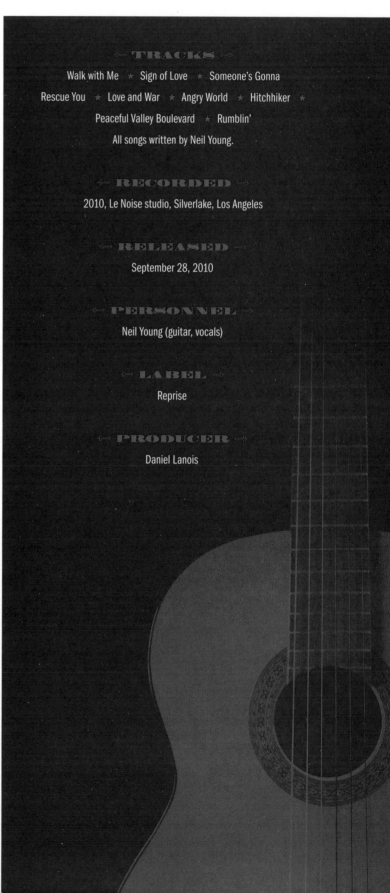

## TRACKS

Walk with Me ★ Sign of Love ★ Someone's Gonna Rescue You ★ Love and War ★ Angry World ★ Hitchhiker ★ Peaceful Valley Boulevard ★ Rumblin'

All songs written by Neil Young.

## RECORDED

2010, Le Noise studio, Silverlake, Los Angeles

## RELEASED

September 28, 2010

## PERSONNEL

Neil Young (guitar, vocals)

## LABEL

Reprise

## PRODUCER

Daniel Lanois

Significantly, in June 2011, as part of the Archives Performance Series, Neil released *A Treasure*, a compilation of live recordings made during his 1984 and 1985 tours with the International Harvesters. Unable to be released at the time, due to Young's ongoing legal problems with Geffen Records, the tracks capture Neil Young with a hand-picked band of country music veterans, epitomizing his close emotional ties to the down-home roots of his music.

Early in 2012, Neil reunited with Crazy Horse for a gig honoring Paul McCartney, promising more dates to come, and at the time of writing announced two new studio projects with the band, including an album of "re-imagined children's songs." Considering the Harvesters release and the Crazy Horse reunion, Neil Young is now clearly at ease with his own past. The chameleon-like changes of style that have marked his artistic endeavors, often at the time presented as a passionate rejection of what had gone before, can now be seen as equally valid parts of a whole.

It's a perspective which Young clearly embraces as the basis of the entire Archives concept, representing a unique life in music spanning six decades—and one that has touched generations of fans and fellow musicians in the process.

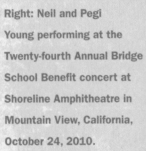

**Right: Neil and Pegi Young performing at the Twenty-fourth Annual Bridge School Benefit concert at Shoreline Amphitheatre in Mountain View, California, October 24, 2010.**

# A Treasure

ALBUM

★ TRACKS ★

Amber Jean ★ Are You Ready for the Country? ★ It Might Have Been ★ Bound for Glory ★ Let Your Fingers Do the Walking ★ Flying on the Ground Is Wrong ★ Motor City ★ Soul of a Woman ★ Get Back to the Country ★ Southern Pacific ★ Nothing Is Perfect ★ Grey Riders

All songs written by Neil Young.

★ RELEASED ★

June 14, 2011

★ RECORDED ★

Live 1984–1985

★ LABEL ★

Reprise

★ PRODUCERS ★

Neil Young ★ Ben Keith

# THE BRIDGE SCHOOL

Of all the various causes supported by Neil Young, none is nearer to his heart than the Bridge School, an educational organization for children with severe verbal and physical disabilities that he and his wife, Pegi, helped found in 1986.

With his two sons Zeke and Ben both diagnosed with cerebral palsy, and his daughter Amber Jean suffering, like Neil himself, from epilepsy, he and Pegi were very aware of the lack of facilities for disabled children. In 1985, finding no school that met the needs of their children, the Youngs and Jim Forderer (another parent of a child with difficulties), in conjunction with Dr. Marilyn Buzolich, a speech and language pathologist, decided to do something about it. They proposed a school in which each child

was given individual attention—a school whose goal was to provide an environment where children with communication needs could develop the abilities and social skills required in later life.

Initially their plans were in danger of collapsing due to a lack of funding, but in 1986 Neil took the initiative by organizing the first of the now-annual benefit concerts for the project. Staged at the Shoreline Amphitheater in Mountain View, California, on October 13, 1986, that original concert featured an all-star lineup including Crosby, Stills, Nash & Young, Nils Lofgren, Bruce Springsteen, the Eagles' Don Henley, Tom Petty, and Robin Williams.

The immediate result was that the Bridge School founders were able to pull together a team of dedicated professionals, working together to teach children with extreme physical and speech problems how to communicate effectively. At its inception, the school was located in an elementary school in Hillsborough, in the San Francisco Bay Area of northern California, and the intention of the courses was for the children to return to their home school districts as soon as it was considered appropriate.

In 1991, the school celebrated its first graduate moving back into the educational mainstream when Thanh Diep entered a sixth-grade class at Horace Mann Middle School in San Francisco. Part of the success of the move, and others that followed, rested on the establishment of a Transition Program that provided support and advice for parents of Bridge School children returning to the general educational system.

After eight years of progress and development, it was decided that the Bridge School should have a permanent home of its own, with a building constructed on the campus of the North Elementary School in Hillsborough. The partnership of the special facility and regular school has been seen as highly

BILL GRAHAM PRESENTS

THE 15th ANNUAL
BRIDGE SCHOOL BENEFIT

NEIL YOUNG
& CRAZY HORSE
DAVE MATTHEWS
PEARL JAM
R.E.M.
TRACY CHAPMAN
BEN HARPER
BILLY IDOL
JILL SOBULE

2001

TWO VERY SPECIAL ACOUSTIC CONCERTS
TO BENEFIT THE BRIDGE SCHOOL
A PROGRAM FOR THE COMMUNICATIVE AND
EDUCATIONAL DEVELOPMENT OF CHILDREN
WITH SEVERE SPEECH AND PHYSICAL IMPAIRMENTS

SATURDAY
OCTOBER 20

SUNDAY
OCTOBER 21

SHORELINE AMPHITHEATRE

Artwork By: Marla Price ©2001 The Bridge School

A poster for the 2001 Bridge School Benefit.

productive for all concerned, and now the Bridge School is cited as a pioneer by other "special needs" schools around the world—as Neil Young explained when he accepted the Allan Waters Humanitarian Award in 2011: "We have a teachers-in-residence program, where teachers come from all around the world and every year we have a visiting teacher from a different part of the world. Then they go back to their countries and we support them."

Neil's most conspicuous support for the school, of course, is the benefit concerts that have been held every year (apart from 1987) since 1986, at the same Shoreline Amphitheater venue. Over the years, the list of performers has come to read like a who's who of rock 'n' roll, with legendary names including Bob Dylan, John Lee Hooker, Pearl Jam, Patti Smith, Tony

Graham Nash, Stephen Stills, Neil Young, and David Crosby at the first Bridge School benefit in 1986.

Bennett, and Elton John all lending their services at one time or another.

In 2011, a compilation of twenty-five recordings, marking twenty-five years of the concerts, was released to critical acclaim. The two-CD set featured Sheryl Crow, Thom Yorke, Norah Jones, Willie Nelson, Jack Johnson, Dave Matthews, Sonic Youth, and others, while a three-DVD set included performances by Bruce Springsteen, Patti Smith, Pearl Jam, David Bowie, Bob Dylan, Paul McCartney, the Who, Tom Petty, Simon and Garfunkel, and—inevitably—Neil Young and Crazy Horse.

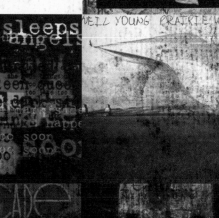
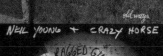

# ✦ Discography ✦

(Title / U.S. Catalog No. / Release Date)

## Albums

### BUFFALO SPRINGFIELD

*Buffalo Springfield* / Atco 33-200 / January 1967

*Buffalo Springfield* / Atco 33-200 / February 1967
(reissue with "For What It's Worth" replacing "Baby Don't Scold Me")

*Buffalo Springfield Again* / Atco 33-2256 / November 1967

*Last Time Around* / Atco SD 33-256 / August 1968

*Retrospective: The Best of Buffalo Springfield* / Atco SD 33-283 /
February 1969

*Buffalo Springfield* / Atco SD 2-806 / November 1973

### CROSBY, STILLS, NASH & YOUNG

*Déjà Vu* / Atlantic SD 7200 / March 1970

*4 Way Street* / Atlantic SD 2-902 / April 1971
(re-released in 1992 on CD with additional tracks)

*So Far* / Atlantic SA 18100 / July 1974

*American Dream* / Atlantic 81888 / November 1988

*Looking Forward* / Reprise 47439 / October 1999

### STILLS/YOUNG BAND

*Long May You Run* / Reprise MS 2253 / September 1976

### NEIL YOUNG

*Neil Young* / Reprise 6317 / January 1969

*Everybody Knows This Is Nowhere* / RS 6349 / May 1969

*After the Gold Rush* / Reprise RS 6383 / August 1970

*Harvest* / Reprise MS 2032 / February 1972

*Journey through the Past* / Reprise 2XS 6480 / November 1972

*On the Beach* / Reprise R 2180 / July 1974

*Tonight's the Night* / Reprise MS 2221 / June 1975

*Zuma* / Reprise MS 2242 / November 1975

*American Stars 'n Bars* / Reprise MSK 2261 / June 1977

*Comes a Time* / Reprise 2266 / October 1978

*Hawks & Doves* / Reprise 2297 / November 1980

*Re-ac-tor* / Reprise 2304 / November 1981

*Trans* / Geffen 2018 / January 1983

*Everybody's Rockin'* / Geffen 4013 / August 1983

*Old Ways* / Geffen 24068 / August 1985

*Landing on Water* / Geffen 24109 / July 1986

*Life* / Geffen 24154 / June 1987

*This Note's for You* / Reprise 25719 / April 1988

*Freedom* / Reprise 25899 / October 1989

*Ragged Glory* / Reprise 26315 / September 1990

*Harvest Moon* / Reprise 45057 / November 1992

*Sleeps with Angels* / Reprise 45749 / August 1994

*Mirror Ball* / Reprise 45934 / June 1995

*Broken Arrow* / Reprise 46291 / June 1996

*Silver & Gold* / Reprise 47742 / April 2000

*Are You Passionate?* / Reprise 48111 / April 2002

*Greendale* / Reprise 48533 / August 2003

*Prairie Wind* / Reprise 49494 / September 2005

*Living with War* / Reprise 44335 / May 2006

*Living with War: "In the Beginning"* / Reprise 43265 / December 2006

*Chrome Dreams II* / Reprise 311932 / October 2007

*Fork in the Road* / Reprise 518041 / April 2009

*Le Noise* / Reprise 525956 / September 2010

## Live Albums

### NEIL YOUNG

*Time Fades Away* / Reprise MS 2151 / September 1973

*Rust Never Sleeps* / Reprise 2295 / July 1979

*Live Rust* / Reprise 2-2296 / November 1979

*Weld* / Reprise 26671 / October 1991

*Arc/Weld* / Reprise 26746 (US) / October 1991

*Arc* / Reprise 9 26769-2 / October 1991

*Unplugged* / Reprise 45310 / June 1993

*Year of the Horse* / Reprise 46652 / June 1997

*Road Rock Vol. I* / Reprise 48036 / December 2000

## Compilation Albums and Box Sets

### BUFFALO SPRINGFIELD

*Retrospective: The Best of Buffalo Springfield* /
Atco SD 33-283 / February 1969

### NEIL YOUNG

*Decade* / Reprise 3RS 224 / November 1977

*Lucky Thirteen* / Geffen 24452 / January 1993

*The Neil Young Heritage* / Reprise W64045 /
September 1982

*Greatest Hits* / Reprise 48924 / November 2004

*The Archives Vol. I, 1963–1972* / Warner/Reprise / June 2009

## CROSBY, STILLS, NASH & YOUNG

CSN [box set] / Atlantic 7567-82319-2 / December 1991

### ARCHIVES SERIES

Live at the Fillmore East 1970 / Reprise 444992 / November 2006

Live at Massey Hall 1971 / Reprise 43328 / March 2007

Sugar Mountain—Live at Canterbury House 1968 / Reprise 516758 / December 2008

Dreamin' Man Live '92 / Reprise 511277 / December 2009

A Treasure / Reprise 527650 / June 2011

# Singles

### SQUIRES

The Sultan/Aurora / V Records 109 / September 1963

### BUFFALO SPRINGFIELD

Nowadays Clancy Can't Even Sing / Go and Say Goodbye / Atco 6248 / August 1966

Burned/Everybody's Wrong / Atco 6452 / December 1966 (withdrawn)

For What It's Worth / Atco 6459 / January 1967

Do I Have to Come Right Out and Say It/Bluebird/Mr. Soul / Atco 6499 / June 1967

Rock & Roll Woman/A Child's Claim to Fame / Atco 6519 / September 1967

Undo Mundo/Merry Go Round / Atco 6572 / March 1968

Kind Woman/Special Care / Atco 6615 / September 1968

On the Way Home/Four Days Gone / Atco 6618 / September 1968

Bluebird/Mr. Soul / Atlantic OS 13074 / May 1971

### CROSBY, STILLS, NASH & YOUNG

Woodstock/Helpless / Atlantic 2723 / March 1970

Teach Your Children/Country Girl / Atlantic 2735 / May 1970

Ohio/Find the Cost of Freedom / Atlantic 2740 / June 1970

Our House/Déjà Vu / Atlantic 2760 / September 1970

Got It Made/This Old House / Atlantic 88966 / January 1989

### NEIL YOUNG AND GRAHAM NASH

War Song/The Needle and the Damage Done / Reprise 1099 / June 1972

### STILLS/YOUNG BAND

Long May You Run/12/8 Blues / Reprise 1365 / July 1976

Midnight on the Bay/Black Coral / Reprise 1378 / October 1976

### NEIL YOUNG

The Loner/Sugar Mountain / Reprise 0785 / December 1968

Everybody Knows This Is Nowhere / The Emperor of Wyoming / Reprise 0819 / March 1969

Down by the River/The Losing End / Reprise 0836 / June 1969

Oh Lonesome Me/Sugar Mountain / Reprise 0861 / January 1970

Oh Lonesome Me/I've Been Waiting for You / Reprise 0898 / March 1970

Cinnamon Girl/Sugar Mountain / Reprise 0911 / April 1970

Only Love Can Break Your Heart/Birds / Reprise 0958 / September 1970

When You Dance I Can Really Love You / Sugar Mountain Reprise 0992 / February 1971

Cinnamon Girl/Only Love Can Break Your Heart / Reprise 0746 / November 1971

Heart of Gold/Sugar Mountain / Reprise 1065 / January 1972

Old Man/The Needle and the Damage Done / Reprise 1084 / April 1972

Heart of Gold/Old Man / Reprise 1152 / November 1972

Time Fades Away/Last Trip to Tulsa / Reprise 1184 / November 1973

Drive Back/Stupid Girl / Reprise 1350 / January 1976

Hey Babe/Homegrown / Reprise 1390 / August 1977

Like a Hurricane/Hold Back the Tears / Reprise 1391 / September 1977

The Needle and the Damage Done/Sugar Mountain / Reprise 1393 / December 1977

Comes a Time/Motorcycle Mama / Reprise 1395 / October 1978

Four Strong Winds/Human Highway / Reprise 1396 / December 1978

Hey Hey, My My (Into the Black) / My My, Hey Hey (Out of the Blue) Reprise 49031 / August 1979

Cinnamon Girl/The Loner / Reprise 49189 (US) / December 1979

Hawks & Doves/Union Man / Reprise 49555 / November 1980

Stayin' Power/Captain Kennedy / Reprise 49641 / February 1981

Southern Pacific/Motor City / Reprise 49870 / November 1981

Opera Star/Surfer Joe and Moe the Sleaze / Reprise 50014 / January 1982

Little Thing Called Love/We R in Control / Geffen 29887 / December 1982

Sample and Hold/Mr. Soul/Sample and Hold / Geffen 20105 / January 1983

Mr. Soul Part 1/Mr. Soul Part 2 / Geffen 29707 / March 1983

Wonderin'/Payola Blues / Geffen 29474 / August 1983

Cry Cry Cry/Payola Blues / Geffen 29433 / October 1983

Are There Any More Real Cowboys?/I'm a Memory / Columbia 05566/ July 1985

Get Back to the Country/Misfits / Geffen 28883 / September 1985

Old Ways/Once an Angel / Geffen 2S753 / November 1985

Weight of the World/Pressure / Geffen 28623 / July 1986

*Mideast Vacation/Long Walk Home* / Geffen 28196 / June 1987

*Long Walk Home/Cryin' Eyes* / Geffen GEF 25 / June 1987

*Ten Men Workin'/I'm Goin'* / Reprise 29708 / April 1988

*This Note's for You/This Note's for You* / Reprise 27848 / May 1988

*Rockin' in the Free World/Rockin' in the Free World* / Reprise 7-22776/ November 1989

*Mansion on the Hill/Mansion on the Hill* / *Don't Spook the Horse* Reprise 9599-21759-2 / September 1990

*Over and Over/Don't Spook the Horse* / Reprise 7599-19483-4 / February 1991

*Harvest Moon/Old King* / Reprise 9-18685-2 / December 1992

*Downtown/Downtown/Big Green Country* / Reprise 9362-43588-2 / August 1995

*Peace and Love/Peace and Love/Safeway Cart* / Reprise 9362-43608-2 / September 1995

*Big Time*/Picture Disc - PRO-CD-8289 (U.S.) / 936 243 731-2 Germany / 9362437312 Australia / 1996

*Let's Roll* / No catalog number. Digital clone (U.S.) / PRO-CD-100829 (US) / PRO2966 Made in Germany / 2001

*Let's Impeach the President* / 2006

*Grey Riders* / Reprise 528147 / 2011

## ⚜ Filmography ⚜

**(All films in which Neil Young was directly involved as composer, director, or producer)**

*Changes* / Composer / 1969

*The Strawberry Statement* / Composer / 1970

*Journey through the Past* / Director / 1972

*Rust Never Sleeps* / Director / 1979

*Where the Buffalo Roam* / Composer / 1980

*Out of the Blue* / Composer / 1981

*Human Highway* / Director / 1982

*Hearts of Fire* / Composer / 1987

*Made in Heaven* / Composer / 1987

*Philadelphia* / Composer / 1993

*Dead Man* / Composer / 1995

*Wing Commander* / Executive producer / 1998

*Greendale* / Cinematographer/producer/composer/director / 2004

*Hearts of Gold* / Composer / 2006

*CSNY/Déjà Vu* / Composer/screenwriter/director / 2008

*Neil Young Journeys* / Composer / 2012

## ⚜ Bibliography ⚜

Betts, Graham / *Complete UK Hit Albums, 1956–2005* [Collins, 2005]

Betts, Graham / *Complete UK Hit Singles, 1952–2004* [HarperCollins, 2004]

Clarke, Donald (Ed.) / *Penguin Encyclopedia of Popular Music* [Viking, 1989]

Crosby, David and Carl Gottlieb / *Long Time Gone: The Autobiography of David Crosby* [Doubleday, U.S. 1988]

Einarson, John / *Neil Young: Don't Be Denied* [Quarry Press, Canada 1992]

Ertegun, Ahmet / *What'd I Say: The Atlantic Story* [Orion, UK 2001]

Hardy, Phil / *Faber Companion to 20th-Century Popular Music* [Faber and Faber, 1995]

Heatley, Michael / *Neil Young: His Life and Music* [Hamlyn, UK 1994]

Jones, Allan (Compiler) / *Classic Rock Interviews* [Hamlyn, UK 1994]

Kahn, Ashley, Holly George-Warren and Shawn Dahl (Eds.) / *Rolling Stone: The Seventies* [Rolling Stone/Little, Brown, 1998]

Kent, Nick / *The Dark Stuff* [Penguin, UK 1994]

McDonough, Jimmy / *Shakey: Neil Young's Biography* [Jonathan Cape, UK 2002]

Miller, Jim (Ed.) / *Rolling Stone Illustrated History of Rock & Roll* [Rolling Stone/Random House, U.S. 1976]

Rogan, Johnny / *Neil Young: Zero to Sixty* [Calidore Books, UK 2000]

Material was also consulted from the following publications and websites: *Billboard, Creem, Los Angeles Times, Melody Maker, Mojo, New Musical Express, Q, Rolling Stone, The Times, Uncut, Washington Post,* 991.com, nypress.com, nyas.org, neilyoung.com, rateyourmusic.com, rocksbackages.com.

# NEIL YOUNG CRAZY HORSE

Unleashed in Los Angeles in 1969, Crazy Horse represented the essence of grunge before the word was ever used in a musical context. The band's long, colorful ride continues because its members have proven to be true rock and roll warriors.

## The current Crazy Horse line-up
(with comments by Neil Young):

**Ralph Molina** (drums/vocals): "Ralph's the quiet one, but he's also very funny. Ralph's steady as a rock."

**Billy Talbot** (bass/vocals): "Billy's the center in some ways, because he plays…the big notes. Billy is a sound, a feeling that's a big part of us."

**Frank "Poncho" Sampedro** (guitar/vocals): "Poncho brings us strength. He has massive amounts of strength…just an unbelievable core of strength. When he's there, it's strong."

**Neil Young** (guitar/vocals): "I always wince when I hear 'Neil Young and Crazy Horse,' because it's really Crazy Horse. I know it's Crazy Horse."

…ogether on stage, Molina, Talbot, Sampedro and Young create a churning tribal dance, …ing off musical explosions streaked with fire, fury and soul. A prime example is the …'s new live double album on Reprise Records, *Year of the Horse*. The…

# ⇥ Quote Credits ⇤

## CHAPTER 1

"There were people dying every day . . . ."
Scott Young quoted in Johnny Rogan *Neil Young: Zero to Sixty* [Calidore Books, UK 2000]

"I used to turn that old record player up full volume . . . ."
Neil Young quoted in Michael Heatley *Neil Young: His Life and Music* [Hamlyn, UK 1994]

"When I finish school . . . ."
Neil Young quoted in Michael Heatley *Neil Young: His Life and Music* [Hamlyn, UK 1994]

"He did it a few times . . . ."
Neil Young interviewed by Cameron Crowe, *Rolling Stone* [February 8, 1979]

"Neil was different . . . ."
Sue Robertson quoted in John Einarson *Neil Young: Don't Be Denied* [Quarry Press, Canada 1992]

"He had a terrific imagination . . . ."
Pamela Smith quoted in Johnny Rogan *Neil Young: Zero to Sixty* [Calidore Books, UK 2000]

"He was definitely the biggest influence . . . ."
Neil Young quoted in Michael Heatley *Neil Young: His Life and Music* [Hamlyn, UK 1994]

"I thought you'd go down, do three takes . . . ."
Ken Smythe quoted in Jimmy McDonough *Shakey* [Jonathan Cape, UK 2002]

"It was good to have it out . . . ."
Neil Young quoted in John Einarson *Neil Young: Don't Be Denied* [Quarry Press, Canada 1992]

"I got into a Dylan thing . . . ."
Neil Young quoted in John Einarson *Neil Young: Don't Be Denied* [Quarry Press, Canada 1992]

"Neil had just discovered Bob Dylan . . . ."
Joni Mitchell quoted in Jimmy McDonough *Shakey* [Jonathan Cape, UK 2002]

"First time we ever played a liquor joint . . . ."
Bill Edmunsen quoted in Jimmy McDonough *Shakey* [Jonathan Cape, UK 2002]

"We used to break loose in it . . . ."
Neil Young quoted in John Einarson *Neil Young: Don't Be Denied* [Quarry Press, Canada 1992]

"There's a band on the stage . . . ."
Ray Dee quoted in Jimmy McDonough *Shakey* [Jonathan Cape, UK 2002]

"The hardest thing I learned to do . . . ."
Neil Young quoted in John Einarson *Neil Young: Don't Be Denied* [Quarry Press, Canada 1992]

"A tall thin guy . . . ."
Bruce Palmer quoted in Michael Heatley *Neil Young: His Life and Music* [Hamlyn, UK 1994]

"They'd Motown us!"
Neil Young interviewed by Cameron Crowe, *Musician* [November 1982]

## CHAPTER 2

"They dumped us . . . ."
Janine Hollingshead quoted in Jimmy McDonough *Shakey* [Jonathan Cape, UK 2002]

"I remembered that Stills . . . ."
Richie Furay interviewed by David Koepp, *Trouser Press* [January 1979]

"Barry put us in the house . . . ."
Neil Young quoted in John Einarson *Neil Young: Don't Be Denied* [Quarry Press, Canada 1992]

"I guess they were quite impressionable . . . ."
Ahmet Ertegun, *What'd I Say: The Atlantic Story* [Orion, UK 2001]

"I think they had me sing . . . ."
Richie Furay quoted in Michael Heatley *Neil Young: His Life and Music* [Hamlyn, UK 1994]

"Buffalo Springfield was very special in so many ways . . . ."
Ahmet Ertegun, *What'd I Say: The Atlantic Story* [Orion, UK 2001]

"put him through the drums . . . ."
Stephen Stills interviewed by Allen McDougall, *Rolling Stone* [March 4, 1971]

"No notice, no nothing"
Jim Fielder interviewed by Leonard Ferris, *Guitar Player* [April 1971]

"Ultimately they didn't do well enough . . . ."
Ahmet Ertegun, *What'd I Say: The Atlantic Story* [Orion, UK 2001]

## CHAPTER 3

"Great . . . .unreal. He was potentially a poet."
Neil Young quoted in Nick Kent *The Dark Stuff* [Penguin, UK 1994]

"Overdubbed rather than played"
Neil Young quoted from 1970 interview at www.canadiancontent.net

"Everybody was curious . . . ."
David Crosby in David Crosby and Carl Gottlieb *Long Time Gone: The Autobiography of David Crosby* [Doubleday, US 1988]

". . . .I picked up the *New York Times* . . . ."
David Geffen in *Atlantic Records: The House that Ahmet Built*, directed by Susan Steinberg [Rhino/WEA 2007]

## CHAPTER 4

"We would play through . . . ."
Nils Lofgren interviewed by Chris Briggs, *Zig Zag* [December, 1973]

"None of the songs here . . . ."
*Rolling Stone* review [September, 1970]

"It was intermission . . . ."
Neil Young interviewed by Bud Scoppa, *Creem* [November, 1975]

"Ever since I left Canada . . . ."
Neil Young recorded at Massey Hall, Toronto, January 19, 1971 [*Live At Massey Hall 1971*, Reprise Records 2007]

"I didn't know Neil Young from Neil Diamond"
Carrie Snodgrass quoted in Jimmy McDonough *Shakey* [Jonathan Cape, UK 2002]

" . . . .put me in the middle of the road
Neil Young, liner notes *Decade* [Reprise Records, 1977]

"I guess at that point I'd attained a lot of fame . . . ."
Neil Young interviewed by Adam Sweeting, *Melody Maker* [September 14, 1985]

"A rag-bag collection . . . ."
Alan Lewis, *Melody Maker* [November, 1972]

## CHAPTER 5

"We tried to do an album and it fell apart"
Stephen Stills interviewed by Cameron Crowe, 1974, quoted in Johnny Rogan *Neil Young: Zero to Sixty* [Calidore Books, UK 2000]

"They were intros to the songs . . . ."
Neil Young interviewed by Adam Sweeting, *Melody Maker* [September 14, 1985]

"The jitteriness of the music . . . ."
Dave Marsh, *Rolling Stone* [June, 1975]

"This is not the work . . . ."
Wayne Robbins, *Creem* [September, 1975]

"One of the most depressing records I've ever made"
Neil Young interviewed by Cameron Crowe, *Rolling Stone* [August 14, 1975]

"There's scattered evidence..."
Ian MacDonald, *New Musical Express* [August 17, 1974]

"As for acoustic guitar . . . ."
Neil Young interviewed in *Guitare & Claviers* magazine [1992]

"We sang on the same mike . . . ."
Nicolette Larson quoted in Jimmy McDonough *Shakey* [Jonathan Cape, UK 2002]

"It didn't take much money . . . ."
Neil Young interviewed by Richard Cook, *New Musical Express* [October 9, 1982]

## CHAPTER 6

"Too big a picture to comprehend . . . ."
Neil Young interviewed by Jimmy McDough, *Village Voice Rock'n'Roll Quarterly* [Winter 1989]

## CHAPTER 7

"Despite pleasant melodies . . . ."
Anthony DeCurtis, *Rolling Stone* review [December, 1988]

## CHAPTER 8

"Our Greendale Tour is now ozone friendly . . . ."
Neil Young quoted in www.renewableenergyworld.com [Edward X. Young, SolarAccess.com News, February 27, 2004]

"Some early listeners have said . . . ."
Neil Young, Warner Bothers press release, October 2007

"Music to be felt more than thought . . . ."
Damien Love, *Uncut* review [UK, 2011]

## BEHIND THE CAMERA FEATURE

"Not many contemporary artists..." Armond White *New York Press* review [February 17, 2004]
"So up close and personal it leaves the audience viewing the rocker through his own spit" David Germain, AP review [September, 2011]

## NEIL YOUNG, ACTIVIST FEATURE

"Johnathan and this car . . . ." Neil Young quoted in the *Wichita Eagle*, 2008
"You know, I thought long ago . . . ." Neil Young quoted in the *Wichita Eagle*, 2008

# ⊹ Picture Credits ⊹

The author and publishers have made every reasonable effort to contact all copyright holders. Any errors that may have occurred are inadvertent and anyone who for any reason has not been contacted is invited to write to the publishers so that a full acknowledgment may be made in subsequent editions of this work.

2: From the collection of Essential Works (background); from the collection of Francesco Lucarelli (bl, cb), from the collection of Cyril Kieldsen; 3: From the collection of Essential Works (background); from the collection of Francesco Lucarelli (tc), UCL Cultural Department (badges, playlist and guest pass bc); all other images from the collection of Cyril Kieldsen; 4: Michael Ochs Archives/Getty Images; 7: Getty Images; 8: UCL Cultural Department; 9: Francesco Lucarelli; 10: John Einarson; 12: UCL Cultural Department; 13: The collection of Cyril Kieldsen; 14: Youngtown Museum; 15: Courtesy of John Einarson; 17: Courtesy of John Einarson; 18: Courtesy of John Einarson; 19: UCL Cultural Department; 20: The collection of Cyril Kieldsen; 21: The collection of Cyril Kieldsen; 23: UCL Cultural Department; 25: Courtesy of John Einarson; 26: UCL Cultural Department; 27: UCL Cultural Department; 28: UCL Cultural Department; 30: UCL Cultural Department; 31: UCL Cultural Department; 33: Nick Warburton; 34: Henry Diltz/CORBIS; 36: Everett Collection/Rex Feature; 38: Michael Ochs Archives/Getty Images; 39: UCL Cultural Department; 40: Redferns/Getty Images; 42: UCL Cultural Department; 43: UCL Cultural Department; 44: Redferns/Getty Images; 45: The collection of Cyril Kieldsen; 46: Michael Ochs Archives/Getty Images; 47: From the collection of Tom Therme; 48: From the collection of Essential Works; 49: From the collection of Essential Works; 50: The collection of Cyril Kieldsen; 51: Redferns/Getty Images; 52: The collection of Cyril Kieldsen; 53: The collection of Cyril Kieldsen; 54: Nick Warburton; 55: UCL Cultural Department; 56: The collection of Cyril Kieldsen; 57: UCL Cultural Department; 58: UCL Cultural Department; 59: The collection of Cyril Kieldsen; 62: Getty Images; 64: The collection of Cyril Kieldsen; 65: Pictorial Press Ltd/Alamy; 66: The collection of Cyril Kieldsen; 67: The collection of Cyril Kieldsen; 68: Redferns/Getty Images; 70: Michael Ochs Archives/UCL Cultural Department; 71: Getty Images; 73: UCL Cultural Department; 74: The collection of Cyril Kieldsen; 75: TS/Keystone USA/Rex Features; 76: Pictorial Press Ltc/Alamy; 81: Redferns/Getty Images; 84: The collection of Cyril Kieldsen; 85: The collection of Cyril Kieldsen; 86: UCL Cultural Department; 87: PETER SANDERS/Rex Features; 88: UCL Cultural Department; 89: UCL Cultural Department; 91: Henry Diltz/CORBIS; 93: The collection of Francesco Lucarelli; 96: Collection of Francesco Lucarelli; 97: WireImage/Getty Images; 98: Michael Ochs Archives/Getty Images; 100: UCL Cultural Department; 101: The collection of Cyril Kieldsen; 102: The collection of Cyril Kieldsen; 103: © Henry Diltz/CORBIS ; 104: The collection of Cyril Kieldsen; 105: The collection of Cyril Kieldsen; 106: The collection of Cyril Kieldsen; 107: The collection of Cyril Kieldsen; 109: The collection of Cyril Kieldsen;

110: NY Daily News via Getty Images; 113: UCL Cultural Department; 114: Ray Stevenson/Rex Features; 116: UCL Cultural Department; 117: RICHARD YOUNG/Rex Features; 118: The collection of Cyril Kieldsen; 120: The collection of Cyril Kieldsen; 121: The collection of Cyril Kieldsen; 122: The collection of Cyril Kieldsen; 123: Redferns/Getty Images; 125: The collection of Tom Therme; 126: The collection of Cyril Kieldsen; 127: The collection of Cyril Kieldsen; 128: Redferns/Getty Images; 130: Michael Ochs Archives/Getty Images; 131: UCL Cultural Department; 133: Redferns/Getty Images; 134: The collection of Cyril Kieldsen; 135: The collection of Cyril Kieldsen; 136: The collection of Cyril Kieldsen; 137: The collection of Cyril Kieldsen; 139: From the collection of Essential Works; 140: The collection of Cyril Kieldsen; 141: The collection of Cyril Kieldsen; 142: The collection of Cyril Kieldsen; 143: Getty Images; 145: Redferns/Getty Images; 148: The collection of Cyril Kieldsen; 149: Redferns/Getty Images; 150: Redferns/Getty Images; 152: Michael Ochs Archives/Getty Images; 153: The collection of Tom Therme; 154: The collection of Cyril Kieldsen; 155: The collection of Cyril Kieldsen; 156: The collection of Cyril Kieldsen; 157: The collection of Cyril Kieldsen; 158: Rex Features; 159: The collection of Cyril Kieldsen; 159: The collection of Francesco Lucarelli ; 160: James Fortune/Rex Features; 161: UCL Cultural Department; 162: The collection of Cyril Kieldsen; 163: The collection of Cyril Kieldsen; 164: The collection of Francesco Lucarelli; 165: Michael Ochs Archives/Getty Images; 166: The collection of Cyril Kieldsen; 167: The collection of Cyril Kieldsen; 168: Redferns/Getty Images; 169: The collection of Cyril Kieldsen; 170: The collection of Cyril Kieldsen; 171: The collection of Cyril Kieldsen; 172: UCL Cultural Department; 173: UCL Cultural Department; 174: Corbis; 176: Michael Ochs Archives/Getty Images; 176: The collection of Cyril Kieldsen; 178: UCL (t); Francesco Lucarelli (below); 179: © Lynn Goldsmith/Corbis; 182: The collection of Cyril Kieldsen; 183: The collection of Tom Therme; 184: The collection of Cyril Kieldsen; 185: The collection of Cyril Kieldsen; 186–87: The collection of Essential Works; 188: The collection of Cyril Kieldsen; 189: The collection of Cyril Kieldsen; 190: The collection of Cyril Kieldsen; 191: The collection of Tom Therme; 192: The collection of Cyril Kieldsen; 193: Francesco Lucarelli; 194: Francesco Lucarelli (b); 194: Corbis (t); 195: The collection of Cyril Kieldsen; 196: The collection of Tom Therme; 197: The collection of Cyril Kieldsen; 198: Time Life Pictures/Getty Images; 199: The collection of Cyril Kieldsen; 200: Redferns/Getty Images; 201: Francesco Lucarelli; 202: The collection of Cyril Kieldsen; 203: The collection of Cyril Kieldsen; 204: The collection of Cyril Kieldsen; 205: MEYER/Rex Features; 206–207: Corbis;

208: The collection of Cyril Kieldsen; 209: The collection of Cyril Kieldsen; 210: The collection of Francesco Lucarelli (l); The collection of Cyril Kieldsen (r); 211: The collection of Cyril Kieldsen; 212: © Caterine Milinaire/Sygma/Corbis; 213: Francesco Lucarelli (t); The collection of Essential Works (b); 214: UCL Cultural Department; 215: Everett Collection/Rex Feature; 216: Redferns/Getty Images; 219: Corbis; 220: UCL Cultural Department (t); The collection of Cyril Kieldsen (b); 221: Time & Life Pictures/Getty Images; 222: The collection of Cyril Kieldsen; 223: UCL Cultural Department; 224: The collection of Cyril Kieldsen; 225: The collection of Cyril Kieldsen; 226: Francesco Lucarelli; 227: © Peter Turnley/CORBIS; 228: The collection of Cyril Kieldsen; 229: The collection of Cyril Kieldsen; 230: The collection of Tom Therme (t); The collection of Francesco Lucarelli (b); 231: The collection of Cyril Kieldsen; 232: The collection of Tom Therme; 233: The collection of Cyril Kieldsen; 234: The collection of Cyril Kieldsen; 235: The collection of Cyril Kieldsen; 236: The collection of Cyril Kieldsen (r); The collection of Francesco Lucarelli (l); 237: REINSTADLER/Rex Features; 238: The collection of Cyril Kieldsen; 239: The collection of Cyril Kieldsen; 240: UCL Cultural Department; 241: UCL Cultural Department; 242: The collection of Cyril Kieldsen; 243: The collection of Cyril Kieldsen; 244: Michael Ochs Archives/Getty Images; 246: The collection of Tom Therme (b); The collection of Francesco Lucarelli (t); 247: The collection of Cyril Kieldsen; 248: The collection of Cyril Kieldsen; 249: The collection of Cyril Kieldsen; 250: Redferns/Getty Images; 251: Getty Images; 252: Sipa Press/Rex Features; 252: Francesco Lucarelli; 253: The collection of Francesco Lucarelli; 256: The collection of Francesco Lucarelli; 257: UCL Cultural Department; 258: The collection of Cyril Kieldsen; 259: The collection of Cyril Kieldsen; 260: UCL (t); Francesco Lucarelli (b); 261: The collection of Cyril Kieldsen; 262: © Mike Cassese/Reuters/Corbis; 263: The collection of Cyril Kieldsen; 264–265: © Jason Moore/ZUMA/Corbis; 266: The collection of Cyril Kieldsen; 267: The collection of Essential Works; 268: The collection of Essential Works; 269: The collection of Essential Works; 270: The collection of Cyril Kieldsen; 271: The collection of Cyril Kieldsen; 272: The collection of Cyril Kieldsen; 273: © ROBERT GALBRAITH/Reuters/Corbis; 274: UCL Cultural Department; 275: © Hans Klaus Techt/epa/Corbis; 276: The collection of Cyril Kieldsen; 277: The collection of Cyril Kieldsen; 278: UCL Cultural Department (t); WireImage (b); 279: The collection of Tom Therme; 280: The collection of Cyril Kieldsen; 281: © Tim Mosenfelder/Corbis; 282: The collection of Cyril Kieldsen; 284–288 From the collections of Cyril Kieldsen and Francesco Lucarelli.

# ⊹ Acknowledgments ⊹

Special thanks to Cyril Kieldsen, Francesco Lucarelli and Tom Therme, for providing many of the images in this book. We apologize for any unintentional omissions and would be happy to insert an appropriate acknowledgment in future editions.

All album and single covers reproduced courtesy of Atco (Warner Music Group), Reprise (Warner Music Group), Atlantic Records, Geffen Records (Universal Music Group), Vapor Records